SOCIAL THEORY

SOCIAL THEORY
AN INTRODUCTION

Jonathan Joseph

NEW YORK UNIVERSITY PRESS
Washington Square, New York

To Maureen, Simon and Sarah

First published in the U.S.A. in 2004 by
NEW YORK UNIVERSITY PRESS
Washington Square
New York, NY 10003
www.nyupress.org

First published in the U.K. by
Edinburgh University Press Ltd
22 George Square, Edinburgh

A Cataloging-in-Publication record for this book is
available from the Library of Congress.

ISBN 0–8147–4277–7 (paperback)
ISBN 0–8147–4276–9 (cloth)

Typeset in Palatino Light
by Pioneer Associates, Perthshire, and
printed and bound in Great Britain by
MPG Books Ltd, Bodmin, UK

CONTENTS

ACKNOWLEDGEMENTS

This book has emerged out of a course I taught at Goldsmiths College, University of London. I would particularly like to thank Len Platt at the department of Professional and Community Education as well as Helen Murphy, James Souter, Paru Raman, Martin Williams and the many students at PACE. I would also like to thank Phil Walden, Jan Selby, Abbas Vali, Bertell Ollman and Ai Saeki. Finally, thanks are due to Nicola Carr, Stuart Midgley and the staff at Edinburgh.

Chapter 1

INTRODUCTION:
THE NORMS OF SOCIOLOGY

The usual division of sociology to be found in introductory texts argues that we have Marx, functionalism, Weber, symbolic interaction-ism and maybe ethnomethodology. This may sometimes be thematised as: functionalism (Durkheim, Parsons), social action theory (Weber, symbolic interactionism, ethnomethodology), and conflict (Marx). Or else we may find a more straightforward division between approaches that are structural (Marx, functionalism) and those that emphasise action (Weber, interactionism). Another way to classify could be according to those theories that emphasise conflict (Marx, Weber) and those that emphasise consent (functionalism, perhaps interactionism).

As we can see, the different approaches to the study of society have been arranged in all manner of ways with the different protagonists finding themselves first on one side, then on another. In other words, such classifications make no sense. The alternative approach adopted by this book is to draw out (to analyse but not classify) according to three themes: conflict, cohesion and consent. This has already been done, somewhat. But, like the above examples, it is done in a classificatory way that creates more confusion than sense. In normal sociology, therefore, we find the following.

According to consensus theory, norms and values are basic elements of social life. Social life depends on solidarity and is based on reciproc-ity, cooperation and commitment. It is argued that social systems rest on consensus, which is the basis on which they are integrated and tend to persist.

Such a view might be found in any number of social theorists – for example Weber's norms, values and legitimate authority, or Habermas's conception of the public sphere and communicative action. But it is the

1

attribution of this theory to functionalism that this book finds most problematic. Indeed, many sociologists have developed criticisms of Parsons and functionalism on the grounds that there is too much emphasis on social equilibrium and an integrated system. Consequently, this body of work displays a conservative tendency to see existing society as functionally justified in so far as it finds equilibrium. Therefore inequalities in status, power and wealth are functionally justifiable in so far as they contribute to the reproduction of the social system.

In response to the problems of functionalism, Conflict theory argues that different interests are the basic elements of social life. Consequently, social life is by its nature divisive and generates opposition, exclusion and social conflict. Social systems tend to be contradictory, rather than well-integrated, and since social life generates structural conflict, the maintenance of social order involves inducement and coercion rather than consensus.

Clearly Marxism can be fitted in here, but also the debate is influenced by a school of conflict theorists, such as Dahrendorf (1959), who are responding specifically to Parsons and who therefore have a narrower focus. Indeed, Dahrendorf disagrees with Marx over the basic source of conflict, which is not property but authority. Functionalism's consensus is therefore really the power of the dominant group over the unorganised mass of the population. What passes for consensus may therefore only be the institutionalised norms and ideas of the dominant group.

The differences between functionalism and conflict theory are now regarded as out of date and will not be developed in this book. However, Dahrendorf's points at least indicate how consensus may be linked to particular interests. This book argues that Gramsci's work is pivotal in exploring this relation. Gramsci's theory of hegemony argues that social cohesion and consent is established on the basis of the interests of the dominant hegemonic bloc – albeit within definite socio-structural limits. Of all the theories covered in this book, while others help us to understand conflict and cohesion, Gramsci's probably provides the only decent account of social consent.

Consent must not be seen as implying some voluntary agreement over rights and obligations, or worse still, some sort of contract theory à la Locke or Hobbes. This book does not deal with the political philosophy approach to such questions although it is useful to note the differences between the political philosophers and social theorists on this question. P. H. Partridge argues that the term 'consent' applies much more to the political philosophy tradition and ideas about political authority, duty and obedience. It refers to relations between members of a political community and the way in which political authority is exercised. 'Consensus' is used much more by contemporary social theorists and has a wider social context. Tellingly, Partridge writes that this term is usually used to explain social order or cohesion (1971: 71).

By contrast, this book will distinguish between 'cohesion' and consensus although it will use the terms 'consensus' and 'consent' interchangeably. Broadly speaking, cohesion will be taken to mean the way in which a group, bloc, order or system is able to maintain itself. It may refer to processes of unification, 'hanging together', maintenance and reproduction. Consensus and consent will relate more to an act of agreement or a process of legitimation or acceptance. This does not have to be voluntary or even conscious; achieving consensus may involve manipulation, duress, habit or conformity. But it does indicate potential differences or divisions within society and the fact that social cohesion does not come automatically. Consensus may exist between conflicting interests or groups while cohesion now comes to mean the degree to which differences can be overcome and integrated into the social system or social order. Both now incorporate a notion of conflict.

This book was written after a study of the concept of hegemony (Joseph 2002) and how this relates to social cohesion and consent. That book attempted to link the issue of consent, and occasional conflict, to the reproduction and transformation of the structures of society. Having come through this route, the way traditional sociology classifies its theories – particularly the general framework that suggests we must choose between conflict (Marx and Weber) and consensus (functionalism) – seems strange. Therefore, a number of sociological norms are called into question by this book. In particular, two are worth emphasising:

1. that functionalism should not be seen as a theory of consensus (or value consensus). It may contain an element of consensus, but it is primarily to be characterised as a theory of systemic cohesion with social conflict playing only a secondary role, thus leaving little need for an active process of consensus building;

2. that to develop a theory of consensus requires the full introduction of Gramsci into the canon of social theory.

I also wish to highlight a number of lesser issues raised here:

3. that Machiavelli is also a thinker of consensus, and not simply of manipulation;
4. that a major problem with Weber is his conflation of legitimacy with domination;
5. that the role of Weber is as significant as that of Marx in influencing the Frankfurt school;
6. that Foucault's approach does, despite his project, imply some degree of consent and legitimacy;
7. finally, that although this book may give the impression that Marx is deterministic (it certainly helps our story by positioning Gramsci and Weber), Marx's approach is more flexible than it appears here and certainly the popular conception has not been sufficiently challenged.

This book will look at Marx from the point of view that he has a theory of the cohesion of society, related to fundamental contradictions that cause conflict. As has been said, Gramsci does then introduce a much stronger notion of consent in examining how hegemony has to be constructed and how legitimacy has to be won. Weber also has an approach to legitimacy which is tied to forms of leadership. Therefore social cohesion and consent comes from people's belief in a legitimate order. But although he is concerned with the way groups understand and interact with each other, Weber's Nietzschean emphasis on power leads to a problematic conflation of legitimacy and domination.

Functionalism places most of its emphasis on the operation of the system. Therefore conflict is viewed as a failing of the system that needs correcting in order to return to equilibrium. Conflict is not the basis of society as it is for Marx, but is a by-product of systemic disorder. The functionalist view that cohesion is the norm is also held by Adorno, Horkheimer and Marcuse, who maintain that society is ever more integrated and dominated by Weber's instrumental rationality. But Habermas challenges this by returning to an idea of consensus that is based on our intersubjective communication. This is seen by many as a utopian approach since it rests on transcendentally established rules of social behaviour. Foucault, among others, offers a challenge to such an approach by concentrating on particular social practices and how these enforce discipline and regulation. Cohesion (consensus) is not attached to the sovereignty model or the state or the legitimacy of a particular ruling group as it is with Marx, Gramsci and Weber. Rather, we conform to social norms through the operation of practices, techniques, and methods that influence our needs and desires. Initially this sort of cohesion is seen as coming from discourse. Foucault's shift to the operation of power opens the door to contested notions that may imply conflict and consent although this is not sufficiently clear.

Indeed, this, it is argued, is the current problem with social theory – that there is not sufficient clarity on the relation between structures and agency and how cohesion and consent are constructed and maintained. Recent approaches such as postmodernism or globalisation theories or risk society seem to reinforce the fragmentations and divisions within society without offering any emancipatory potential. Yet social cohesion and consent continues to operate and the leaders of society continue to operate in their own ways. The conclusion will suggest that uncertainty, diversity and fragmentation are actually the new forms of cohesion and consent – utilised by the ruling groups to justify their own position. The point of reading the chapters in between is to discover how they might be challenged.

Chapter 2

MARX AND ENGELS:
CONFLICT AND CONSENT

1. THE ECONOMIC BASIS OF SOCIETY

The most striking thing about the Marxist account of society is that it takes as its starting point the material basis of society and examines how this material basis is organised by means of an economic mode of production. Karl Marx and Friedrich Engels develop a theory of history and society – historical materialism – that moves away from the usual concerns such as the deeds of great people, the occurrence of important events and even the political life of societies and concentrates instead on the underlying conditions that help produce such events. In order to understand the development of human society it is necessary to understand the fundamental role played by production. Through production the members of society are able to satisfy their basic wants and needs – the need for food, clothing and shelter as well as other, more developed tastes – so the process of production is the means by which societies reproduce the basic material conditions necessary to sustain their existence.

Marx argues that human history is that of different modes of production, of different ways in which the basic economic relations of society are organised. Thus the organisation of the process of production is a necessary feature of all societies, but the way in which these relations are organised assumes a particular historical form. Marx writes that 'the mode of production in material life determines the general character of the social, political and spiritual processes of life' (1975a: 425). Historically we can point to different modes of production such as the communal system of primitive society, the slave system of ancient society, the serfdom of feudalism and the wage-labour economy of capitalism. This, then, is the most basic principle of the Marxist theory of social organisation – society is organised around the dominant mode of production.

The capitalist mode of production is based on generalised commodity production and wage-labour. The purpose of Marx's *Capital* is to explain the economic laws of the capitalist mode of production as well as outlining the origins of capitalism and its future decline. *Capital* is an attempt to outline both the workings of capitalist society and to explore the contradictions that will lead to its demise. It starts with an analysis of the commodity, an object that through its qualities satisfies human needs, but which is produced, however, in order to be exchanged. When an object assumes the form of a commodity it thereby acquires an exchange value based on its relation to other commodities. However, Marx's analysis of commodity production is concerned with moving away from the appearance of commodities in their exchange relations in order to examine the social conditions that underlie them. His study of commodity production leads to an analysis of the social relation between capital and labour.

The capitalist system is based on the pursuit of profit leading to the accumulation of greater amounts of capital. Marx's task in *Capital* is to explain how the production and exchange of commodities lead to profit and accumulation. He does this through his labour theory of value. According to this theory the value of a commodity is equal to the amount of human labour used to produce it. The value of an article is equal to the amount of labour time socially necessary for its production (Marx 1976: 129). The capitalist who wishes to produce exchange values capable of generating profit must therefore employ labour. Workers, in exchange for their labour, are paid a wage. In effect, the worker's labour itself becomes a commodity to be exchanged for money. However, there is something unique about this commodity – it is capable of producing value over and above its own value. What the capitalist is buying is not the actual amount of labour performed by the worker, but the worker's labour-power or capacity to work for a given period of time. During this time the capitalist must ensure that the worker can produce more value than what is given back in wages. So through the wage-labour relation a form of exploitation takes place which forms the basis for capitalist profits. The key to capitalist production is to be able to generate surplus value. This surplus is based on the difference between the value the workers produce, and what they receive in wages.

What is unique about the capitalist system is that this relation of exploitation appears as fair or at least free. Unlike previous forms of class exploitation such as direct enslavement or the forcible payment of rent to the feudal lord, capitalism is based on the voluntary sale of the worker's labour-power to the capitalist. How voluntary this actually is is of course questionable. The mass of workers are forced to sell their labour-power to the capitalist because they do not have ownership of the means of production and must therefore find work in order to survive. However, this represents an economic rather than a political compulsion, allowing the representatives of the capitalist class to claim that each individual is free to do as they wish and make the best of their particular abilities. Indeed, the exploitation involved in wage-labour is concealed and often presented as a fair exchange, as is reflected in the popular saying 'a fair day's work for a fair day's pay'. The wage-form therefore acts as a kind of mystification, concealing the real level of exploitation. Consequently it can be argued that not only does the capitalist system have a built-in form of exploitation, but it also has a built-in consensual element that leads to workers accepting and freely consenting to the exploitation of their labour-power. The capitalist system generates its own ideological legitimation.

This goes some way towards explaining how capitalism, in its most general sense, generates both social division and inequality (between capitalists and workers) and yet conceals and legitimates these divisions. We will later explore the consequences of this in terms of the genera-tion of the social ideologies that secure this consent to the rule of capital. However, we can see the basis of this in such elementary things as the way capitalism organises the production process. Capitalism brings with it a new stage in the division of labour within the produc-tion process. This has the effect not only of destroying the social bonds and feelings between different people, but also of undermining the free spirit of the individual. The routinisation of production turns the worker into little more than an automaton:

> The habit of doing only one thing converts him into an organ which operates with the certainty of a force of nature, while his connection with the whole mechanism compels him to work with the regularity of a machine. (Marx 1976: 469)

These workers must operate alongside actual machines and adapt themselves the a mechanised process. The result is the destruction of any individual creativity and feeling, something which extends beyond the sphere of production and enters into social life so that the

> division of labour seizes upon, not only the economic, but every other sphere of society, and everywhere lays the foundation for that specialisation, that development in a man of one single faculty at the expense of all others. (Ibid., p. 474)

As if the pressure to fit in with the routinised work of the machine and the factory were not enough, workers come under further pressure from other workers. Chief among these are the unemployed or what is called the reserve army of labour. By overworking those who are employed the capitalist system creates numbers of unemployed or reserve labour, which in turn puts pressure on those who are employed to keep their jobs at all costs. Workers are divided between those who have jobs and those who do not, but who constitute a threat to those who do. In addition, competition exists between the employed, between different branches of production and between rival firms. This further adds to the coercive power of the system and piles the pressure on those who are forced to sell their labour-power in order to survive.

We will see later how Marx's discussion of the division of labour relates to his discussion of alienation so that the potentially creative and satisfying aspect of human labour is turned into an arbitrary, alien and objective force. Humans are compelled to subordinate themselves to a production process that divides them up and treats them as little more than appendages of the machine. In turn, the products that human beings help to create later confront them as alien, objective entities. The division of labour is therefore much more than a technical issue. It is bound up with the demands of the capitalist system, the private ownership of the means of production and the constant need to create more capital. And the effects go beyond the economic process itself and affect all forms of social relations – the relations between people and their products, between people and themselves and between themselves and others.

2. CLASSES AND CLASS CONFLICT

Our discussion of these economic questions has revealed Marx's

analysis to have a particularly objective focus. Thus social division and
social consensus are created not so much by individual people but by
the system itself. According to this general description of the process of
capitalist production it is not so much the individual capitalist who is
responsible for social exploitation, but rather capitalism itself.
Likewise, if people consent to the rule of capital, this is not so much
because they are coerced into doing so by the ruling class, but more
because the mystifying character of the wage relation conceals the
process of exploitation. In keeping with this objective approach we can
say that different classes are determined on the basis of their place in
the mode of production. Therefore, under capitalism classes can be
defined on the basis of the ownership or non-ownership of the means
of production. In a short chapter in *Capital* the working class is defined
as wage-labourers or the owners of mere labour power while the capitalists, as the owners of capital, derive their income from profit (Marx
1981: 1025). However, Marx's analysis of class is richer than this and
includes a more subjective or dynamic element too. Indeed, although
we could choose to interpret Marx in a one-sided way and declare that
society (or more specifically the economic basis of society) determines
class, we could also turn this around and claim that class determines
society. At least this is the intention of Marx and Engels themselves
when they open the *Communist Manifesto* with the declaration: 'The
history of all hitherto existing society is the history of class struggles'
(Marx and Engels 1973: 67).

However, despite the centrality of class to a Marxist analysis Marx's
actual writings on class are notoriously sketchy. His proposed chapter
on class in *Capital* gets no further than forty lines. This brevity has led
to a number of debates over the importance of such issues as subjective class consciousness, labour productivity and the creation of surplus
value. Nevertheless, it is possible to make out a general theory of class
from what Marx has written.

The *Communist Manifesto* is a good place to begin our examination
of Marx and Engels' conception of class since this famous pamphlet
does more than simply describe class relations – it is also an active
attempt to mobilise the working class. At the time of its writing strong
workers' movements had emerged, such as Chartism in Britain and the
revolutionary socialism of Auguste Blanqui in France. Meanwhile,
although the German working class was much weaker, Marx and
Engels were anticipating a revolution in Germany more radical than

those of Britain and France that would sweep away the old order. The *Communist Manifesto* therefore attempts to combine a historical materialist analysis of society with an outline of the necessary tasks facing the working class and their organisations.

The first section of the *Manifesto* is entitled 'Bourgeois and Proletarians' and introduces us to two social groups, 'the owners of the means of social production' and the 'modern wage-labourers who . . . are reduced to selling their labour power' (ibid., p. 67). Marx and Engels note that classes have existed throughout history. However, capitalism has created new classes, new conditions of oppression and new forms of struggle. The bourgeoisie is itself the product of a long course of development resulting from a series of revolutions in the mode of production. Marx and Engels are at pains to stress that historically the bourgeoisie has played a progressive revolutionary role, putting an end to 'feudal, patriarchal, idyllic relations' and bringing together the means of production, collectivising the population and advancing political centralisation and modernisation. And because capitalism is a dynamic system (based on competition and the drive for profit), the bourgeoisie cannot afford to stand still but must continually revolutionise the relations of production. In just one hundred years, the *Manifesto* argues, capitalism has created more massive productive forces than all preceding generations put together.

But flowing from this are the negative conditions of the proletariat's existence. The constant revolutionising of production forces the proletariat into conditions of ever-greater exploitation, while the constant drive to expand capitalism turns more and more people into proletarians. This includes large sections of the peasantry as well as the lower stratum of the middle class, which sinks slowly into the ranks of the working class as its members are forced to sell their labour power to survive. The *Manifesto* argues that the distinctive feature of capitalism is that it has simplified class relations so that 'society as a whole is more and more splitting up into two great hostile camps, into two great classes directly facing each other: bourgeoisie and proletariat' (ibid., p. 68).

This does, however, provide the key to social change. The collectivisation and urbanisation of the working class gives it its potential power and makes it more aware (certainly more aware than the isolated peasantry and the self-interested middle classes) of its common experiences and interests. While the other classes remain bound to the

existing order, 'the proletarian movement is the self-conscious, independent movement of the immense majority, in the interest of the
immense majority' and ultimately the gravedigger of capitalism. (ibid.,
pp. 78, 79) In class terms, therefore, social cohesion is undermined by
the historical process.

The weakness of the account in the *Manifesto* is the presumption
that the development of capitalism will lead to the homogenisation of
the working class into one large (and revolutionary) group while
underestimating the divisions that exist within classes. The development
of capitalism may well lead to a growth in the size of the working class
and to a polarisation between the proletariat and bourgeoisie, but it
also develops a stratification within these classes. These divisions may
be based on a combination of factors such as economic interests,
political motivations and ideological effects – distinctions which are
noted by Marx in other analyses. These differences were also later
addressed by Gramsci and Poulantzas in their discussion of the need
to create a hegemonic unity between these different class fractions.
Weber also addresses these in his criticism of Marx's reduction of social
groups to economic relations and his theory of the determining
capacity of such things as social status, prestige and political authority.
Likewise, Dahrendorf argues that as soon as ownership is separated
from factual control, authority relations become more significant
(1959: 136). There has been a change in the composition of the groups
engaged in conflict. The problem with the account in the *Communist
Manifesto*, then, is that it assumes too much homogeneity, too much
cohesion, within classes.

The development of capitalism into a more and more complex
economic system brings with it more and more intricate social relations.
It would have been impossible for Marx, writing in the nineteenth
century, to have fully anticipated some of the complex social relations
that we have to consider today – for example the post-colonial world
system, the growth of the state sector, the rise of labour and social
democratic organisations and ideologies and the growth in skills,
technology, information and specialised knowledge production.
However, on a world scale it is possible to maintain that a polarisation
is continuing between a growing working class (a working class
growing in areas like Brazil and Korea) and a rich ruling class.

However, this theory of class polarisation has become controversial
because it is linked to Marx's theory of immiseration, according to

which the dynamics of the capitalist system lead to increased misery for the masses and an ever-declining standard of wages. Many commentators have challenged this theory and when it is applied to the living standards of workers in the West it seems to be untrue – although the misery suffered by many in the semi-colonial world tells a different story. But in any case, it is not clear that Marx is arguing that workers suffer an absolute decline in their wages or standard of living, but rather, suffer a relative decline in relation to the overall level of profits. Therefore wages and profits stand in an inverse ratio to one another.

> If capital is growing rapidly, wages may rise; the profit of capital rises incomparably more rapidly. The material position of the worker has improved, but at the cost of his social position. The social gulf that divides him from the capitalist has widened. (Marx 1952: 37)

Marx compares this situation to the possession of a house which may be small but satisfies all social demands. But if a palace arises beside the house it now shrinks to the status of a hut (ibid., p. 32). So although wages and living standards may rise, the gap in status and possessions between rich and poor also widens, leaving the workers in a relatively worse position. Whether this theory is true or not depends on how we interpret Marx. It might be argued that during the post-war period state intervention led to a narrowing of the gap in the West. However, Marx's theory is meant to be a general economic theory, not an analysis of each concrete situation. It is true that other factors such as state intervention may alter this general trend. But recent surveys show that the gap between rich and poor has once again widened and it is no accident that this coincides with new cuts in state intervention and a turn to the policies of economic neo-liberalism.

This still leaves the problem of different social layers, most notably the so-called middle class. Marx's argument is that the intermediate layers are increasingly disappearing or being dragged down into the working class. This is certainly true of the peasantry but could also be said about white-collar workers. For example many clerical and office jobs have become technicised, routinised and deskilled. Clerical workers no longer require the same levels of knowledge and skills and have suffered a loss of status and prestige (not to mention a relative loss of earnings) as a result. For many white-collar jobs a process of 'proletarianisation' has taken place. Marx would therefore argue that the majority of people belong to the working class in the sense that whatever they do (and whether in sociological terms they are described as working-class manual labourers or middle-class professionals) they are still selling their labour-power in return for a wage. Other writers, most notably Weber, have tried to introduce other factors into the definition of social groups, such as social status, prestige, honour, function and political role. However, Marx himself does introduce a subjective factor into the definition of class when he talks of a 'class in itself' and a 'class for itself'.

This may well be a leftover from his days as a follower of the German philosopher G. W. F. Hegel, but it does bring with it a Hegelian dynamism which breaks the notion of class from a static, purely economic context. Here class is seen as an active social relation based on specific interests, actions and consciousness. Class is not simply given by a group's economic position but is conditioned and reformed through the political process of class struggle:

> Economic conditions had first transformed the mass of the people of the country into workers. The combination of capital has created for this mass a common situation, common interests. This mass is thus already a class as against capital, but not yet for itself. In the struggle . . . this mass becomes united, and constitutes itself as a class for itself. The interests it defends become class interests. But the struggle of class against class is a political struggle. (Marx 1963: 173)

Hence there is a political or social dimension to class determination based on conflict and struggle. Class is not imposed statically but is reproduced through the different social relations that people enter into as well as the struggles that they engage in. Here we find an account of how social cohesion relates to a group. The unity and cohesion of a social group does not flow from economic conditions alone, but is forged through concrete experiences and struggles. This viewpoint is developed by the English historian E. P. Thompson in *The Making of the English Working Class*, although there is a danger in his work of losing any kind of objective, economic definition of class. However, perhaps the point to make here is that we need to distinguish between the determination of class in an economic sense (based on people's relations to the means of production) and the development of class consciousness, which shapes the outlook of a group and which is all-important when it comes to taking action.

3. THE STATE

Rather like the writings on class, it is difficult to find a single overriding conception of the state in Marx and Engels. Rather, it has been left to their followers to develop various interpretations that draw on different aspects of their writings. We will briefly examine three different conceptions – the early writings on the abstract nature of the state and its relation to civil society, the idea of the state as a class instrument and the notion of the state as a factor of social cohesion.

Early writings

In these writings, before he became a communist, Marx engages with the arguments of Hegel, who distinguishes between the state or political society and civil society, which comprises the economic sphere and private relations. For Hegel, because civil society, as an arena of particular needs and self-interest, is potentially divisive, the state must act to ensure that the general or universal interest prevails. Like Rousseau, Hegel believes that the state stands above particular groups and interests to represent the collective interest, thus ensuring social cohesion and consensus.

Marx criticises Hegel's view that the state acts to guarantee the universal interest. His argument is that the state is run by a bureaucracy which, rather than defending the universal interest, actually develops its own interests. Hegel's philosophy attempts to present the state as the realisation of free spirit. Yet Hegel himself became a supporter of the Prussian absolutist state, something hardly distinguished by its liberalism and which, as Marx points out, acted to guarantee the interests of a small group – the property-owning Junker class. So rather than representing the universal interest, the state bureaucracy represents the particular interests of certain groups, while attempting to disguise these as the universal interest: 'The bureaucracy must therefore protect the *imaginary* universality of particular interests, i.e. the corporation mind, in order to protect the *imaginary* particularity of the universal interest' (Marx 1975b: 107).

The early works treat the state as an abstract system of political domination that denies the social nature of people and alienates them from genuine involvement in public life. The state instead comes to represent a few private interests, in particular those based on private property. Marx sees this as a recent development linked to the growth of capitalism: 'The abstraction of the *state as such* was not born until the modern world because the abstraction of private life was not created until modern times. The abstraction of the *political* state is a modern product' (ibid., p. 90). This is clearly moving towards a class conception. Later Marx collaborates with Engels who is developing his own views on the state and their joint work *The German Ideology* links the rise of the state to the social division of labour and the development of class society.

The state as a class instrument

The idea of the state as a class instrument is most notably stated in Marx and Engels' comment in the *Communist Manifesto* that 'the executive of the modern state is but a committee for managing the common affairs of the whole bourgeoisie' (Marx and Engels 1973: 69; for a similar expression see also Marx and Engels 1965: 79–80). Here the state is regarded as a direct representative of the economically dominant class. If the economy is held to be the basis of society then the state is seen as the main body of the political superstructure. In particular, the state is regarded as an instrument of coercion and administration that backs up the exploitation of labour by capital with coercion and control in the political sphere. Marx talks of 'the instrument of that class rule – the state, the centralised and organised governmental power' (1974a: 250).

One well-known instrumentalist interpretation of Marx is Ralph Miliband's *The State in Capitalist Society*, which argues:

> In the Marxist scheme, the 'ruling class' of capitalist society is that class which owns and controls the means of production and which is able, by virtue of the economic power thus conferred upon it, to use the state as its instrument for the domination of society. (Miliband 1973: 23)

In particular the instrumentalist view stresses the fact that the state is a coercive instrument that can be used as a tool by the ruling class to gain political acceptance of its economic power. The criticism of this view is that by stressing coercion it leaves little room for a sophisticated account of how consent is achieved through more subtle means. A theory of consent would also recognise that a diverse range of interests needs to be appealed to, whereas the instrumentalist view tends to assume that the two main classes are fairly cohesive and that they act on clear interests. In Miliband this instrumentalist view of the state is combined with elite theory (see Chapter 3), which is used to show how the ruling class can rely on the selection of a reliable state personnel who will serve their interests.

Miliband argues that Marx and Engels 'never departed from the view that the state was above all the coercive instrument of a ruling class' (ibid., p. 7). However, this view might be questioned by some of Marx's historical studies. As we will examine next, Marx's writings on the regime of Louis Bonaparte suggest that, because of rival factions within the ruling class, the French state rose above these differences and assumed a more autonomous nature under the authoritarian control of a single dictator. Indeed Miliband himself draws parallels between this situation and that of fascist Germany, where again the ruling class had to make do with a dictatorship which promised to defend its economic interests, but over which it had no genuine control (ibid., p. 85). However, the instrumentalist view of the state might also be questioned by events at the other end of the class spectrum. These were the events surrounding the Paris Commune of 1870 when the workers of Paris rose up and established their own regime. The aim of the Commune was to abolish private property and establish a socialised system of production under the control of a democratically elected government. However, the economic ruling class eventually managed to bloodily suppress the Commune and re-establish its own dictatorship.

Although Marx's study of these events contains many instrumentalist metaphors, *The Civil War in France* contains the important statement explaining the failure of the Commune that 'the working class cannot simply lay hold of the ready-made state machinery, and wield it for its own purposes' (Marx 1974a: 206). This indicates that although sections of the capitalist class may seek to use the state as their own instrument, it cannot be used by just any social group. The working class cannot, therefore, use the existing state as an instrument for its own rulership.

Rather, it must smash the existing state and establish a new one that is better suited to defending a system of common ownership (what becomes known as the dictatorship of the proletariat and which is developed in Lenin's writings, particularly *The State and Revolution*). This suggests that the state is more than just an instrument of the dominant group or class but has a more deeply inscribed character based on its relation to the economic system. In other words, the capitalist state is capitalist not simply because it is under the control of the bourgeois class but because of its intrinsic relationship to the capitalist system. This explains why it is possible for groups like the fascists, Bonapartists, Islamic populists and other sections of the petite bourgeoisie to come to power without threatening the overall class character of the state (which remains capitalist). This view of the state has a functional rather than an instrumental emphasis based on its relation to the mode of production.

The state as a guarantor of social cohesion

This third position sees the state as a guarantor of social cohesion. In particular, it recognises that cohesion within society is not guaranteed by economic developments, but that the state must act as a mediator between the economic and political spheres. The state becomes historically necessary once society moves beyond a basic subsistence level of production. Its development may well be linked to the rise of class society; however, it might be also argued that, regardless of this fact, the state also has a socially necessary function in relation to such factors as the distribution of surplus product, the regulation of different interests and the mediation of different conflicts. It argues that the state must function in the best interests of the economic mode of production – that is, under capitalism, the state must act in accordance with the demands of private property and the market economy. However, if this seems a rather mechanical view, it is precisely because there is no absolute guarantee of smooth functioning between the economy and the ruling class that the state must play a unifying role.

This can be seen in Marx's study of France in *The Eighteenth Brumaire of Louis Bonaparte*. Here capitalism was riven by different factional interests which in turn had different political representatives – for example the financial bourgeoisie was represented by the Orleanist monarchy. Marx argues that under Louis Philippe and the parliamentary republic the state was the instrument of the ruling class, but under Louis Bonaparte it seemed to attain an autonomous position. He then goes on to add that Bonaparte does in fact represent a social class as well, but this class is that of the small peasant and not the ruling class. This clearly goes against the view that the state is simply the instrument of the economically dominant class. In fact Marx argues that the ruling class had lost its vocation to rule. Into this void steps the figure of Bonaparte, causing Marx to remark that 'France therefore seems to have escaped the despotism of a class only to fall back beneath the authority of an individual' (Marx 1973b: 236).

The conclusion to be drawn from this study is that the Bonapartist state was necessary in order to hold things together when class and fractional conflicts could not be resolved. So power fell into the hands of the state executive, which assumed an autonomous or parasitic character. However, although the state arose above the different fractions of the ruling class, it was still required to respond to the overall needs of capitalist development. Although the case of Louis Bonaparte is an exceptional one, this view of the state as a factor of social cohesion can be applied more generally to describe the process whereby the state seeks to resolve or contain the conflicts between different groups and interests in order to protect the general needs of the economic system – to resolve class conflicts in order to further capitalist interests. Such a view, as we shall see, can be found in the work of Nicos Poulantzas, who draws on Gramsci's notion of hegemony to show how the state attempts to hold the social order together – to resolve social conflicts and secure consent. This indicates that the functioning of the capitalist economy is not guaranteed but has to be socially secured and that it is the state that attempts to perform this necessary function.

This is the clearest case of a political or state-centred (rather than economic) process of social cohesion to be drawn from Marx's work. Nevertheless, Perry Anderson has argued that Marx's work still suffers from being too narrowly focused on a peculiar dictatorial state and that he failed to analyse the British parliamentary state under which he lived. Marx tends to generalise Bonapartism as a typical rather than exceptional form of state. 'The result is that Marx never produced any coherent or comparative account of the political structures of bourgeois class power at all.' (Anderson 1979: 114) This lack of sufficient material on the political structures of bourgeois class power means it is necessary to supplement Marx's views on the state with a more developed position on the operation of bourgeois democracy and the institutional complexity (and durability) of the modern state. Anderson and Poulantzas both turn to Gramsci in order to develop this position.

Finally, Engels' book *The Origin of the Family, Private Property and the State* has also been influential in historically situating the rise of the state and linking it to the growth of class society and the development of the family. Engels argues that the state has not existed from all eternity and that there have been early societies that did without state power. However, 'at a certain stage of economic development, which necessarily involved the split of society into classes, the state became a necessity because of this split' (Engels 1978: 210). This occurs once human labour is able to produce more than is necessary for the maintenance of the producers, so the state is linked to the production, protection and distribution of this surplus. Most generally, the state is an organisation of the possessing class for its protection against the non-possessing class, the means by which the most powerful economic class becomes the politically dominant class:

> Thus the ancient state was, above all, the state of the slave-owners for holding down the slaves, just as the feudal state was the organ of the nobility for holding down the peasant serfs and bondsmen, and the modern representative state is an instrument for exploiting wage labour by capital. (Ibid., p. 208)

We can see that this is an instrumental perspective but also an institutional and genealogical approach that links the development of the state to changes in wider society. Most interesting is the link Engels makes to the institution of the family, an aspect of society neglected by Marx. He argues that the emergence of private property requires a monogamous nuclear family which is capable of organising the inheritance of private property by producing children of undisputed parentage and guaranteeing the supremacy of the male line. With this comes the increased exploitation of women since household management now becomes a private affair and the wife becomes the chief servant of the household. While the man becomes the main wage-labourer, the woman of the family is confined to domestic slavery (ibid., p. 85). Thus Engels shows how the division of labour within society is more than just a class issue but is also linked to a system of patriarchal relations. If classical Marxism is strong on questions of class conflict, it is often weak on other cases of social division such as those based on gender and race. More recently, some feminist scholars have attempted to develop aspects of Engels' analysis and move Marxism away from a simple class-based analysis in order to examine other forms of social division and conflict and other structures of domination such as the patriarchal one.

4. IDEOLOGY

Ideology is commonly assumed to describe a set of ideas or beliefs, or different theories, outlooks and worldviews. However, for Marxists it has a negative connotation best expressed in Engels' remark that ideology is false consciousness. At the very least ideology is said to be partial or misleading. If this is so, then the task for the Marxist theory of society is to account for the production of ideology and to explain its inadequacy.

Marx's early writings link ideology to the concept of alienation, where human beings become separated from their true essence. A concept of alienation stays with Marx throughout his work, but in the early writings where his view of alienation or estrangement is not yet tied to a full economic analysis, it takes a more humanist form. The idea here is that society denies our true species-being, our essence as people living and producing within nature and alongside each other. The essence of the true community lies in our activity; however, with the development of private property we become estranged from the products of this activity. Hence private property acts as an alien mediator and

> through this *alien mediator* man gazes at his will, his activity, his relation to others as at a power independent of them and of himself ... Hence this *mediator* is the lost, estranged *essence* of private property, private property *alienated* and external to itself; it is the *alienated mediation* of human production with human pro-duction the *alienated* species-activity of man. (Marx 1975c: 260–1)

In this early work the idea of estrangement from our true human essence plays a much stronger role than in the later writings. But by focusing on the role of private property in civil society Marx is develop-ing the basis of an economic analysis, although this is based on the role of private property in a more general sense and not on the specific economic ideas associated with the production of surplus value. But Marx does connect the processes of wage-labour, trade and exchange to the production of an alienated consciousness so that 'in the process of exchange men do not relate to each other as men, *things* lose the meaning of personal, human property' (ibid., p. 261).

This theme is continued in the *Economic and Philosophical Manuscripts*, where Marx argues:

> The object that labour produces, its product, stands opposed to it as *something alien*, as a *power independent* of the producer . . . it is the *objectification* of labour . . . In the sphere of political economy this realisation of labour appears as a *loss of reality* for the worker, objectification as *loss and bondage to the object*, and appropriation as *estrangement*, as *alienation*. (Marx 1975d: 324)

So production and ideology are bound together as part of the same process. And it is difficult for workers to reflect on the nature of this process because while they are suffering from the loss of control over the production process they simultaneously suffer from a loss of reality in their heads. The worker produces capital and capital produces the worker, not just physically but also mentally. Through estrangement workers find themselves confronted with the objectified powers of their own essence but in the form of objectified, alien objects. These ideas were also developed by the Hungarian philosopher György Lukács, who talks of this process as 'thingification', whereby the real objects of human labour confront people as independent things.

This 'thingification' represents ideology in its most general sense, but what of the accompanying beliefs or ideologies that reinforce this state of estrangement? We have already examined Marx's views on the way in which the separation of civil society from political society leads to the state playing a mystificatory role. In reality the state represents only the interests of the property-owning few. But it puts itself forward as representing the interests of the whole community. Although the state has considerable coercive powers, its consensual aspect is equally dangerous, for it promotes the illusion of community, citizenship and universal rights when in fact these rights belong only to those who have money and property. The state actually serves the interests of a few, but in order to do so it must create the illusion that it is serving the many.

It does this in an abstract, legalistic way while at the same time alienating most people from genuine involvement in public and political life.

So alienation carries over from the economic system into the political sphere of the state and other social institutions such as the legal system and, as Engels shows, the family. It also carries over into religion, which is said to justify and reinforce alienation by shifting people's consciousness away from the problems of daily life towards higher things while also making a virtue out of misery and suffering. Religion offers comfort but not a solution to social problems, it does not cure but instead deadens the pain:

> *Religious* suffering is at one and the same time the *expression* of real suffering and a protest against real suffering. Religion is the sigh of the oppressed creature, the heart of a heartless world and the soul of soulless conditions. It is the *opium* of the people. (Marx 1975e: 244)

Religion can clearly be called an ideology in the sense that it offers a false or mystifying viewpoint while leaving the real relations of the world intact. In fact, more than this, religion is a product of these real relations. It is no accident that religion exists, for, 'this state and society produce religion, which is an *inverted consciousness of the world*, because they are in an *inverted world'* (ibid., p. 244).

In *The German Ideology* Marx and Engels explain ideology in more detail. They continue to talk of ideology as an inversion, but it is an inversion based on material life:

> If in all ideology men and their circumstances appear upside down as in a *camera obscura*, this phenomenon arises just as much from their historical life-processes as the inversion of objects on the retina does from their physical life-process. (Marx and Engels 1965: 37)

The production of ideas and conceptions in our consciousness is interwoven with our material activity. Such things as morality and religion, although they have the semblance of independence, are really the product of (imperfect) material intercourse. Marx and Engels write that the phantoms formed in the human brain are sublimates of our material life processes (ibid., pp. 37–8).

However, there is a danger of this portrayal of ideology as an inversion of the world becoming slightly mechanistic. A well-known passage in *The German Ideology* has sometimes been interpreted to show that the dominant ideas in society are a direct (but inverted) reflection of economic relations. This is combined with an instrumentalist approach that shows the ideas of the ruling class to be an uncomplicated reflection of capitalist production:

> The ideas of the ruling class are in every epoch the ruling ideas: i.e. the class which is the ruling *material* force of society, is at the same time its ruling *intellectual* force. The class which has the means of material production at its disposal, has control at the same time over the means of mental production . . . the ruling ideas are nothing more than the ideal expression of the dominant material relationships. (ibid., p. 61)

This passage need not be interpreted in such a way, however. It could instead be seen as an expression of the fact that those classes who have control over economic and material resources are better placed to dominate social, cultural and political life. This is not to say that the leading ideas in these domains neatly reflect the dominant economic interests – indeed, we have argued that the ruling class is itself divided into different fractions so that there is no straightforward 'interest' to represent. But the fact that certain groups have access to economic resources does mean that they can influence the political and cultural sphere (as a study of newspaper proprietorship clearly shows). So we can say that the economic structure of society does tend to produce the ruling ideas, but how these ideas are expressed or articulated depends upon many other social, cultural and political factors.

If the description of ideology as an inversion of real relations causes problems of interpretation, then the later work in *Capital* constitutes a shift in emphasis. The ideas associated with our social relations are no longer described as unreal or upside-down but rather as partial and misleading. If we apply Marx's distinction between essence and appearance we can say that ideology represents the way that things appear to us in our day-to-day interactions but that this appearance may not be the whole picture. In this way the capitalist system may appear to be based on free and fair exchange. The real essence of capitalist relations – the production of surplus value – remains hidden.

The concept of alienation in *Capital* is now given a more a precise definition. It is no longer simply the estrangement of human essence by private property but the way that workers are dominated by social forms that are real and yet hide their true natures. We have already discussed how the wage-form hides the real nature of the production process and the extraction of surplus labour from the producer. Marx also talks of the fetishisation of the commodity-form:

> The mysterious character of the commodity-form consists therefore simply in the fact that the commodity reflects the social characteristics of men's own labour as objective characteristics of the products of labour themselves, as the socio-natural properties of these things . . . It is nothing but the definite social relation between men themselves which assumes here, for them, the fantastic form of a relation between things. (Marx 1976: 164–5)

So with the theory of commodity fetishism we see again how for Marx it is the capitalist system itself that produces its own ideology, its own means of securing cohesion and consent. It is in fulfilling this cohering function that ideology is often conceived of, within the Marxist tradition, as a sort of social cement that holds the different aspects of the social system together, the mortar to fill the gaps between the bricks.

Of course the capitalist system would not exist without the people who make it work. But the reproduction of the system is in large part a product of the system and does not depend on the efforts of individual capitalists to ensure ideological cohesion. Social forms such as money, capital, the commodity and the wage are real but at the same time mystifying forms that conceal the essence of capitalist relations through their surface appearances and create the illusion of free and equivalent exchange. This of course does lead to a debate as to whether these illusory forms are in themselves sufficient to ensure the maintenance of the capitalist system. It tends to be accepted that Marx and Engels view social cohesion and consent as deriving primarily from the economic basis of society and the functioning of the capitalist system itself. However, in the political works the ideological effects of the processes of production and exchange are supplemented with a range of ideologies generated in the class struggle. But on the whole their account of ideology does tend to emphasise its negative rather than positive effects, and it has been left to future Marxists such as Lenin and Gramsci to give a fuller account of the processes by which different classes actively use ideology to advance their interests in conflict and to secure their interests through consent.

5. POULANTZAS'S READING OF COHESION AND CONSENT

So Marx and Engels do not really have an explicit theory of cohesion and consent in the way, for example, that Gramsci does. But their work does provide a crucial starting point for theorists who do seek to make this aspect more prominent. That they can do so is because Marx and Engels' work has an implicit account of cohesion and consent, and aspects that we have covered – the cohesive function of capitalist production, the mystifying ideology that it produces, the commodification of social life – provide a good basis for developing a more explicit theory. Most of all, it is the idea of the state as a factor of social cohesion that presents the greatest opportunities, but again, as this theory is in need of more explicit elaboration, we will turn, in this section, to the work of the Greek Marxist Nicos Poulantzas, as an example of the possibilities present in Marx's work.

Marx's account of the situation in France shows that the bourgeoisie was prepared to lose its control of the state apparatus, because the strong executive under the control of Louis Bonaparte was better able to guarantee its continued domination and social power. Poulantzas uses Marx's analysis of France to argue that the state, rather than being the instrument of any one class, is relatively autonomous and that this autonomy allows it to play the role of organising the different classes and class fractions, intervening to arrange compromises among the dominating classes and between these and the dominated classes. The state has a general function in managing class contradictions. In this way it secures social cohesion and maintains the necessary conditions for the reproduction of the mode of production.

The state must secure the cohesion of a class-divided society. This is a necessary social function that is not reducible to the narrow interests of any one particular group. That the state is able to act as a factor of social cohesion is due to its autonomy from the economic sphere. Poulantzas makes much of Marx's point about capitalism separating the worker from the means of production and this provides the basis for the autonomy of the political sphere. Unlike previous modes of production, under capitalism it is no longer necessary to secure exploitation by political means and the state is not directly implicated in organising economic production. This relative autonomy in fact allows the state to present itself as the representative of the 'general interest' in the way suggested by Marx and Engels. It is able to stand above competing and divergent economic interests, or, if necessary, to present these interests as the popular will. This is important ideologically as 'the state assumes a specific autonomy *vis-à-vis* these [socio-economic] relations, in putting itself forward as the representative of the unity of the people/nation' (Poulantzas 1973: 135).

The autonomy of the state apparatus from the economic class struggle is also important because it means that the economically dominant class does not have to correspond to the politically dominant class. Political domination does not flow automatically from the economic situation. Rather, it has to be achieved, leaving this process open to hegemony. The concept of hegemony implies that domination and leadership have to be achieved, and the state becomes crucial as a site where this hegemony is established. The state must act as the cohesive factor in the unity of a social formation, but how this is achieved is a political rather than merely an economic matter. Hence 'the capitalist state, characterised by hegemonic class leadership, does not *directly* represent the dominant classes' economic interests, but their *political interests*: it is the dominant classes' political power centre, as the organising agent of their political struggle' (ibid., p. 190).

It can be seen from the use of the plural that there is no one unified ruling class, but rather a plurality of class fractions, each with different interests. This goes against the view in the *Communist Manifesto* that society is more and more splitting up into two great classes. In fact it is the classes themselves that are splitting up, with fractions formed on the basis of different interests, powers and relations within classes, determined by economic, political and ideological factors. Given these divisions, social cohesion becomes all the more important. The state becomes the site of the construction of what Poulantzas calls a power bloc:

The capitalist state and the specific characteristics of the class struggle in a capitalist formation *make it possible* for a 'power bloc', composed of several *politically dominant* classes or fractions to function. Amongst these *dominant* classes or fractions one of them holds a particular *dominant role*, which can be charaterised as a *hegemonic* role. (Ibid., p. 141)

State power corresponds to the interests of the power bloc. However, this power bloc is not straightforwardly reducible to class interests but is a product of the complex process by which hegemony is constructed. The state's role is to act as the factor of political unity of the power bloc under the protection of the hegemonic group:

> The unity of the capitalist state stems from the fact that it represents the political unity of the people-nation and that it constitutes the political unity of the power bloc under the protection of the hegemonic class or fraction. (Ibid., p. 303)

The state is able to play this role of organising and unifying the bourgeoisie and representing its long-term interest in so far as it has relative autonomy from particular fractions and interests. This is possible because the state is separated from the means of production. Once the cohesion of the dominant class fractions has been achieved, the consent of the broader masses must be mobilised. The capitalist state is described as an institutional ensemble with the function of organising hegemony within the power bloc and mobilising active consent to this. This process of securing social cohesion and consent falls under Gramsci's description of an 'unstable equilibrium of compromise'. Poulantzas interprets this in the following way:

1. compromise – power corresponds to hegemonic leadership and economic sacrifices;
2. equilibrium – political power sets limits and tries to balance political interests;
3. unstable – limits to equilibrium as affected by political conjuncture. (Ibid., p. 192).

The role of the state is to ensure the social formation's cohesion by keeping the struggles within the limits of the mode of production:

> The principal role of the state apparatus is to maintain the unity of a social formation by concentrating and sanctioning class

domination, and in this way reproducing social relations, i.e. class relations. Political and ideological relations are materialised and embodied, as material practices, in the state apparatuses. (Poulantzas 1978a: 24–5)

Poulantzas goes on to divide these state apparatuses into two types. The repressive state apparatuses include the police, army, prisons, judiciary, civil service, etc, while the ideological state apparatuses include educational, religious, cultural, informational, trade union, family and other bodies that contribute to the reproduction of social relations. Such an approach suggests that the state comes to play an increasingly important role in everyday life, utilising a diverse array of apparatuses to secure cohesion and consensus within society.

In fact Poulantzas's later work tends to emphasise, perhaps overemphasise, the tendency towards interventionist and exceptional forms of state. Implicitly rejecting Marx's distinction between political society and civil society, he argues that the state now cuts across all forms of life and that state institutions and apparatuses are embodiments of class relations and practices. He argues that this period of what he calls monopoly capitalism requires an interventionist state with a strong or authoritarian character. These 'exceptional' states are marked by their increased control over social life and the economy and the rise of bureaucracy and administrative apparatuses. Like the writers of the Frankfurt school, Poulantzas argues that the increasingly dominant role of the state accompanies the economic domination of monopoly capital. There is a change in the role of state apparatuses and political parties and a breakdown of the boundaries between public and private spheres.

Like the Frankfurt school and the work of Weber, Poulantzas's position becomes increasingly pessimistic, focusing as it does on the shift away from the legitimacy of popular sovereignty towards legitimacy of state bureaucratic administration. Nevertheless, some optimism can be derived from the fact that he shifts from a structuralist position to a relational view of the state. In other words, the fact that the state is divided by class contradictions leads to the view that the state is not a thing, but a set of relations. The state is not an intrinsic entity, a thing, an instrument or a subject; 'it is rather a relationship of forces, or more precisely the material condensation of such a relationship among classes and class fractions' (Poulantzas 1978b: 128). The fact that the state is a social relation means that class struggles are inscribed into the state. The state no longer stands above class relations; these are inscribed into its very nature. The state becomes the centre for the exercise of power and it is Poulantzas's hope that the state can be transformed by popular struggles against authoritarian dictatorship.

6. CONCLUSION: SOCIAL CHANGE

It is important that we end this chapter by addressing Marx and Engels' ideas on social change, for this, after all, was the goal of their life's work. We will do this by assessing the basis for social conflict, the breakdown of consent and the outcome of struggle. We can also draw out what appear to be the dual dynamics of Marx and Engels' analysis – the systemic properties of capitalism itself and the actions and consequences of class struggle.

We have studied the dynamics of the capitalist system in terms of some of the intrinsic properties and inherent powers of its different structures, relations, mechanisms and processes. Marx's method of studying the capitalist system at this level is to examine some process or mechanism in the abstract so, for example, he advances the proposition that commodities exchange at their values and that these values are based on the amount of socially necessary abstract labour that has gone into making them. However, Marx extends this analysis into the social domain so that not only does the capitalist system produce commodities, it also produces ideas about commodities or commodity fetishism. These ideas are as much an inherent part of the capitalist system as the commodities themselves and they explain at an abstract level how it is that workers fail to recognise commodities as products of their own labour or why it is that the mystifying character of the wage relation leads workers to consent to the extraction of surplus labour. In this sense coercion and consent are built into the capitalist system.

All this makes the capitalist system look like an invincible machine. But at the same time Marx argues that the capitalist system has inherent weaknesses and contradictions. One of the most basic contradictions is the tendency of rate of profit to fall. Capitalism is based on the need for profit, which in turn is based on the extraction of surplus value. Marx argues that although labour is the source of surplus value, there is a historical tendency for the amount of labour (or what he calls variable capital) to decline as a proportion of total capital, thus reducing that proportion of capital capable of producing surplus value and hence profit. This is a contradiction, because it is actually the desire to extract increasing amounts of surplus value that leads the capitalist to spend more money on machines and other forms of fixed capital that can increase the productivity of labour. In a competitive environment this reduces costs per unit and gives the producer an edge over any rivals. But ultimately it is not factories or machines that create profit for the capitalist but the exploitation of unpaid labour. And while the innovative capitalist may initially benefit from the use of improved technology, the benefits of this soon disappear as the improvements become generalised across the industry. Meanwhile the increased spending on fixed capital leads to longer-term costs, such as depreciation, that take their toll on the rate of profit.

The tendency of the falling rate of profit is controversial but is accepted by most Marxists. Other theories of crisis have provoked debates between different schools of Marxism. However, all these theories of crisis are founded on the recognition that the free nature of capitalist production creates unstable or anarchic conditions that undermine the smooth flow of production and circulation. One such theory is that the anarchy of the capitalist system leads to crises of overproduction, where different capitalists or indeed whole sectors or industries are unable to sell their goods, so that output exceeds demand. Recent examples of this are the huge lots full of unsold cars. The more controversial theory of underconsumption suggests that since the wages workers receive are considerably lower than the value of what they produce, they cannot afford to buy back what they produce, thus generating a gap in demand. Other theories are based on the idea of a wage squeeze, whereby a rise in real wages (brought about by the organised activities of workers) leads to a fall in the rate of profit. More generally, we could say that conflicts emerge from the contradiction between the social nature of production and the private appropriation of capital.

These contradictions are also described at a general historical level that connects developments in the economic mode of production to developments in class conflict and the possibilities of social revolution. Marx is attempting to show that social revolution is a historical necessity based on certain historical principles. The most famous example of this approach is his 1859 preface to *A Contribution to the Critique of*

Political Economy. Here Marx argues that the economic mode of production conditions social, political and intellectual life, but that at a certain stage the further development of capitalism comes into conflict with the existing set of social relations so that 'from forms of development of the productive forces these relations turn into their fetters. Then begins an era of social revolution' (Marx 1975a: 425–6). For some this is the most precise account of Marx's theory of historical materialism. For others it represents a crude, mechanical and deterministic approach that leaves little scope for human agency. We will explore this issue further in the next chapter.

To put this in terms of our main theme, it would seem that the production of social cohesion and the generation of consent seem to be built into the capitalist system itself, particularly in the process by which workers consent to sell their labour-power, which in turn reproduces capitalist relations and generates ideologies that justify this process. But Marx also argues that the capitalist system has other built-in tendencies of a more damaging nature and that these generate social conflict. Explained in this way, the breakdown of social cohesion and consent would seem to be a result of the inherent failings of the capitalist system itself rather than anything more political or conscious. In fact it could be said that social consent flows from social cohesion and that consent only becomes an issue once cohesion has broken down.

Marx's more objective, systemic and perhaps mechanical accounts of social conflict and social change are nevertheless supplemented with a much more agential, creative and dynamic theory of class struggle. This is particularly evident in the passage we cited from *The Poverty of Philosophy* where Marx explains how large-scale industry concentrates a group of workers into a class and gives them the potential to resist the power of capital. He argues that this is not enough and that class needs to establish itself on a political level, that the struggle of class against class is a political struggle (Marx 1963: 172–3). Earlier in this book, Marx gives an account of how the bourgeoisie came to power and smashed the old forms of state and civil society. It came to power for two reasons – first that antagonisms were already present in the old feudal order, but also because it was prepared to take political action to overthrow that order and establish its own rule. But on coming to power the bourgeoisie finds itself in a similar position to the old classes that it replaced:

In the course of its historical development, the bourgeoisie necessarily develops its antagonistic character . . . As the bourgeoisie
develops, there develops in its bosom a new proletariat, a modern
proletariat; there develops a struggle between the proletarian
class and the bourgeois class . . . From day to day it thus becomes
clearer that the production relations in which the bourgeoisie
moves have not a simple, uniform character, but a dual character;
that in the selfsame relations in which wealth is produced, poverty
is produced also; that in the selfsame relations in which there is
a development of the productive forces, there is also a force
producing repression. (Ibid., p. 122–3)

History develops by means of contradictions which give rise to
conflicts which give rise to revolutions. And thus we have it that
'revolutions are the locomotives of history' (Marx 1973a: 46). But if
conflict leads to power, it is still necessary to consolidate this power by
means of consent. As well as the consent automatically generated by the
capitalist mode of production, a class consensus is necessary. This we
have described as the way in which the particular interests of the ruling
group or class are articulated as the general or universal interests:

For each new class which puts itself in the place of the one ruling
before it, is compelled, merely in order to carry through its aim, to
represent its interest as the common interest of all the members
of society, that is, expressed in ideal form: it has to give its ideas
the form of universality, and represent them as the only rational,
universally valid ones. (Marx and Engels 1965: 62)

Marx and Engels argue that history does progress and that each suc-
cessive ruling group must establish an ever greater degree of consent
or hegemony: 'Every new class, therefore, achieves its hegemony only
on a broader basis than that of the class ruling previously, whereas the
opposition of the non-ruling class against the new ruling class later
develops all the more sharply and profoundly' (ibid., p. 63).

The working class must also take power by putting itself forward as
the leading power and by representing the universal interest. Because
bourgeois society is firmly linked to the capitalist mode of production
and the repressive form of the state, revolution will be a difficult
process. The working class is economically disenfranchised in the sense

that it does not have ownership over the means of production, but its place in the production process means that by acting collectively it can directly affect production and thus bring down capitalist society. This is in contrast to groups like the peasantry and other middle layers who may also come into conflict with the capitalist system but who are more dispersed and have fewer economic levers. Some sections of the bourgeoisie – particularly the intellectuals – may also come over to the side of revolution. But the rest of the bourgeoisie will not give up without a fight. And since they can draw on the repressive machinery of the state, revolution is likely to be a violent business.

What happens after the revolution? Does the historical process repeat itself and a new antagonism develop in relation to working-class rule? According to Marx and Engels it does not, because for the first time in history the working class does genuinely represent the universal interest. After the revolution, class differences and hence class conflicts begin to fade. Indeed, for Engels even the state starts to disappear:

> *The proletariat seizes power and to begin with transforms the means of production into state property*. But it then puts an end to itself as proletariat, it thus puts an end to all state differences and class antagonisms, and thus also to the state as state ... The government of persons is replaced by the administration of things and the direction of the process of production. The state is not 'abolished', *it withers away*. (Engels 1976: 362–3)

Marx and Engels hold a dialectical philosophy; for them, social progress is based on social contradiction and social conflict, leading to revolutionary change. This process is said to end with the victory of the proletariat, the abolition of social conflict. With the end of conflict, the coercive nature of the state withers away as it is no longer required, and society, for perhaps the first time, becomes truly consensual:

> In a more advanced phase of communist society, when the enslaving subjugation of individuals to the division of labour, and thereby the antithesis between intellectual and physical labour have disappeared; when labour is no longer just a means of keeping alive but has itself become a vital need; when the all round development of individuals has also increased their productive

powers and all the springs of co-operative wealth flow more abundantly – only then can society wholly cross the narrow horizon of bourgeois right and inscribe on its banner: From each according to his abilities, to each according to his needs! (Marx, 1974b: 347)

Chapter 3

ANTONIO GRAMSCI:
THEORIST OF HEGEMONY

―――⊃⊂――――

1. THE REACTION AGAINST ECONOMIC DETERMINISM

The Italian Marxist Antonio Gramsci is famous for his concept of hegemony, which stresses that rulership cannot be based solely on coercion but also requires a large degree of consent. We have argued that these views are also present in Marx and Engels in that they explain the role of ideology within society both at the level of the power of the ideas of the ruling class and as an intrinsic product of the capitalist system itself. What is distinctive about Gramsci's approach is that he shifts the emphasis away from a narrow focus on the economic basis of society and emphasises the importance of 'superstructural' factors – like politics and culture – in maintaining social cohesion.

In particular, Gramsci is seeking to reject the mechanical materialism of the social democratic parties of the Second International. Writers such as Karl Kautsky and Georgy Plekhanov had developed historical and dialectical materialism in such a way as to give society a rigid structure comprising a number of different layers, starting from the economic base and building upwards. Ignoring the more sophisticated socio-economic analysis of *Capital*, mechanical materialism tends to focus on the five pages of historical generalisations contained in Marx's preface to *A Contribution to the Critique of Political Economy*, where it is stated:

> In the social production of their existence, men inevitably enter into definite relations, which are independent of their will, namely relations of production appropriate to a given stage in the development of their material relations of production. The totality of these relations of production constitutes the economic structure

of society, the real foundation, on which arises a legal and political superstructure and to which correspond definite forms of social consciousness. (Marx 1975a: 425)

Such a model can certainly be seen as schematic and it has led to the kind of wedding-cake model which sees political, legal, cultural and ideological relations as standing on top of an economic base. It is also economically determinist in the sense that it overemphasises the power that the economic base has in determining the rest of social life. Everything, ultimately, can be reduced to the question of the economic mode of production and the balance between the productive forces (means of production and labour power) and the relations of production (classes and ownership). Further, the preface gives primacy to the productive forces, suggesting that these shape the development of productive relations, which in turn develop the social relations at the level of the superstructure. This determinism then assumes a historical character so that

> at a certain stage of development, the material productive forces of society come into conflict with the existing relations of production . . . From the forms of development of the productive forces these relations turn into their fetters. Then begins an era of social revolution. (Marx 1975a: 425–6)

Although it is not necessarily wrong to see the economic structure of society as the main driving force of history, interpreters of Marx have erred in giving this a one-sided and mechanical emphasis. The historical process is reduced to a single economic (or even technological) development. Yet this schema poses more questions than it answers. What exactly does the economic structure consist of? If we are referring to the process of social production, then this contains a number of relations which are not purely 'economic' but are of a more 'superstructural' nature. The most problematic of these relations is the legal structure, which, it can be argued, belongs to the superstructural sphere of political, ideological or ethical relations but which could equally be said to be part of the economic base because capitalism is founded upon property rights and relations. Other important social structures and institutions pose similar problems, for surely such things as the family, education and training, welfare, indeed the state itself, cannot be reduced to either the economic or the superstructural. All of these could be said to reinforce consensus at the superstructural level, but equally, they are important factors in the reproduction of capitalist relations of production.

This raises questions, not only about the distinction between base and superstructure but also about the distinction between forces of production and relations of production. Marx's preface suggests that the productive forces develop to ever-greater degrees until, at a certain stage, they come into conflict with social relations. However, we have started to question whether these forces can be separated from wider social relations. Surely the productive forces do not develop autonomously, but only develop within the context of particular social relations. Rather than returning as fetters to further development, the relations of production are there from the beginning. Consequently, it is pretty much impossible to follow through the argument and decide at which point the relations of production become a fetter. This is obviously problematic given that the preface claims that social revolution is dependent on this contradiction. The truth is that this schema has proved to be of no real help to Marxists when analysing actual history. Again, taking another schematic passage from the preface, Marx writes:

No social order is ever destroyed before all the productive forces for which it is sufficient have been developed, and new superior relations of production never replace older ones before the material conditions for their existence have matured within the framework of the old society. (Marx 1975a: 426)

However, this is contradicted by actual Marxist practice. In 1917 Lenin led a socialist revolution in what was still a backward, semi-feudal country with an emerging but still weak capitalist system and only a small working class. According to the mechanical materialists of the Second International, a fully socialist revolution was only possible in the advanced capitalist countries of the West. For them, a revolution in Russia was not possible until it had completed its capitalist development. For Bolshevik leaders such as Lenin and Trotsky, however, the backwardness of Russia made revolution a greater possibility. The combination of backward feudalism and weak capitalism, a condition described as combined and uneven development, made social revolution possible provided it was given strong and determined leadership (here, for Lenin, the term 'hegemony', rather than emphasising consensus, stresses the leading and directing role of the party). This indeed occurred and led the young Gramsci to declare that the revolution in Russia was a 'revolution against *Capital*'.

> In Russia, Marx's *Capital* was more the book of the bourgeoisie than of the proletariat. It stood as the critical demonstration of how events should follow a pre-determined course: how in Russia a bourgeoisie had to develop, and a capitalist era had to open, with the setting up of a Western-type civilisation, before the proletariat could even think in terms of its own revolt, its own demands, its own revolution. But events have overcome ideologies. Events have exploded the critical schemas determining how the history of Russia would unfold according to the cannons of historical materialism. (Gramsci 1977: 34)

Thus Gramsci claims that the Bolsheviks reject Karl Marx but live Marxism. Instead of a predetermined schema, Gramsci stresses an active conception of history that 'sees as the dominant factor in history, not raw economic facts, but man, men in societies, men in relation to one another, reaching agreements with one another, developing through these contacts (civilisation) a collective, social will' (ibid., pp. 34–5). Of course Marx, as we have seen in his political writings, also stresses a more active and socially based theory of history. Rather than talking of a revolution against *Capital*, it would be more correct for Gramsci to describe events in Russia as a revolution against the 1859 preface and the mechanical determinism of the Second International theorists. In fact writers like Kautsky and Plekhanov opposed the Russian Revolution because they saw it as premature and because history had not run its full course. But their impeccable commitment to the 'principles' of historical and dialectical materialism in theory meant a rejection of revolutionary politics in practice.

Like Lenin, Gramsci is concerned to return the active element to Marxist theory. His comments on the Russian revolution shift emphasis from away from 'objective' economic or historical developments towards a study of the interaction of social beings. This is important when dealing with such issues as social development, class conflict, the structures and institutions of consensus and consent in political and civil society and the question of social change. Paradoxically, Gramsci's emphasis on the importance of actual historical develop- ments requires him to reject the prevailing assumptions of historical materialism and its reduction of history to iron laws of development. But Gramsci does not altogether break from prevailing theory; he maintains Marx's base/superstructure and forces/relations formulas, but tries to shift their emphasis. Later, in the *Prison Notebooks* he returns to the passage in the preface when he talks of the

> two fundamental principles of political science: 1. that no social formation disappears as long as the productive forces which have developed within it still find room for further forward movement; 2. that a society does not set itself tasks for whose solution the necessary conditions have not already been incubated, etc. It goes without saying that these principles must first be developed critically in all their implications, and purged of every residue of mechanism and fatalism. (Gramsci 1971: 106–7)

Having examined Gramsci's view of the Russian revolution we may well wonder why he still believes that the preface contains funda- mental principles and how it can be possible to purge this view of its mechanistic fatalism. Gramsci's answer is to relate developments at the economic level to such things as the equilibrium of political forces and the development of culture and ideas. This then leads to a development of his theories of hegemony, historical bloc and passive revolution. In doing so it might be claimed that Gramsci maintains the base/super- structure distinction, but shifts the emphasis towards the political, ideological and cultural superstructure. This indeed occurs, but it leads to a radical tension that has preoccupied many subsequent Marxist and Gramscian commentators.

2. MACHIAVELLI AND THE MODERN PRINCE

Gramsci's Italian background leads him to draw on the ideas of Niccolò Machiavelli in order to develop a practical and action-based approach to politics and history. His approach is one of 'immediate political action' and Gramsci claims that Machiavelli's conception of the world is based on a 'philosophy of praxis' which emphasises the role of purposeful action. This might be contrasted with the mechanical, deterministic Marxism that Gramsci was criticising. While these views left little scope for human action or creativity, Machiavelli's approach is described as a 'neo-humanism' which 'bases itself entirely on the concrete action of man, who, impelled by historical necessity, works and transforms reality' (Gramsci 1971: 249). This helps enforce Gramsci's belief in human will as Machiavelli 'is not merely a scientist; he is a partisan, a man of powerful passions, an active politician, who wishes to create a new balance of forces and therefore cannot help concerning himself with what "ought to be"' (ibid., p. 172).

The Florentine diplomat was concerned with the instability of the Italian city states and wished to see Italy restored to its former greatness. This requires the rulers to adopt a clear strategy that can create civil unity and order. To do so, the ruler may draw upon different tactics, employing both force and consent in order to maintain power and influence. It appears that Machiavelli favours force when he writes that 'it is desirable to be both loved and feared; but it is difficult to achieve both and, if one of them has to be lacking, it is much safer to be feared than loved' (Machiavelli 1988: 59). However, his examples of force are almost exclusively derived from ancient society whereas his discussion of his own society draws much more on the idea of consent or 'civil principality'. Despite his best-known work being called *The Prince*, Machiavelli's writings, in particular the *Discourses*, reveal him to be a modern republican who is interested in less direct forms of rulership and is concerned about popular governance. A broader consent can be developed on the basis of custom and tradition, laws and justice, the dominance of the towns and the middle classes and, above all, through civic virtue and the institutionalisation of popular power. Power should operate through various social institutions and through civil society. In this way, states can 'develop their roots, trunks and branches, and will [not] be destroyed by the first chill winds of adversity' (ibid., p. 23). Here we find a clear precursor to Gramsci's concept of hegemony.

Machiavelli inspires the practical aspect of Gramsci's Marxism, but this has its limitations. Just as Marx found inspiration from Hegel, so Gramsci is influenced by the Italian Hegelian philosopher Benedetto Croce. Through Croce Gramsci is able to situate practical activity within a wider context; history is the dialectic between the practical and the ideal, it is unified by spirit and represented by the progress of liberty. Gramsci also draws on the one notable Italian Marxist of this time, Antonio Labriola, who introduces the term 'philosophy of praxis' to describe Marxism. Gramsci later uses this term in his *Prison Notebooks* in order to evade the prison censors; however, it also captures the spirit of Gramsci's approach, which is to reject the mechanical or 'scientific' aspect of Marxism in favour of an emphasis on historical actions and human will.

This emphasis is also derived from Georges Sorel, whose conception of revolutionary activity is based on a rejection of 'scientific Marxism' in favour of the spontaneity of the masses. As a syndicalist, Sorel sees the general strike as an act of creativity that attempts to overcome the moral collapse of society. His notion of myth describes the ideal that inspires the masses to overcome society. Gramsci believed that Sorel's notion of myth could be combined with Machiavellian politics and he argues:

> Machiavelli's *Prince* could be studied as an historical exemplifica-
> tion of the Sorelian myth – i.e. of a political ideology expressed
> neither in the form of a cold utopia nor as learned theorising,
> but rather by the creation of a concrete fantasy which acts on a
> dispersed and shattered people to arouse and organise its collec-
> tive will. (Gramsci 1971: 125–6)

What Gramsci finds problematic in Sorel is the lack of direction and leadership. In his early days in Turin, Gramsci had embraced the revolutionary syndicalism and spontaneism of the factory councils. But the failure of these projects, combined with the development of Gramsci's understanding of Russian Bolshevism and its emphasis on the role of the political vanguard, led Gramsci away from Sorelian politics and towards questions of political direction and leadership. As he notes, 'every "spontaneous" movement contains rudimentary elements of conscious leadership, of discipline' (ibid., p. 197). Again, Gramsci finds support for his view in the work of Machiavelli.

The prince in Machiavelli's work is not a real prince but a theoretical abstraction or ideal type. His intention is to form a collective will out of the mass of the people but under the clear direction of a leadership and programme. Gramsci believed that this factor was missing from Italian history and that the prince's task to unify society was still to be achieved. In this sense the role of Machiavelli's prince must now pass on to the Communist Party or 'modern prince', which must attempt to awaken and develop a national-popular collective will based on its political and ethical leadership.

We can see, therefore, how Gramsci shifts emphasis away from mechanistic Marxism towards an active and dynamic politics. Machiavelli is not a cold-blooded political scientist but an advocate of moral and political action. Politics, for Machiavelli, is the art of the possible. What Machiavelli brings to Marxism is a politics of statecraft, of tactics and strategy. Power will not fall into the hands of the Communist Party as a result of objective economic developments, but must be won through conflict and consent. The Communist Party must turn itself into an intellectual force capable of forging a new political will that is universal and total. It must first bind together an alliance of different groups and interests and offer a leadership which will lay the basis for a new state power.

> The modern prince must be and cannot but be the proclaimer and organiser of an intellectual and moral reform, which also means creating the terrain for a subsequent development of the national-popular collective will towards the realisation of a superior, total form of modern civilisation. (ibid., p. 133)

The clear difference between the two philosophers is that Machiavelli's prince is already in power whereas Gramsci's modern prince must struggle to gain that position. Machiavelli advocates a strategy for the ruling class in order to modernise Italy, while Gramsci's modern prince is initially only an aspiring ruler although it must also learn how to maintain power once it is won. Philosophies, Gramsci believes, reflect the class standpoint of the bearer, and in this sense there is a radical distinction between the philosophies of the two thinkers.

The philosophy of the modern prince is Marxism. However, Marxism must win support from the masses. In creating a counter-hegemonic force, the Communist Party must transform existing consciousness and gain an acceptance of the communist worldview. This corresponds to Machiavelli's emphasis on the need to develop a popular will. But it must be combined with the more calculating aspects of Machiavelli's advice so that the modern prince can assess the possibilities inherent in a given situation and decide how best to act. The prince gives way to the party, but the party must learn how to replace the state.

3. HEGEMONY: STATE AND CIVIL SOCIETY, COERCION AND CONSENT

Marx, following Hegel, sees the private sphere of civil society as belonging to the same domain as the economic structure, while the state belongs to the superstructure. In Gramsci, although the economy remains as the 'base', it seems that civil society joins the state as part of the superstructure. This is not entirely clear, however, as Perry Anderson points out (1976: 12–13). First, Anderson explains, Gramsci has a model in which the state and civil society are contrasted with one another so that 'when the State trembled a sturdy structure of civil society was at once revealed' (Gramsci 1971: 238). According to this view the state is only one of the structures in society and behind it stands the complex mechanisms of civil society that buttress and support it.

But Gramsci's work contains two other formulations as well. Another model has it that rather than being distinct, the state encompasses civil society so that 'State = political society + civil society, in other words hegemony protected by the armour of coercion' (ibid., p. 263). A further view maintains that the state does not simply encompass civil society but is identical to it: 'By "State" should be understood not only the apparatus of government, but also the "private" apparatus of "hegemony" or civil society' (ibid., p. 261).

The existence of these differing distinctions between the state and civil society leaves us with two options. The first is to recognise with Anderson that there are serious conflicts and tensions in Gramsci's writings and that we should be careful when reading him. This is certainly true, but it should certainly not amount to a rejection of what he has to say. A more worthwhile approach is to use Gramsci's 'antinomies' as an excuse to break from the straitjacket of analytical precision and recognise that the conflicts in Gramsci's work reflect in some way the tensions in society itself. Gramsci's lack of clarity in outlining the roles and functions of state and civil society is an inevitable consequence of the fact that in more advanced capitalist societies the spheres of state and civil society become increasingly entwined. Thus Gramsci's 'confusion' of the realms of state and civil society actually represents a theoretical advance or a transcendence of a more serious problem, which is orthodox Marxism's tendency towards a rigid separation of the two spheres. For as Gramsci's writings make clear, the traditional distinctions between state or political society and civil society, or between base and superstructure, are only analytical distinctions and to fully understand the different spheres, it is necessary to take a more integrated and dialectical approach to the question of their relation.

This leads to the central concept in Gramsci's vocabulary, that of hegemony. Roughly speaking, hegemony refers to the level of consent reached in civil society as opposed to the more coercive sphere of political society or the state. We know that there are problems formulating hegemony in this way as the two domains cannot really be separated. It can be argued that hegemony or consent is not confined to civil society but is also generated by the parliamentary institutions of the political sphere. Nevertheless, the distinction between the more coercive aspects of class domination (as represented by the repressive bodies of state power) and the consensual aspects of wider society is well outlined in Gramsci's distinction between the situation in the East (in particular Russia) and that of the more developed West. Accounting for the reasons why revolution occurred in Russia, but why transformation in the West is more difficult, he writes:

> In the East the State was everything, civil society was primordial and gelatinous; in the West, there was a proper relation between State and civil society, and when the State trembled a sturdy structure of civil society was at once revealed. The State was only an outer ditch, behind which there stood a powerful system of fortresses and earthworks . . . (Gramsci 1971: 238)

This sturdy structure in civil society represents the mechanisms by which social consent is developed and maintained. Gramsci's point is that in Russia this aspect of society was weak and power was more closely reliant on coercion and conflict. Thus the task for revolutionaries in the East was to muster enough force to take state power. However, in the West it is necessary for revolutionaries to gain consent within civil society in order to confront the powerful fortresses and earthworks that the bourgeoisie has at its disposal.

In making this contrast between East and West, Gramsci is developing a distinction between force and consent or between the coercive apparatus of state power and the consensual institutions of civil society. Again, it might be claimed that this distinction owes more to Machiavelli than it does to Marx, although this is perhaps a bit unfair to Marx and Engels and in particular to their detailed political writings. However, these writings tend to focus on specific moments of crisis (such as the rise of Bonapartism and the suppression of the Paris Commune) where force comes to the fore. Subsequent interpreters have often failed to acknowledge the exceptional nature of these moments of state crisis and have therefore been unable to confront the main absence in these writings – the operation of 'normal' consensual institutions of bourgeois society. Consequently, many interpretations of the political writings of Marx and Engels tend to emphasise the instrumentalist conception of the state as an 'armed body of men' or a committee of the bourgeoisie and an instrument of coercion without paying due attention to the question of social cohesion and consensus. This in turn is usually combined with the economic reductionist view that the state and civil society are in any case merely epiphenomena of the economic mode of production. In contrast to this tendency in classical Marxism to overemphasise force and downplay consent and to emphasise the economic at the expense of the political and cultural, Gramsci talks of Machiavelli's centaur, a hybrid creature that is half animal and half human so that the animal part corresponds to force, violence and authority, while the human half represents consent, civilisation and hegemony (ibid., p. 170).

Machiavelli distinguishes between rulership by force and rulership through the moral and intellectual power that he calls *virtù*. As he says in *The Prince*, 'there are two ways of contending; one by using laws, the other, force. The first is appropriate for men, the second for animals' (Machiavelli 1988: 85). To become dominant and civilised it is necessary to possess moral and intellectual authority. However, the centaur is a combination of both human and beast and the two halves cannot exist separately of each other. It is not a matter of choosing consent over force, but of how they combine. We can see an example of this combination in Gramsci's statement on the role of parliamentary democracy, where he writes:

> The 'normal' exercise of hegemony on the now classical terrain of the parliamentary regime is characterised by the combination of force and consent, which balance each other reciprocally without force predominating excessively over consent. Indeed, the attempt

is always made to ensure that force will appear to be based on the consent of the majority. (Gramsci 1971: 80)

However, this statement is complex in a number of ways. First, it undermines the usual distinction between hegemony and coercion and suggests that hegemony in fact combines consent with force. Secondly, it undermines the view that hegemony is exclusively confined to the sphere of civil society and that the state is primarily a coercive body. According to this quote, the state, and in particular its parliamentary apparatus, is also based on hegemony and consent. The state, now conceived as much more than just the coercive instrument of the ruling class, plays the role of securing the unity of the dominant group and spreading this consensus through society. In other words, the state, instead of being contrasted with hegemony, should be seen as the main organiser of hegemony and the body by which consensus is developed throughout the whole of society.

The state is the ultimate means by which the unity and rulership of the dominant group can be achieved and it certainly puts at their disposal a considerable coercive apparatus. But at the same time the state has an ethical function in that it is an important means by which the ruling group gets across its ideas, norms, values and worldview. For Marx, the state acts to present the interests of the ruling class as the general interest. For Gramsci, this must be done in an organic way through the various institutions of civil society and through the leading and directing role of the state. Hegemony operates through an institutional ensemble and is based on the leadership of a certain group or combination of groups. This occurs in all spheres and Gramsci is keen to stress the cultural aspect of this when he writes that 'every state is ethical in as much as one of its most important functions is to raise the great mass of the population to a particular cultural and moral level'. But he continues by saying that this level also 'corresponds to the needs of the productive forces for development' (ibid., p. 258).

We must come to the conclusion, therefore, that the state, civil society and the economy are inseparably linked and that the process whereby hegemony develops, rather than being limited to a particular sphere, operates across a wide terrain. This is even more the case in the West, where Gramsci argues that the brute force of the state gives way to the more subtle mechanisms of social control and consensus. Hegemony corresponds to the construction, organisation and distribution of this consensus through and beyond the state and civil society. The supremacy of a social group is maintained in two ways – as domination and as intellectual and moral leadership. This role is realised through the state while, by definition, those groups who do not enjoy state power are destined to be fragmented, subaltern and subject to domination. Gramsci breaks from economic determinism by arguing that hegemony does not flow automatically from the economic position of the dominant group, but that it has to be constructed and negotiated and that it has to take into account the interests of those groups over which it is to be exercised. But although Gramsci rejects crude determinism, he does not deny the importance of the economy in shaping this process and argues that 'though hegemony is ethical-political, it must also be economic, must necessarily be based on the decisive function exercised by the leading group in the decisive nucleus of economic activity' (ibid., p. 161). Again we see the unique position of Gramsci, of someone who is trying to maintain the importance of the economy while rejecting economism and who is trying to stress the significance of culture and ethics while avoiding slipping into the culturalism many interpreters attribute to him. He is trying to balance force with consent, state with civil society, structure with superstructure, while ultimately his efforts cry out for these distinctions to be transcended.

4. HEGEMONY: HISTORICAL BLOC AND PASSIVE REVOLUTION

The idea of hegemony as social consent to be balanced against the role of force is important, but it would be wrong to reduce hegemony to this relation, as it concentrates too much on the relation between social groups so that one group is seen as dominant (through coercion or consent) while the other is dominated, one group leading while the other is led. This is sometimes the interpretation given to Gramsci's related notion of the historical bloc, which is seen as the way in which a dominant group constructs a ruling alliance incorporating some groups into the ruling bloc while offering concessions and incentives to others. However, Gramsci has a deeper, more structural conception of the historical bloc which sees it not simply in terms of the relation between groups but also as the relation between groups and social structures. Returning to familiar terminology, but using it in a new context, he writes: 'Structures and superstructures form an "historical bloc". That is to say the complex, contradictory and discordant *ensemble* of the superstructures is the reflection of the *ensemble* of the social relations of production' (Gramsci 1971: 366).

So although the historical bloc concerns the relation between different social agents, this must be seen within the context of the relationship between the economic structure and the politico-ethical superstructure, a relation which is realised through the activity of different social groups. By relating the historical bloc to the question of hegemony, Gramsci is attempting to give the base–superstructure relation a more dynamic character. Social hegemony is not given but must be constantly reproduced and developed. The historical bloc represents the complex interaction of various social and historical forces, ideas and relations.

The structural nature of the historical bloc means that groups are limited in the role that they can play. Gramsci avoids the voluntarist view that any social group can put itself forward as leading. For a group to become hegemonic it must have behind it the economic, political and cultural conditions that allow it to emerge as a leading force. Although this role may emerge within civil society, to become hegemonic it must be developed through the state, which plays a vital role in the development of hegemony and the historical bloc. As Gramsci says: 'The historical unity of the ruling classes is realised by the state, and their history is essentially the history of States' (ibid., p. 52). The state helps forge a unity between the different components of the ruling bloc. Rather than being automatic, class rulership must be constructed and maintained. The state acts as the institutional terrain on which this process of construction and negotiation takes place, but at the same time, it also plays a vital organisational role in relation to other social structures. As we have stressed, hegemony represents not only the relation between groups, but also the relation between groups and structures. A powerful hegemony will therefore be more than just the domination of one group or bloc over another, it will also be about the way that the ruling group can cultivate its rulership in relation to other social processes. Of particular importance is the relation between the state and the economic sphere. As Gramsci says of developments in Italy: 'Through the legislative intervention of the State, and by means of the corporative organisation – relatively far-reaching modifications are being introduced into the country's economic structure in order to accentuate the "plan of production"' (ibid., p. 120).

This point is raised in the context of an elaboration of another of
Gramsci's important concepts, that of passive revolution, and relates to
the way in which groups may strengthen their position by acting in
accordance with wider social developments. Like many of his other
concepts, passive revolution is not straightforward and contains two
aspects. First, ruling groups or blocs may maintain their position on
the back of deeper or underlying developments. In the context of Italy,
Gramsci is referring to changes in the economic sphere where the
industrialisation of the north and the introduction of new methods of
production were radically altering social life. However, the passive
revolution is passive as well as revolutionary in that the ruling group
cultivates social change without mass participation. Although socially
everyone is affected by these changes, politically this process represents the conscious exclusion of popular participation. It is hoped that
by cultivating broad social changes, direct popular involvement can be
avoided. It is revolution without revolution.

Gramsci argues that the situation of passive revolution is often
characteristic of a weak rather than a strong hegemony. Often the
ruling bloc lacks security and is under threat from other social forces.
The purpose of the passive revolution is to offer concessions in order to
ward off the threat of emerging forces, cultivating social developments
and offering the bare minimum of reform in order to gain consent from
the masses while outflanking those forces that might offer a more
radical alternative. The passive revolution is the manipulation of a
developing situation by the ruling group based on taking advantage of
underlying changes while absorbing the opposition. These forces often
cultivate the notion of modernisation or transformation, but the real
aim of the passive revolution is the maintenance of the status quo.

However, Gramsci believes that the consequences of Italy's passive
revolution were serious, leading to a weak state, hegemony and ruling
class. The new Italian state was founded on a restrictive hegemonic
base, while the compromise between the urban industrial north and
the agrarian south was responsible for a weak political unity. Ultimately, for Gramsci, the Risorgimento was a failure and an indication
that not all historical blocs are able to achieve a high level of hegemony. Gramsci is concerned to explain the weakness of the Italian
historical bloc partly in order to develop an understanding of the way
that fascism was able to exploit the crisis. He explains the rise of
fascism in terms of a hegemonic crisis where the masses become

detached from their traditional parties and beliefs. He talks of a crisis of authority and writes:

> If the ruling class has lost its consensus, i.e. is no longer 'leading' but only 'dominant', exercising coercive force alone, this means precisely that the great masses have become detached from the traditional ideologies, and no longer believe what they used to believe. (Ibid., p. 276)

The rise of fascism (or Caesarism – a term that incorporates Marx's understanding of Bonapartism) is due to the failure of the ruling class to act combined with a failure of the masses to remain passive. Instead of the gradual change of passive revolution, a dangerous and violent situation emerges, in this case under the directorship of a 'man of destiny' (ibid., p. 210). Fascism is not so much the cause of the crisis but the consequence of a deeper crisis of hegemony in Italian society. It is part of a process where 'as soon as the dominant social group has exhausted its function, the ideological bloc tends to crumble away; then "spontaneity" may be replaced by "constraint" in ever less disguised and indirect forms' (ibid., pp. 60–1). So fascism emerges as a product of a hegemonic crisis but is not, itself, able to create a new hegemony. Rather than establishing a new social hegemony, Caesarism is a standoff reflecting a deep-seated imbalance between hegemony and force, coercion and consent.

5. HEGEMONIC STRATEGY: WARS OF POSITION AND MANOEUVRE EAST AND WEST

So far we have been concerned to stress that although Gramsci rejects the cruder versions of economic determinism, he is keen to maintain the importance of structural situations ranging from the economic to the cultural and political. In rejecting economic determinism Gramsci also rejects the view that social classes are straightforwardly defined. Classes are not homogeneous blocs with shared ideas and interests but are determined by a range of social, cultural, political and economic factors, creating various fractions and strata within classes. It is for this reason that social rulership is constructed rather than given. Ruling blocs must be put together from a range of different class strata. Hegemonic projects are both possible and necessary because of this

complex social stratification and the diversity of agents. The organisation
of different fractions of classes and their interests around a hegemonic
project makes strategy a vital aspect of the social process.

In his studies of Italian history Gramsci examines the development
of political projects around the Risorgimento and later the rise of
fascism, but he relates these to the social and historical context in order
to understand their potential and limitations. To understand these
events we must distinguish between the hegemonic conditions that
exist (such as the economic situation, the development of civil society
and the historical weakness of the ruling class) and the actual articulation of hegemonic projects by particular groups and fractions. The term
'hegemonic project' can be applied to the aims and actions of these
groups and the various tactics and strategies that are deployed in order
to achieve them. But, as Gramsci's passage on social crisis makes clear,
these projects must be understood in their economic and political
context:

> Incurable structural contradictions have revealed themselves
> (reached maturity), and despite this, the political forces which are
> struggling to conserve and defend the existing structure itself
> are making every effort to cure them, within certain limits, and to
> overcome them. (Gramsci 1971: 178)

Structural conditions provide the background conditions for political forces to struggle in order to conserve a situation that is to their
advantage. Their hegemonic projects are both motivated by these
structural contradictions and limited or undermined by them. Likewise,
if it is the case that certain groups are struggling to preserve a particular situation, then there will be other groups who are struggling to
transform a situation. We therefore have a scenario where two groups
or bloc may be battling against each other in order to preserve or
change a situation but where each group may be helped or hindered
by social developments, crises and contradictions and other structural
conditions.

In order to conceptualise this relationship between hegemonic
projects and the social terrain on which they must operate Gramsci
deploys his famous terminology of trenches, earthworks and fortifica-
tions. As we have already noted, the conception of the state as an outer
ditch beyond which stand the various earthworks of civil society is

used by Gramsci to indicate the complexity of the structure of the West in comparison to the East. This has important strategic connotations in that the conservative forces in the West can utilise these defences in order to protect their hegemony. Those forces attempting to win power must therefore engage in a complex battle. To make this point Gramsci distinguishes between two types of strategy: the war of positions and the war of manoeuvre. The latter is a frontal assault that might be compared to the seizure of power by the Bolsheviks in 1917. This was possible because, as Gramsci says, the state was primordial while civil society was gelatinous (ibid., p. 238). However, in the West a more prolonged and tactical battle is necessary which must be conducted through the institutions of civil society. In the West there is a better balance between the state and civil society and between the economy and the state – in other words, Western society enjoys greater levels of cohesion and integration. The complexity of civil society means that ideological struggle becomes important. Those forces that hope to win state power must already play a leading role in civil society and must already be culturally, politically and ideologically influential: 'A social group can, and indeed must, already exercise "leadership" before winning governmental power' (ibid., p. 57).

Gramsci was not alone in making such a contrast between the East and the West. The Bolshevik leaders were themselves well aware of the differences, as is shown by Lenin's claim that:

> The whole difficulty of the Russian revolution is that it was much easier for the Russian revolutionary working class to start than it is for the West European classes, but it is much more difficult for us to continue. It is more difficult to start a revolution in West European countries because there the revolutionary proletariat is opposed by the higher thinking that comes with culture, while the working class is in a state of cultural slavery. (Lenin 1961: 464)

Like Gramsci Lenin argues that it is necessary to take cultural and political factors into account when assessing the possibility of taking power. Along with culture we can talk about the influence of science, technology and education. All these make winning power more diffi-cult, but at the same time, once power is won, it is easier to maintain as the ruling group now has on its side the fortresses and earthworks of civil society. For these reasons, as Lenin recognises, holding onto power in Russia was more difficult. It could be said that the Bolsheviks managed to win political hegemony, but were unable to establish a strong enough social hegemony. The later development of Stalinism in the USSR was a reflection of the dominance of the state over civil society.

As the examples of Russia and Italy indicate, strong hegemonic rule is dependent upon the exercise of power through the structures of civil society. To win this power, the forces of counter-hegemony must engage in a complex tactical battle to capture the support of the masses and undermine the power of the ruling bloc. Again, this emphasis on tactics and strategy derives from the influence of Machiavelli. The revolution-ary party as the modern prince must operate on a diverse social terrain, uniting various different social groups, political forces and interests. Marxism, for both Gramsci and Lenin, becomes infused with the art of statecraft. Both emphasise the real tasks facing the Marxists, the problems of mobilising and coordinating different classes and class fractions. Both realise the difference between frontal assault and a more tactical understanding of the mechanisms of power. However, Gramsci does get something wrong when he criticises Trotsky as being a theorist of frontal attacks in a period when they lead only to defeats. Trotsky, like Lenin, also stresses the differences between East and West and writes in strikingly Gramscian terms that it is

> necessary to understand that it will not be possible to overthrow the bourgeoisie automatically, mechanically, merely because it is condemned by history. On the highly complex field of political struggle we find, on the one side, the bourgeoisie with its forces and resources and, on the opposing side, the working class with its various layers, moods, levels of development, with its Commu-nist Party struggling against other parties and organisations for influence over the working masses. In this struggle the Communist Party . . . has to manoeuvre, now attacking, now retreating, always consolidating its influence, conquering new positions until the favourable moment arrives for the overthrow of the bourgeoisie. (Trotsky 1974: 7)

The war of positions is like siege warfare and requires 'exceptional qualities of patience and inventiveness'. But once won it is 'decisive definitively' (Gramsci 1971: 239). Like a war of colonisation, it is a slow struggle of territorial conquest. To win power it is necessary to forge a new will out of diverse forces. Some sections of the counter-hegemonic bloc may be difficult to mobilise – the peasantry for example is territorially dispersed and lacks homogeneity. For Gramsci, the counter-hegemonic alliance is not an alliance of equals – the different component parts of the alliance must be led and directed by the working class and the party. However, this is not a top-down process. The party's relationship to the class must be an organic one so that 'the essential task is that of systematically and patiently ensuring that this force is formed, developed and rendered ever more homogeneous, compact, and self-aware' (ibid., p. 185). The party should be an expression of the real experiences of the masses and for this reason Gramsci places great emphasis on the role of those he calls organic intellectuals, who are a part of the masses but can play a leading and directing role. Marxism needs to go beyond its scientific analysis and so among the masses to win over hearts and minds.

6. IDEOLOGY AND THE ROLE OF THE INTELLECTUAL

Orthodox Marxism, as we have argued, tends to concentrate on the dominant character of the ruling class as given by its economic position. Hegemony is a radical alternative to this view that emphasises the importance of conscious direction, moral and intellectual leadership and the need to construct and develop consensus. The power of ideological control is based on the ruling class conveying its beliefs and values. Hegemony is about the assertion of cultural and moral supremacy through persuading people to accept the beliefs and values of the ruling group. For this reason Gramsci spends a lot of time examining cultural processes, something neglected by Marx, who tended to view consciousness as a more spontaneous and uniform development.

Gramsci links the development of consciousness to the existence of intellectuals and the realisation of hegemony. He believes that

> Every social group, coming into existence on the original terrain of an essential function in the world of economic production, creates together with itself, organically, one or more strata of intellectuals which give it homogeneity and an awareness of its own function not only in the economic but also in the social and political fields. (Gramsci 1971: 5)

These intellectuals are organic because they are closely tied to class positions. They are not, as Weber would argue, a distinct social stratum or group. Nor are they an elite group with special interests. Gramsci does talk of the traditional, professional intellectuals such as academics and the clergy, who may have (or aspire to) some sort of autonomy. In Italy, the imbalance between the north and the south meant that southern intellectuals tended to play traditional roles such as clerics and state administrators. The northern intellectuals are more organic and are associated with political parties, the workforce and the towns.

This distinction between traditional and organic intellectuals is based on the importance of social function. The role of the intellectual has as much to do with organisation as does with ideas. As Gramsci says:

> By 'intellectuals' must be understood not those strata commonly described by this term, but in general the entire social stratum which exercises an organisational function in the wide sense – whether in the field of production, or in that of culture, or in that of political administration. (ibid., p. 97)

The functioning of the intellectual is bound up with the process of hegemony and the need to transmit ideas and cement and unify the ruling bloc. Gramsci relates the function of the intellectual to the organisation of knowledge, which in turn is related to the wider organisation of society and the sphere of production. This organisational role in developing social cohesion is bound up with the development of a collective will. Here again we find an active, dynamic conception of history: 'One cannot make politics-history without this passion, without this sentimental connection between intellectuals and people-nation' (ibid., p. 418). This has organic and strategic connotations in that it is necessary to 'stimulate the formation of homogeneous, compact social blocs, which will give birth to their own intellectuals, their own commandos, their own vanguard – who will in turn react upon these blocs in order to develop them' (ibid., pp. 204–5).

Different social groups have their own conceptions of the world, which are manifested in their actions. There is an important link between these conceptions or worldviews and hegemonic position. Those groups lacking independence and autonomy will be ideologically subordinate to the hegemonic group and will adopt their worldview as their own. Philosophy and politics are linked together in that 'philosophies', for Gramsci, are tied up with the leading role of intellectuals in shaping organic blocs and normative action. Above all they are a particular elaboration of worldviews, derived from hegemony in the sense that they are the expression of groups seeking domination or moral leadership. Philosophy is history in action and the philosopher is the intellectual who modifies the environment and the relations humans are engaged in. That is why, for Gramsci, Marxism is more like a philosophy than a science. It is a guide to action. The philosophy of praxis

> consists precisely in asserting the moment of hegemony as essential to its conception of the state and in attaching 'full weight' to the cultural factor, to cultural activity, to the necessity for a cultural front alongside the merely economic and merely political ones. (Gramsci 1995: 345)

In fact, these various processes – cultural, economic, political, and intellectual – are interlinked, and a successful political party must critically relate to them all:

> With the extension of mass parties and their organic coalescence with the intimate (economic-productive) life of the masses themselves, the process whereby popular feeling is standardised ceases to be mechanical and causal ... and becomes conscious and critical. (Gramsci 1971: 429)

This critical function is not restricted to the role of the revolutionary party in modern society. We could also look at the revolutionary potential of the ideas and movements of the Reformation and Renaissance. Gramsci compares the two, claiming that the Reformation was a cruder but broader and more popular national movement. It produced new religious teachers who were innovative, mobilising and capable of penetrating the everyday life of the masses. It was a religious movement but one that combined a new morality with a popular revolution. The Renaissance, by contrast, was much narrower, and although it was potentially more progressive in its humanist ideology, it was confined to an aristocratic elite and not translated into a popular worldview. It failed to produce organic intellectuals. Therefore, although it may not have been as sophisticated as the Renaissance, the Reformation in fact had more impact on intellectual development and paved the way for the Enlightenment. It was the religious worldview of the Reformation that was ultimately responsible for the modernisation and secularisation of Europe.

Generally, however, religion plays a backward social role, creating the impression of a natural, God-given order. Religion as a way of everyday life might therefore be seen as a variant of common sense, an important concept in Gramsci's understanding of the relationship between ideology and everyday life. Common sense relates to various myths and superstitions, mentalities, feelings and sentiments and plays a passive but pacifying role, being quietly absorbed and internalised by the masses. It is therefore implicit in our day-to-day practical activity, but at the same time it limits our understanding of the world and gives a disjointed and episodic view of social life. Common sense is not an explicit ideology of the ruling class but is something more organic which we inherit from the past and often uncritically absorb, its effect on the individual being almost psychologistic.

Although Gramsci gives common sense this negative function, he does see it as an important first stage in an alternative hegemonic project. Common sense relates to practical problems, but it is unable to resolve them because it lacks a critical attitude. The philosophy of praxis is critical of existing modes of thought but it must first base itself on existing culture and common-sense views and make critical existing modes of activity in order to supersede them. Politics must base itself on the relation between common sense and philosophy. The basis for a radical politics is a critical consciousness of what one already is. It is about recognising our place in the world and our belonging to a particular grouping. Consciousness of being part of a hegemonic force is the first step in transforming our consciousness and going beyond common sense. This might be related to Machiavelli's concept of *virtù*, based on a conscious and purposive will actively engaged in the world.

Gramsci uses the term 'catharsis' to describe the development of consciousness within a person or a group. He describes this as the passage from the purely economic to the ethical–political. It is the movement from structure to superstructure in consciousness. Catharsis is like the realisation of human freedom where

structure ceases to be an external force which crushes man,

assimilates him to itself and makes him passive; and is transformed into a means of freedom, an instrument to make a new
ethico-political form and a source of new initiatives. (Gramsci
1971: 367)

Catharsis is like the historical process taking place inside people's
heads. Indeed, having made the point that the historical bloc is the
combination of structure and superstructure Gramsci also believes that
'Man is to be conceived as a historical bloc of purely individual and
subjective elements and of mass and objective or material elements
with which the individual is in an active relationship' (ibid., p. 360).
More generally it can be said that hegemony itself is the overcoming of
the economic–corporative moment and the movement to a new level
of class consciousness and cultural and intellectual understanding.

Jorge Larrain has written an interesting book on Marxism and
ideology which argues that there are two conceptions of ideology,
one negative, the other positive. As has been argued in the previous
chapter, Marx's conception of ideology and his theory of commodity
fetishism is linked to the effects of the capitalist system itself. For
Larrain, Marx's conception of ideology is negative in that it involves a
distortion and misrepresentation of the real situation; in particular,
'ideology refers to a limited material practice which generates ideas
that misrepresent social contradictions in the interest of the ruling
class' (Larrain 1983: 27). In Marx this negative conception of ideology
is most closely associated with economic relations – for example, the
distorting effect of the wage-form and commodity-form. But Gramsci's
discussion of common sense is somewhat similar in that it is also a
negative conception of ideology based on a passively received consciousness that mystifies the real contradictions of social life. However,
Gramsci adds something by stressing the cultural side of this social
consciousness. Ideologies are related to the economic, but they are also
cultural and political; they are a key organic part of the historical bloc
that unites structure and superstructure.

However, this rather more structural or organic conception of
ideology is accompanied by a more positive conception of ideology. As
Gramsci puts it:

It seems to me that there is a potential element of error in
assessing the value of ideologies, due to the fact . . . that the name

ideology is given both to the necessary superstructure of a particular structure and to the arbitrary elucbrations of particular
individuals . . . One must therefore distinguish between historically
organic ideologies, those, that is, which are necessary to a given
structure, and ideologies that are arbitrary, rationalistic, or 'willed'
(Gramsci 1971: 376–7).

Here ideology is taking on a positive role. As Larrain remarks in relation to both Gramsci and Lenin, 'ideology now refers to class political
ideas instead of referring to the masking of contradictions' (Larrain
1983: 64). Gramsci argues that ideologies should be analysed historically and as part of the superstructure:'they "organise" human masses,
and create the terrain on which men move, acquire consciousness of
their position, struggle, etc.' (Gramsci 1971: 377). In other words, social
cohesion and consent is not simply a passive effect of the system
(whether economic or cultural) but is something that has to be posi-
tively achieved through the actions of people. And because ideology
is the terrain on which the ruling class must achieve consent, it is also
an important field of conflict where alternative ideologies, worldviews
or hegemonic projects may be advanced. By linking ideology to hegemony Gramsci gives us a more detailed and developed understanding
of the politics of consensus and conflict which stresses the fact that
the consensual aspect of ideology is never given but always has to be
achieved.

7. RECENT APPLICATIONS: HISTORICAL, CULTURAL AND ECONOMIC THEORY

This chapter concludes by briefly looking at how Gramsci's ideas have
inspired two recent debates. First we will look at the cultural and historical debates surrounding the nature of the English Revolution, then
we shall look at the development of Gramsci's theory of Fordism.

It has been argued that Gramsci adds a degree of complexity to
the Marxist understanding of bourgeois society. Rulership comes not
simply from the dominant economic position of the ruling class, nor
from the simple exercise of coercive force, but must be based on the
construction of social consent. The controversial analysis of the English
Revolution carried out by Perry Anderson and Tom Nairn puts this
theory into practice by arguing that English history and culture should

be understood in terms of a disjuncture between the economically dominant class and the dominant political bloc.

The Nairn–Anderson thesis argues that British capitalism lacks innovation and dynamism owing to a backward-looking and anachronistic social and political culture. This can be traced back to the earliness of the English Revolution and the fact that social and political change was based on an historic compromise. Because of the earliness of the revolution, the emerging capitalist class was not yet strong enough to fully secure its victory over the landed classes. Instead, the Civil War led to a compromise between the emerging bourgeoisie and the old feudal classes. It was a bourgeois revolution by proxy. It is true that this paved the way for the momentous development of capitalism, but it also produced a new ruling class that was heavily influenced by aristocratic residues. Seeing this new historical bloc in terms of Gramsci's formulation of structure and superstructure, Anderson argues:

> After a bitter, cathartic revolution, which transformed the structure but not the superstructures of English society, a landed aristocracy, underpinned by a powerful mercantile group, became the first dominant capitalist class in Britain ... the bourgeoisie won two modest victories, lost its nerve and ended up by losing its identity. (Anderson 1992: 29)

Thus the new historical bloc led to a rapid development of capitalism but ultimately began to restrict further development. The archaic state was not helped by the development of Britain's imperial role, which reinforced the traditional institutions. When economic problems did develop, the state apparatus was therefore ill-equipped to deal with them. Britain's historical bloc was feudalistic and 'gentlemanly' in its outlook, imbued with a set of beliefs, values and traditions that were inappropriate for the development of modern capitalism. British capitalism was ultimately undermined by British culture, politics and state and civil society; by Eton, Oxbridge and the House of Lords; and by its amateurish personnel, who failed to develop a modern, progressive worldview.

This in turn had its effect on the development of the working class so that 'in England, a supine bourgeoisie produced a subordinate proletariat. It handed on no impulse of liberation, no revolutionary values, no universal language' (ibid., p. 35). In Gramsci's terms, the British working class developed as a corporate class – that is, a class that accepts its position within the system and is unable to transform itself into a hegemonic group. It has a limited consciousness of its role, enshrined, in this case, in the structures of British labourism. However, this view of Anderson's is contested by a number of British historians, in particular E. P. Thompson, who argues that the Anderson–Nairn model of a hegemonic (and aristocratic) ruling class and a subordinate, corporatist working class is too schematic. Likewise, the focus on the dramatic episode of the English Revolution fails to do justice to the complexities of history. Thompson's alternative is to introduce a history from below that focuses on popular movements, customs and traditions. This approach is more subjective and cultural and less structural than that of Anderson and Nairn. It argues that 'hegemony is not just imposed (or contested) but is articulated in the everyday intercourse of a community' (Thompson 1993: 345). Here Thompson is moving towards a more cultural definition of hegemony, an approach that is shared by the Marxist cultural critic Raymond Williams. Like Thompson, Williams argues that hegemony must be related to what he calls the structure of feeling, which is made up of various cultural values and traditions. Challenging the accepted metaphor he argues that this, in fact, is the true material base of society (Williams 1982).

These approaches were themselves accused of being too culturalist with too much focus on shared experiences, meanings and values at the expense of objective social relations like class. To an extent, however, both sides were making similar points; that is, that they emphasised the role of politics and culture in shaping historical development. The danger of these approaches is that they overemphasise the historico-cultural aspect of the hegemonic process at the expense of the economic, which, after all, is the accepted basis of the Marxist approach. An alternative application of Gramsci's ideas to modern society was developed by the Fordist and regulation approaches, which drew on Gramsci's writings on the organisation of the production process and its effects on wider society.

Gramsci's terms 'Fordism' and 'Taylorism' describe the reorganisation and modernisation of the production process in line with new developments in technology and management. The Ford motor company best reflects the use of new techniques of conveyor-belt mass production leading to a new consumer-based society. For Gramsci these developments have a wider social character which he describes as Americanism. In the US, the lack of an aristocratic or parasitic class sediment (in contrast to what Anderson claims is the case in Britain) made it easier to develop a modern society based on the rationalising drive of capitalist production methods. Here, Gramsci's claim is that hegemony is born in the factory (Gramsci 1971: 285). The specialisation of the production line leads to an increasingly complex division of labour which requires a type of social education and training. These help enforce political and ideological control, while persuasion – in the form of high wages, social benefits and consumer goods – is backed up with coercion in the form of attacks on the trade unions and other forms of workers' self-organisation. In other cases – in western Europe, for example – workers may be co-opted by giving their political organisations and trade unions a more active role in the historical bloc. But in both cases corporatism prevails so that the majority of workers are not in a position to advance their own demands. Gramsci writes that Americanisation requires a particular environment, social structure and type of state (ibid., p. 293). The Fordist state plays an active role in developing the economy and civil society. The interventionist or regulatory role of the state is backed up with underlying changes in economic production and the co-option of the organisations of the working class. Fordism, therefore, might be seen as a particular example of passive revolution:

> Through the legislative intervention of the State, and by means of the corporative organisation . . . relatively far-reaching modifica-tions are being introduced into the country's economic structure in order to accentuate the 'plan of production' element; in other words, that socialisation of and co-operation in the sphere of production are being increased, without however touching (or at least not going beyond the regulation and control of) individual and group appropriation of profit. (Ibid., p. 120)

Gramsci goes on to argue that in Italy this passive revolution is attempting to develop the productive forces of industry under the leadership of the traditional ruling classes. Such an example highlights the errors of those (for example, Norberto Bobbio) who believe that Gramsci emphasises the political and cultural superstructure rather than the economic structure. Gramsci analyses the development of superstructure in accordance with structure where 'what is involved is the reorganisation of the structure and the real relations between men on the one hand and the world of the economy or of production on the other' (ibid., p. 263). But at the same time, this combination of factors undermines the view that economic forces are all-powerful. Economic processes are tendencies that are affected by counteracting forces (Gramsci 1995: 429); therefore Taylorism and Fordism, while confirming the importance of the economic structure, are also examples of attempts to overcome these tendential laws (ibid., p. 433).

Americanism and Fordism reflect a growing rationalisation of society that permeates all aspects of popular life. It develops a tendency towards standardisation and conformity, including ways of thinking and acting. This is encouraged by the development of a mass media, a bureaucratic apparatus, and a popular-culture industry. It affects everything from culture to consciousness to morals and values. It could be argued that after the Second World War these changes were institutionalised by means of a passive revolution. Such a view is compatible with the theories put forward by the regulation school, which argues that the post-war period is characterised by a new regime of accumulation; in other words, that a number of deep social changes have occurred which are organised into a regime that helps facilitate the accumulation of capital. In particular, this period is characterised by a new form of state regulation based on the interventionist policies of Keynesianism, corporatism, nationalisation and welfarism. The era of Fordism is based on the state playing an active role in the economy and civil society in the belief that this is the best way both to advance the accumulation of capital and to secure consensus in civil society. This can be linked back to Gramsci's view that

> the state must be conceived of as an 'educator', in as much as it tends precisely to create a new type or level of civilisation. Because one is acting essentially on economic forces, reorganising and developing the apparatus of economic production, creating a new structure, the conclusion must not be drawn that superstructural factors should be left to themselves, to develop spontaneously . . . The state, in this field too, is an instrument of 'rationalisation', of acceleration and of Taylorism. (Gramsci 1971: 247)

However, this view of state intervention is now being reconsidered in light of the free-market policies of the 1980s. For many regulation theorists there has been a shift towards a post-Fordist regime of accumulation based on the deregulation of markets and the flexibility of production methods. For other analysts of post-war politics, the notion of periods of Fordism and post-Fordism is problematic in that it lays too much stress on the ability to regulate capitalism and wider society. It suggests that the contradictions of the capitalist mode of production and the dynamic of class conflict can both be resolved by some sort of institutional fix (see Joseph 1998 and Marsh et al. 1999). But this is to give regimes of accumulation too much power. It is to forget that Gramsci's notions of the integral state and the passive revolution are founded on the weakness of the bourgeoisie rather than on some inherent ability of capitalism to reorganise itself.

Ultimately, therefore, despite all the claims that have been made for him, Gramsci is not an advocate of culture or consensus or regulation. He is a revolutionary who believes that politics involves social conflict. In case there is any doubt, he writes: 'The philosophy of praxis . . . does not aim at the peaceful resolution of existing contradictions in history and society but is rather the very theory of these contradictions' (Gramsci 1995: 395). But to know how to act in a revolutionary way it is necessary to understand the importance of consensus as well as conflict. A revolutionary policy must therefore wait for the right moment – for a structural crisis or a breakdown in the hegemonic apparatus. And if it is to do this well, then it must be capable of building up its own hegemonic support if it is to move beyond conflict and establish a firm basis for its rule.

Chapter 4

ÉMILE DURKHEIM AND
FUNCTIONALISM

——— ◦⊂ ———

1. THE EMERGENCE OF POSITIVISM

The main themes of functionalist sociology are social cohesion, social equilibrium, regulation, integration and organisation. Society is seen as a bounded, self-maintaining system while social institutions and practices are seen in terms of their function in performing a social requirement and must be understood in terms of how they contribute to maintaining the social whole. Functionalist sociologists look at how social equilibrium is maintained and how society meets its needs and requirements. In particular, this makes from a strong emphasis on the idea of social cohesion.

As we shall see in the following sections, Émile Durkheim argues that social cohesion in small-scale societies depends on what he calls the collective conscience, expressed in religious beliefs and reinforced by ceremony, bringing people together in solidarity. Modern society evolves away from this type of solidarity and the hold of the collective conscience is weakened. However, for Durkheim, the paradox of modern societies is that as they become more individualised so they become more integrated. This, we will discover, is due to the nature of the division of labour.

Durkheim's approach contains a dual focus on normative and structural factors. Social order comes from a core of institutionalised values that are held in common. It is important to recognise the moral order that imparts shared values to the members of society. However, if we think of this in terms of the themes of this book, this institutionalisation of common values can be seen in terms of social cohesion, but less so in terms of a more active process of social consent. Durkheim tends to neglect individual agency and holds an oversocialised conception

66

of the human agent. It is often said that his is an integrated and harmonious view of society. There is little need for a concept of consensus
because there is little in the way of conflict, or at least, where there is
conflict, this is to be resolved through the adaptation of the system.

In the work of Talcott Parsons this becomes an evolutionary theory
of social change where systems develop in relation to changes in the
environment. Society is seen as a self-regulating system with a kind of
adjustment mechanism that keeps it in a state of equilibrium. This
has led to the widely held view that functionalist sociology is socially
conservative and this is certainly an easy claim to make in relation to
Parsons, whose work reflects the viewpoint of the post-war United
States and thus makes little reference to Marx or other radical theories.
However, Durkheim is more sympathetic to socialism and is influenced by the French utopian socialist Henri de Saint-Simon. But again,
it is Saint-Simon's evolutionary view of society (and his rationalism)
that most impresses Durkheim. Against Marx, Durkheim seems to
endorse order and stability rather than conflict or change. He is radical
in his own way, for example in his opposition to property inheritance,
and might be said to be communistic without being revolutionary.

As well as the influence of Saint-Simon, there is also the strong
influence of positivism and the idea of establishing a social science of
objective facts. Unlike Marx or Weber, Durkheim had little political
involvement and he defines his project in academic terms as a founder
of a discipline – sociology. In the 1870s France was undergoing big
intellectual changes, with great stress on science and the notion of
social progress. Combine the two and we get an emphasis on the role
of the scientific study of society in order to resolve social ills and aid
social progress.

Auguste Comte, in outlining his scientific methodology, strongly
opposed speculative and metaphysical approaches. From this Durkheim
inherits the idea of the importance of establishing a sociology free from
metaphysics, while laying down clear rules and methods to distinguish
it from other disciplines. Sociology is regarded as a science which
develops an overall view of society while examining different degrees
of crystallisation of social life. Sociology the is study of institutions and
the beliefs and modes of collective functioning: 'One may term an
institution all the beliefs and modes of behaviour instituted by the
collectivity: sociology can then be defined as the science of institutions,
their genesis and their functioning' (Durkheim 1982: 45).

Another positivist to influence Durkheim is Herbert Spencer. His advocacy of the free market leads to the view that social cohesion naturally follows from individual interests, that cohesion comes from spontaneous individual activity. Durkheim replies that the social cohesion provided by this individual activity is only momentary and superficial. Rather, it is the new occupational specialisation that is replacing the old collective conscience. As Steven Lukes says, this allows social cohesion to be reconciled with increased individualisation (Lukes 1973: 147).

Positivism stresses the importance of facts and these exist outside the individual. Social facts exist independently of our concepts and are known through empirical investigation. So although facts may consist of 'manners of acting, thinking and feeling', these are 'external to the individual . . . invested with a coercive power by virtue of which they exercise control over him' (Durkheim 1982: 52). Examples of this control would include legal, moral, religious and financial beliefs and practices. Durkheim goes on to argue that 'what constitutes social facts are the beliefs, tendencies and practices of the group taken collectively' (ibid., p. 54).

The Rules of Sociological Method looks at how each discipline must study its own particular field through careful treatment of empirical evidence. Durkheim's own study of suicide is based on the positivist method of establishing a causal relation based on empirical regularities, in this case to understand the social 'fact' of suicide. He looked at public records in different countries and how different rates might indicate various different causes. The suicide rate is a regularity of a factual nature and it is this rate, rather than the individual case, that the social scientist should study. This requires an 'objective' and detached researcher who is capable of remaining emotionally neutral and who works to establish precise scientific concepts. These are then applied by Durkheim in a functionalist manner so that 'we must determine whether there is a correspondence between the fact being considered and the general needs of the social organism' (ibid., p. 123).

Durkheim is also very much a rationalist and is concerned with the classification of science into an order of complexity. The positivistic method is seen as strongest in the most developed sciences – the natural sciences and mathematics. Durkheim's ambition is to put the social sciences on the same footing: his positivism centres on the extension of the scientific method to study of society. However, because his model is derived from the natural sciences their influence is strongly felt. Biology and medicine, for example, influence Durkheim's typology of different social forms. Evolutionary biology influences the view that 'societies are only different combinations of one and the same original society' (ibid., p. 116), while medical science influences Durkheim's distinction between normal and pathological behaviour. Durkheim sees as pathological some of the central aspects of modern society such as anomie or the lack of norms of behaviour, feelings of alienation and even social conflict. We can see that this is quite a dangerous approach, with Durkheim claiming: 'The principal purpose of any science of life, whether individual or social, is in the end to define and explain the normal state and distinguish it from the abnormal' (ibid., p. 54). This definition of normal and pathological, rather than explaining society, would seem to ideologically justify and reinforce it, helping to construct what Foucault would describe as a new discursive order.

Durkheim is opposed to an individualistic emphasis as might be found in utilitarianism with its rational acting individual. He argues the need to look at the wider system of social rules within which action takes place. Society is prior to the individual and forms an organic whole: 'society is not the mere sum of individuals, but the system formed by their association represents a specific reality which has its own characteristics' (ibid., p. 129). One of the ways in which Durkheim expresses this is through the idea of the collective conscience or collective habits which 'are expressed in definite forms such as legal or moral rules, popular sayings, or facts of social structure . . . they constitute a fixed object, a constant standard which is always to hand for the observer' (ibid., p. 82). Durkheim talks of collective representations as the condensation of the beliefs and values of a society: 'what collective representations express is the way in which the group thinks of itself in its relationships with the objects which affect it' (ibid., p. 40).

By classifying social beliefs and actions in such a way we see that Durkheim establishes a layer of social reality. Durkheim describes his study of the form and structure of society as a social morphology. He describes three different levels which may be listed as:

1. morphology – the substratum of collective life – volume, distribution and density of population, material objects – instruments, machines, raw materials, etc.;

2. institutions – the normative sphere – more or less formal legal and moral rules and norms, morals, religious dogmas, political forms, economics, professional roles, collective habits and routines;
3. collective representations – symbolic – societal values and ideals, various opinions, legends, myths, religious representations, emerging values and opinions.

Kenneth Thompson argues for a comparison between Durkheim's levels and Gramsci's stratified deposits that make up common sense, and Foucault's layers of discourse and regimes of truth (Thompson 1986: 21). We can also see similarities with a structuralist approach, with each layer exercising a degree of constraint. The structuralist aspect of Durkheim's morphology might be compared with the work of the Annales historians whom it inspired, presenting a multi-layered model with different layers of structure. There is a need to go beneath the surface layers to the deeper layers of society – the impersonal norms of thought and action. As Durkheim says: 'We must strip away that surface of ideas in order to penetrate to the deep things that they express more or less unreliably' (Durkheim 1982: 168).

2. RELIGION AND THE COLLECTIVE CONSCIENCE

In contrast to Weber, Durkheim's approach to religion is functional rather than substantive. Rather than looking at its content, he looks at how religion performs an essential social function in maintaining social cohesion through belief systems. Society needs religious functions to be performed in one way or another and therefore religion is real, if not in terms of its content, then in terms of its necessary social role so that 'all are true after their own fashion: All fulfil given conditions of human existence, though in different ways' (Durkheim 1995: 2). Thus religion is not an individual but a social thing providing us with beliefs, states of opinion, representations, rites and rituals:

> Religion is an eminently social thing. Religious representations are collective representations that express collective realities; rites are ways of acting that are born only in the midst of assembled groups and whose purpose is to evoke, maintain, or recreate certain mental states of those groups. (Ibid., p. 9)

Durkheim's mention of collective representations is important in defining what religion is. These collective representations provide us with a conception of ourselves, of each other and of our relations with the natural world. They are based on cooperation between people and are the combination of different ideas and feelings that have accumulated (ibid., p. 15). The collective or common conscience describes the beliefs and sentiments that are shared in common by members of society. Durkheim's use of the French term *'conscience'* implies both conscience and consciousness. This means a concern not just with cognitions – as might be the concern of positivism – but also with the beliefs and morals that give meaning and purpose to action, and which structure social life. The collective conscience creates common conditions of existence. It is not an expression of individual consciousness but something objective that develops according to its own laws. With the development of a collective conscience our morality is universalised.

Religion is the main form of collective conscience, imposing a uniformity of beliefs and actions: 'all known religions have been systems of ideas that tend to embrace the universality of things and to give us a representation of the world as a whole' (ibid., p. 140). Religious forces may also be seen as the sentiments of the group projected outwards and objectified so that 'religious forces are in fact only transfigured collective forces, that is, moral forces; they are made of ideas and feelings that the spectacle of society awakens in us' (ibid., p. 327).

Religion is fundamental to the classification of the external world. The social organisation of the group becomes the basis for the mental organisation of their ideas. Central to all religions is a set of fundamental representations and modes of ritual conduct. Rituals, as well as proving a basis for collective action, thus reinforcing collective beliefs, provide the basis for the social group's understanding of time. In primitive societies the division of time into days, weeks, months and years is based on rites, rituals, festivals, ceremonies and so on. This indicates religion's relation to underlying aspects of social life. Religion can be defined as a system of beliefs and rites, that is to say, of ideas, attitudes and actions towards sacred things. Beliefs are representations that express the nature of sacred things, rites are the rules of conduct regarding how we act towards these things. This unifies the groups and makes the members feel they are united by a common faith:

A religion is a unified system of beliefs and practices relative to sacred things, that is to say, things set apart and forbidden – beliefs and practices which united into one single moral community called a Church, all those who adhere to them. (Ibid., p. 44)

Religion divides the world into two domains – sacred and profane. We relate to the sacred through beliefs, rituals and rites, while the profane is opposed to the sacred and subordinate to it. The sacred must be protected – by taboos, prohibitions and so on – while the spiritual is separated from the everyday. Things are made sacred when they are set apart and forbidden or when they are kept within the bounds of specific actions. Religious and profane life each have their own space and time. The relationship between the sacred and profane is thus one of antagonism and mutual exclusivity. A basic social function of religion is to maintain this separation and lay down a system of beliefs, rules and prohibitions.

Or at least, this is the role that religion used to play. Durkheim's study attempts to define the social role of religion and how this role may be in decline. His looks at the role religion plays in primitive societies where the collective conscience is strong, but notes how the collective conscience has been progressively weakened by modern developments and in particular by the division of labour.

Shocking though it may have been at the time, Durkheim argues that primitive religions (*The Elementary Forms of Religious Life* concentrates on Australia), like all religions, 'fulfil the same needs, play the same role, and proceed from the same causes' (ibid., p. 3). The main difference is that primitive religions have more intellectual and moral uniformity. Above all, religion's function in simple societies is as the main basis of social solidarity.

Totemism is the most elementary form of religion. The members of the group or clan take a tribal name which makes them family members and designates them as a social group. The people are held to be of the same essence as if united by blood ties. They recognise the duties and obligations towards each other, obligations that may include aid, vengeance and mourning. The group projects its own sacredness onto nature. From this arises the classification of the world into groups and categories. Religious organisation is the basis of group organisation, which is the basis for categorisation.

Totemism unites the social group around a sacred object, from which derive obligations and rites of worship. The totem becomes an emblem that represents the group. It represents the collective beliefs and social practices of the group to the individuals who belong to it. This extends to customs, rituals and sacred practices. Totemism supports a set of interdicts – rules and prohibitions and moral compliances. The positive ones secure relations between the members of the group and reaffirm the sacredness of the totem. Negative interdicts are prohibitions in relation to the natural world, human perception and contact with the totem. Violations of these constitute an attack on the sacred. The totem is the emblem of the clan and through it the clan group is hypostasised and represented to the imagination. The totem or the emblem is what gives the clan society its basic form of social cohesion. The clan society is not tied to a locality, nor to a leader or strong central authority, and therefore there is a need to rally round a symbol (ibid., pp. 234–5). The sentiments of the collective fix themselves on the totem, which is 'the symbol of both the god and the society' (ibid., p. 208). Religion is the expression of the self-creation of human society and a 'society is to its members what a god is to its faithful' (ibid., p. 208).

Religion does offer the believer answers to questions about human existence and the nature of the universe while lifting the believer above the human condition and the miseries of everyday life. But its role is just as much to reinforce the normal way of things, as Durkheim suggests when he says:

> Religious conceptions aim above all to express and explain not what is exceptional and abnormal but what is constant and regular. As a general rule, the gods are used far less to account for monstrosity, oddity, and anomaly than for the normal march of the universe. (Ibid., p. 26)

However, Durkheim is quite clear that societies have moved on from their more primitive forms and that the normal march of the universe has changed. He addresses this in his account of the decline of religion in modern societies and we will see in the next section that the decline of religion is a consequence of the reduced significance of the mechanical solidarity of primitive society. Although religion 'still maintains grip over the soul' science tends to replace religion in areas requiring cognitive and intellectual functions (ibid., p. 431). In contrast to Weber's theory of rationalisation, the individual progressively becomes emancipated, acquiring new and greater freedoms with the development of new rights and beliefs. Like Weber, Durkheim believes the modern world becomes increasingly rationalistic, with the changing nature of belief systems leading to more diverse and complex social processes. But 'the more we advance, the more profoundly do societies reveal the sentiment of self and unity' (Durkheim 1964: 173). The source of this is the division of labour: 'It is the division of labour which, more and more, fills the role that was formerly filled by the common conscience. It is the principal bond of social aggregates of higher types' (ibid., p. 173).

3. THE DIVISION OF LABOUR

Durkheim writes that 'social life comes from a double source, the likeness of consciences and the division of social labour' (1964: 226). In this way he investigates the links between the individual and society, examining the nature of social bonds and their function in the social cohesion of society. A particularly important concept is that of social solidarity – the social bonds that tie us together, the system of relations linking individuals to the social whole. Solidarity looks at social integration and how individuals are linked to other groups. These social links change as the social division of labour develops and society becomes more advanced. Durkheim, like Marx, looks at economic exchanges. But he argues that social interaction goes beyond such exchanges and that the sociologist needs to study the wider social unity. He is concerned with how social solidarity develops from pre-industrial to industrial societies, and he expresses this through the use of the terms 'mechanical' and 'organic'.

Mechanical solidarity is found in less advanced societies where the collective conscience is strong and consequently where there are common roots of identity and similarity. There is no distinction between the individual and collective conscience and the individual is enmeshed in the social whole with no autonomy. Members share the same perceptions and functions and solidarity is based on likeness. Religion is the dominant belief system that unites people through common practices. These practices in turn form the basis for collective rules and customs and obligations which affect all aspects of social life. Society is dominated by shared beliefs and sentiments with little differentiation between individuals.

The kinship group forms the dominant social institution, with social cohesion based on familial and domestic ties. There may be politico-familial groups or tribal or clan groups based around communal property. Members of the clan are joined by bonds of kinship and acknowledge reciprocal obligations. The organisation of society into tribes corresponds to what Durkheim calls the segmental structure of mechanical solidarity, where society is made of small groups or segments organised into tribes with close proximity to one another and where the division of labour is along domestic and political lines. The structure of these segmental societies is like the rings of an earthworm, which are integrated into one body. As societies become more advanced the segments turn into organs with more specialised functions. Advanced societies are characterised by industrialisation and increased division of labour with specialised functions and autonomous social bodies. Solidarity now comes from occupation rather than kinship and social links are based on contracts. Common beliefs and practices start eroding and there emerges a more political and legal form of centralised power with specialised judicial and administrative functions.

Organic solidarity therefore bases itself on a more specialised form of social relations with individuals linked more to each other rather than to society as a whole. The division of labour makes individuals more reliant on each other and, in particular, on the economic functions that different people perform. As organic solidarity increases, society becomes more and more based on the interdependence of its members, whether through economic activities or through other specialised functions like political or legal ones. As these functions become more specialised there are fewer shared understandings between people, or at least, social bonds become based on contract rather than religious beliefs or customs. Links based on common likeness also gradually slacken as religious doctrines decline and social relations become secular and political. The collective conscience is weakened and 'the common conscience consists less and less of strong, determined sentiments. Thus it comes about that the average intensity and mean degree of determination of collective states are always diminishing' (Durkheim 1964: 167). In place of collective states, individual personality becomes more and more important. And although the collective conscience does not vanish, 'it more and more comes to consist of very general and very indeterminate ways of thinking and feeling, which leave an open place for a multitude of individual differences' (ibid., p. 172).

4. LAW, ECONOMY AND STATE

That social bonds become more like contracts indicates the importance of law. This is important for social cohesion, for law reproduces the principal forms of social solidarity with different forms of law corresponding to different types of social solidarity. The main distinction Durkheim makes is between penal and contractual law, with penal law based on repressive sanctions and contractual law based on restitutive sanctions. The penal aspect of law predominates in the less advanced societies while the restitutive aspect is stronger in modern societies.

Penal law is about doing harm. This is often physical but it can involve restricting freedom or reducing social honour. It reinforces social cohesion through the setting of examples. Penal law is more in keeping with mechanical solidarity and is a response to crimes that go against the common conscience or against prevailing social rules, common customs or core beliefs. Repressive force is used in proportion to the given offence and is a severe and swift 'public vindication'. It mobilises the collective population in moral outrage and is affirmed at the moment it is contradicted in that punishment expresses a 'unanimous aversion' to the crime, and 'serves to heal the wounds made upon collective sentiments' (Durkheim 1964: 108). Under penal law, punishment is an emotive response to transgression. The origin of the penal–repressive approach is religious and it serves to maintain collective sentiments in order to preserve the power of social cohesion. Punishment's 'true function is to maintain social cohesion intact, while maintaining all its vitality in the common conscience' (ibid., p. 108).

By contrast, modern society develops the cult of the individual and judicial law recognises individual freedoms and rights. The division of labour brings into being new, more specialised roles and encourages individual talents. Organic solidarity binds people together through contracts rather than through the common conscience. Judicial law is based on contracts between individual parties rather than between individuals and society. Written law prescribes obligations to others and establishes the sanctions if violated. It is less about social cohesion of society as a whole, more about specialised or restitutive sanctions. The aim of these is not to inflict harm but to return things to their normal state and to reestablish what has been disturbed. Organic societies therefore are restitutive rather than repressive and aim not so much to punish as to secure compensation for damage. Restitutive sanctions are based on specialised social institutions which become autonomous as a consequence of the developed division of labour. Along with the more specialised system of social organisations – courts, tribunals, administrative bodies and so on – are specialist officials like judges and lawyers.

This illustrates the more general issue, which is that modern societies become more socially differentiated. Mutual relations arise from the division of labour and legal rights form the basis for a moral framework that secures social cohesion. As society becomes more socially differentiated – economically, legally, politically and morally – common interests are shared, not between all members of society, but between smaller units. Individuals break free of the social claims and allegiances of less developed societies and become more selective of their particular beliefs and values. With increasing social density, individual ideas come to dominate over collective ones and people's own needs and wants became more significant than society's. The collective conscience, which was responsible for strong social cohesion, now becomes weaker and more highly generalised in that 'it more and more comes to consist of very general and very indeterminate ways of thinking and feeling which leave an open place for a growing multitude of individual differences' (ibid., p. 172).

But despite the fact that 'all social links which result from likeness progressively slacken'(ibid., p. 173), social cohesion does not break down. As Durkheim puts it: 'In sum, since mechanical solidarity progressively becomes enfeebled, life properly social must decrease or another solidarity must come in to take the place of that which has gone' (ibid., p. 173). That other form of social solidarity comes from the role of the division of labour and the contract system. In fact, due to specialisation, we become increasingly dependent on other people. So, just at the occupational level, 'far from serving to emancipate the individual, or disengaging him from the environment which surrounds him, it [collective conscience] has, on the contrary, the function of making him an integral part of a whole' (ibid., p. 398). But Durkheim also has in mind a system of moral regulation that accompanies the division of labour. We will look briefly at how he conceives of social and economic crises in relation to this moral cohesion.

It is argued that social cohesion is based on the regulation of society and that this regulation needs moral as well as social institutions. Durkheim clearly sees social cohesion as a positive thing and holds an evolutionary notion of its development, although he is not as bold as the positivists in asserting this. Indeed, he breaks with the positivist view of social evolution in so far as he believes that the evolution of societies is dependent upon successful moral and social integration. His account of society leaves space open for social conflicts although his is not a conflict theory of society, as it might be for Marx. Conflict is not the essence of the social system; rather, it exists as a problem of social cohesion that must be resolved through greater social and moral regulation.

If class struggles and other social disturbances reflect a lack of social cohesion, this is not entirely due to the division of labour, as a Marxist might claim. Rather, this has more to do with the fact that the growth of new divisions of economic functions has outpaced the development of corresponding forms of moral regulation. Whereas for Marx economic conflict is a fundamental aspect of capitalist society, for Durkheim it is the product of unregulated economic expansion.

An example of this is what Durkheim calls the anomic division of labour, which is particularly prevalent during crises and commercial failure. Social cohesion is affected as social solidarity breaks down and individuals cannot understand the functions of society as a whole. With the anomic division of labour it becomes difficult to maintain relations between people. Another case is termed the forced division of labour, which occurs when jobs are allocated on the basis of unequal power relations rather than through free choice. In Durkheim's view strong social solidarity is spontaneous, therefore with a forced division of labour individuals cannot enjoy their natural place in the social system. The distribution of social functions is not based on the distribution of natural talents, and such a system, rather than establishing social cohesion, only meets the needs of particular social groups.

Therefore, the modern failure of economic life stems from a lack of regulation and anarchic social relations, particularly when economic growth is not matched by the growth of moral regulation. For this reason, Durkheim argues against what he sees as the socialist view by claiming that social crisis is not primarily economic and that it will not be resolved by socialist measures like the redistribution of wealth. In fact, he argues, socialism is itself a product of the social crisis in modern society, not a solution to it. The ideas of modern socialism can arise only in those societies with an advanced division of labour. By contrast, communism can be related to a variety of different societies since it is concerned with the more basic question of how individuals are cohered into a group. Therefore, crisis is not primarily economic but moral, as is reflected in the process of anomie or normlessness. The solution to such problems is not to concentrate production in the hands of the state, as Marx suggests, but to foster organic solidarity through the spontaneous generation of norms. Without this the division of labour is artificial and forced and we get the modern crises of anomie and the forced division of labour.

The resolution of these problems lies not with a change in the social order but with social reform and reconstruction. The division of labour leads to new laws and beliefs that have to be coordinated. Although we have seen that Durkheim opposes the Marxist emphasis on the role of the state and believes in the need for spontaneous social solidarity, he does see the state as playing an important role in maintaining social cohesion through its regulative powers. The paradox of Durkheim's system is that as societies become more complex and the collective conscience becomes weaker, social cohesion remains strong because of the new emphasis on the rights of the individual. The state, reflecting the increased specialisation and complexity of society, is itself a specialised institution whose role is to offer regulation and direction. The expansion of the state in modern societies can be linked to the development of moral individualism. With the increasing division of labour, the state becomes more important as the institution responsible for the protection and maintenance of individual rights. Its role is to be able to guide society while ensuring justice and offering protection to the individual. The state has a special function in preserving social unity out of the diversity of functions. Its own distinctive functions concern policymaking, law and government. The state interacts with the rest of society, ensuring that society becomes more consciously directed, as opposed to being the product of unthinking custom and tradition. Democracy depends on how this interaction with the rest of society develops. In this two-way process, if the collective conscience represents the 'social mind', the state represents the 'social ego'.

5. SUICIDE AND ANOMIE

Anomie has already been mentioned as one of the modern social ills. It is also addressed in Durkheim's work on suicide, along with what he calls egoistic and altruistic suicide.

Suicide is regarded as a pathological response to the civilisation of society. Its causes are not psychological but are located within society. The act of suicide is a consequence of a social condition and suicide often corresponds to a serious upheaval in the organic conditions of society. In Durkheim's view, 'suicide varies inversely with the degree of integration of the social groups of which the individual forms a part' (Durkheim 2002: 167). Social integration refers to bonds between the individual and society. These bonds are commonly held views and values that act as a check on individualism and focuses the individual outside the self. Social bonds act to impose restrictions and constraints on individuals so that their weakening leads to a situation where society 'no longer then possesses the authority to retain them in their duty if they wish to desert' (ibid., p. 168). Such bonds are important to the regulation of individual wants and needs; without them we get anomic and egoistic forms of suicide.

Egoistic suicide occurs when the individual is not sufficiently integrated and it is a result of too much individuation and a weakening of the social fabric. If the individual is thrown to their own resources there is a greater chance of suicide. Individuals retreat into themselves and detach themselves from society. The individual ego asserts itself over the social ego and the individual personality over the collective one. Consequently, individual goals replace common goals and individuals withdraw from collective life. Counters to this process are familial, religious and political–national ties. However, the natures of religion and the family have changed and they no longer have the same preservative influence.

The soldier is also a member of a strongly unified group which functions like a family. Yet the suicide rate among the military is much higher than average. Here the causes are the opposite of individualism. Within the military there is feeble individuation and, as with lower societies, traditionalism is strong and a more primitive morality prevails. So in contrast to egoistic suicide, altruistic suicide results from too much social integration. The bond between the individual and society is excessively strong owing to such things as customs or social honour. Suicide is almost like a social duty or obligation, where pressure is brought upon the individual by society to avoid disgrace. Among types of altruistic suicide, obligatory altruistic suicide bases itself on social expectation, while optional altruistic suicide places fewer demands but links suicide to prestige and virtue. Finally, acute altruistic suicide embraces the joy of sacrifice and the renunciation of life.

As we have seen, social integration can be brought about through religion by linking individuals to things beyond them, while placing them under restrictions and constraints. Religion creates a bond between a community of believers. However, the strength of these bonds varies between different religious groupings and Durkheim's empirical data reveals how the suicide rate is much higher among Protestants than among Catholics. Catholics are more accepting of religious demands and hold to fixed and unchanging customs and practices; Protestants adopt a more critical attitude towards formal doctrine, thus undermining religious discipline. Protestantism promotes a spirit of free enquiry and has a less strongly integrated church. By contrast, the Catholic Church has a more traditional hierarchy based on the authority of priests and the enforcement of dogma. Consequently, Protestants have more control over their religious practices and observances, and are more critical and reflective in relation to their beliefs. They thus develop more religious autonomy and individualism. People start to withdraw from religious society as religious beliefs lose their authority and become less binding.

As religion plays less of a role in the life of individuals, social bonds get weaker and attachment to the community declines. With Protestantism, the religious act of confession is replaced with self-reflection and ritual is minimised. This self-reflection loosens the hold of religious doctrine and encourages greater self-reliance and hence egoism. The problem is that this egoism comes at the expense of social integration in that once the obligations of religious teaching are questioned, social cohesion starts to break down. This explains higher suicide rates, for 'man seeks to learn and man kills himself because of the loss of cohesion in his religious society' (Durkheim 2002: 123).

The family is another potential block on suicide. It provides us with ties to the conjugal group, bonds of friendship and shared experience. Family life reduces egoism, as commitment is focused on the family rather than the individual. Obligations to the family integrate the individual into the family group, gives them social responsibilities, and thus lessen the focus on oneself. According to Durkheim's study, suicides vary according to whether people are in families and according to the size of the family. Greater social cohesion comes from the large family with its historical memories and sentiments and its greater shared experience.

These older forms of regulation such as religion and the family start to fail, but new functional substitutes may not be forthcoming, leading to social disequilibrium and anomie. Anomie refers to the absence of law, deregulation or the failure of regulating norms. Production becomes deregulated due to rapid industrialisation, causing an irregular harmony of functions. Rapid economic change may give rise to new interests that have yet to reach equilibrium. Anomic suicide may occur during economic crisis. But suicide during a crisis is not due to economic hardship but because of the problems of social equilibrium. Durkheim links anomic suicide to shifts in the regulatory mechanisms in society, in particular those responsible for social equilibrium. In a traditional society, religious institutions set limits and provide a framework of meaningful constraints. Modern society replaces this with free enterprise, and the economy with its spirit of competition replaces religion as the dominant social institution. Economic development frees social activity from regulation by replacing religion and removing social limits. As religion is replaced by economic and industrial ends, desires get expressed through material wants. In modern societies these desires increase but social restraints are reduced.

Anomie therefore refers to the decline in the regulatory powers of society or in those social functions that set limits on our needs and wants. Society sets limits on our wants through a moral framework of restraint and so anomie refers to a decline in such social regulatory mechanisms. People have well-being when their needs are proportionate to their wants. Otherwise they develop feelings of disappointment and failure. Without social limits on our needs and wants, individuals exceed the means at their disposal and become frustrated. If society does not regulate and restrict our needs and wants we strive for that which we cannot obtain. Suicide rates reflect such moral disturbance and the loss of social regimen.

Durkheim is often held responsible for the structural–functional theory of later generations and we can find in his concept of anomie the basis for the work of structural–functionalists like Talcott Parsons and Robert Merton. They look at how these moral rules are the basis of social life and how they function to control or discipline our impulses. This draws on a biological model where social structure acts to control people's basic instincts and urges. Functionalism makes a distinction between healthy and pathological forms of social organisation, drawing on Durkheim's distinction between the normal integrated society and the pathological conditions that deviate from this. The next section will look at the work of Parsons and Merton and how they concern themselves with social cohesion through the issues of groups' expectations and achievements, moral regulation, anomie and deviance.

6. THE FUNCTIONALIST SOCIOLOGY OF TALCOTT PARSONS

North American functionalism maintains that social cohesion comes from socialised conformity to particular social rules and cultural norms. The influence of Durkheim can be seen in the account of how social order is internalised, with stress on the normative aspects of social relationships. This internalised moral order relates to the collective conscience or system of common values beyond the individual level that forms the basis of social order and collective solidarity. Functionalist sociology looks at normative rules that shape social action or at how this social action is guaranteed by a system of shared norms and values.

The functionalism of Talcott Parsons concerns itself with 'placing dynamic motivational processes in this context of functional significance for the system' (Parsons 1991: 22). We will look at these motivational processes in more detail later, but first it is worth stressing the structural or systemic aspect of this approach. As Parsons says:

> Every social system is a *functioning entity*. That is, it is a system of interdependent structures and processes such that it tends to maintain a relative stability and distinctiveness of pattern and behaviour as an entity...To this extent it is analogous to an organism. (Parsons 1954: 143)

This understanding of the social system is reminiscent of Durkheim's view that the social system is a living organism like the human body. Such organisms need preservation mechanisms and in the case of the social system this is a built-in self-righting equilibrium that ensures the status quo. We can understand the importance of various social processes in so far as they fulfil the role of supporting social cohesion. Therefore, various dynamic factors and processes 'are important insofar as they have functional significance to the system, and their specific importance is understood in terms of the analysis of specific functional relations between the parts of the system and between it and its environment' (ibid., p. 217). Something 'either "contributes" to the maintenance (or development) of the system or it is "dysfunctional" in that it detracts from the integration, effectiveness, etc., of the system' (ibid., p. 218). This is a more 'structural' version of the normal/pathological distinction in Durkheim. Processes within a social system either provide order or dysfunctionality.

Parsons's arguments about the functional role of religion; and more generally, ideology, are also developed from Durkheim's work. Parsons takes Durkheim's theory of religion further with a functional explanation of religion's role. Religion acts to foster shared values and operates as a mode of motivational orientation. It constitutes a central unifying belief system that is basic to maintaining social solidarity. It also serves as the basis for the provision of ethical principles as well as negative sanctions. The collective acts of ceremony and ritual serve to promote social solidarity. Ceremony sets collectivity in motion, bringing groups together in celebration. Religion, therefore, is a belief system, but it is not primarily cognitive like science. Rather, it rests on an evaluative interest and a commitment to action. It gives answers to problems of meaning and serves to legitimate moral norms. In comparing religion to ideology, Parsons argues that both ideologies and religion are belief systems, but religious beliefs are distinguished by their non-empirical cognitive references in relation to the supernatural order. More generally, the social order depends on a consensus of shared values and ideology provides this. Ideology may be said to be a system of beliefs held in common by members of a collectivity. It provides a level of evaluative commitment and serves as a primary basis for cognitive legitimation of patterns of value orientation. What is interesting to note here is how Parsons's theory of ideology is strongly defined in relation to the activities and beliefs of a collective or group rather than in relation to social structures. We will later see that social structures are themselves given a non-material basis and are reduced to the ordered activities of social agents.

It can be seen that there is a strange double influence affecting Parsons's theory. On the one hand, the functionalism of Durkheim is evident; on the other, the social interactionism and action theory of Weber is present. This means that Parsons focuses at the level of individual and group action while trying to give this a structural or systemic grounding. Parsons is concerned with how human behaviour becomes constant and how relationships solidify over time. Social structure means the institutionalisation of cultural patterns, notably value orientations. The cultural system gives coherence to these norms and mediates and regulates communication and mutual orientation and interaction. Culture is therefore defined as 'patterned or ordered systems of symbols which are objects of the orientation of action, internalized components of the personalities of individual actors and institutionalized patterns of social systems' (Parsons 1991: 327).

The functionalism of Parsons takes over when breaking the social system down into its various aspects and examining the relationship between what he calls the personality system (and the process of socialisation), the cultural system (of normative structures and need dispositions) and the realm of symbolic meanings. Culture is assessed in terms of its usefulness for system maintenance, as is social solidarity. This too is a normative aspect of the social system based on common value orientations. Solidarity involves relations between the individual and the collective and entails issues of loyalty and responsibility. Loyalty is the 'uninstitutionalised precursor of solidarity' which is converted into the institutionalised obligation of the role expectation. The institutionalised role involves patterns of solidarity obligations whereby we comply with common or moral rules.

An aspect of Parsons's functionalism is the view that the social system must satisfy certain functional prerequisites if it is to survive. These four needs or requirements are:

1. each system must adapt to its environment (adaption);
2. each must have a means of mobilising its resources to achieve its goals and obtain gratification (goal attainment);
3. the system must maintain internal coordination of its parts and develop ways of dealing with deviance. It must hold itself together (integration);
4. the system must maintain itself in a state of equilibrium (latency or pattern maintenance).

All social systems must meet these requirements in order to maintain themselves. Adaption is concerned with obtaining resources from the external environment distributing them within the system. Goal attainment refers to the features of the system that serve to establish its goals and mobilise people in support of them. Integration is concerned with maintaining social cohesion and solidarity and coordinating the subsystems to maintain the unity of the system. Latency or pattern maintenance concerns the way that motivational energy is generated and stored.

To meet such functional requirements, various subsystems develop. For example, the cultural subsystem should be understood in terms of the function of integration, while the economy performs the function of adaption. The economy is concerned with the production of utility to meet the needs of society along with other subsystems such as the political (goal attainment) and the cultural–motivational system (latency). The later work of Parsons looks at the relationships between the four action systems. These different systems are related through the exchange of symbolic information; for example, the relation between the economy and other subsystems is mediated by the money relation. In the political sphere this is power, while the socialisation subsystem depends upon commitment. New developments have increased the differentiation of the four action systems and the elements within them, each of them gaining some functional interdependence, but also developing new mechanisms of integration. There has been an enhancement of the adaptive capacity of each subsystem in relation to its environment and Parsons chooses to illustrate this by highlighting three types of historical revolution. There is economic development through the Industrial Revolution, political development through the French and American revolutions, and there is the educational revolution, which furthers the rationalisation of knowledge and the changes in the cultural and occupational subsystems. These historical revolutions have produced many developments but have also posed major problems for social integration (Parsons 1977: 53).

Parsons has a structural–functional explanation of historical change which is analogous to the way a cell divides and multiplies. Simple societies are like the simple cell that then divides and multiplies into different subsystems. A new subsystem differentiates itself and goes through a process of adaptation and reintegration and a more general system of values is established. This model can be applied to the transition from agrarian to industrial society, where there was a separation of the economic from the socialisation system (reflected in the separation of work into offices and factories), with the family no longer acting as the main unit of production. Work is now carried out more efficiently and effectively in the new units while the family is able to carry out its socialisation functions more effectively without economic responsibilities. Social integration involves the coordination of new subsystems, the development of a new economic hierarchy, and the integration of people into wider political and social communities. Social evolution is seen as a process of ever-increasing differentiation of social institutions.

Parsons defines social institutions as the clusters of stable interactions such as may be found within the family. This institutionalisation of patterns of action creates social order and relates to the moral cohesion of society in so far as 'institutions . . . are patterns governing behavior and social relationships which have become interwoven with a system of common moral sentiments' (Parsons 1954: 143). Social cohesion works through institutionalised roles and motivational processes. The social system is described as a network of interactive relations and its most important institutions are those that pattern our relations through the definition of status and roles. The main functional issue for the system is the regulation of our interests and this is explained in relation to the various levels of the social system, which include: 1. all living systems; 2. systems of action; 3. subsystems of action such as personality and cultural, biological and social systems; 4. further subsystems including the political system, socialisation system, economy and societal community; 5. subsystems of these such as the capitalisation subsystem, production subsystem and organisational subsystem.

Social cohesion and social development depend on functional prerequisites for system integration. A key part of this is the motivation of social actors in accordance with requirements of the role system. Parsons is therefore concerned with the psychological aspect of social life in terms of the dispositions of social agents, their internalisation of social norms and their performance of a role. This is related to social structure and the restrictions placed on role expectations and how normative regulation attempts to control actors' relationships. He looks at how the actions of agents is shaped by need gratification or the need-disposition system, where agents respond normatively to their environment. People act according to their need dispositions and their internalisation of cultural patterns.

For Parsons the most elementary unit of the social system is the act.

That the social system is regarded as a system of interdependent action processes seems rather individualistic. It is argued that 'a social system is a mode of organisation of action elements relative to the persistence or ordered processes of change of the interactive patterns of a plurality of individual actors' (Parsons 1991: 24). The structure of relations between individuals is essentially the structure of the social system (ibid., p. 25). Meanwhile structures are described in terms of achievement patterns and status roles. They are to be understood in terms of the activities of social agents and such things as goal selection and occupational aspiration. But these actions are located within the system and so our status role is defined in terms of our functional significance for the system. Action should thus be understood not primarily in terms of motivation, but in terms of the consequences for the system. Durkheim is concerned with the actor's environment and systems of action and how they limit us. We are located within a system of status roles or a network of social positions to which expectations of behaviour and rewards and sanctions are attached. This is the basis of our institutionalisation.

Mechanisms of social control are exercised against tendencies to violate these role expectations. The socialisation process involves mechanisms of value acquisition, instruction, reward and punishment. The moral code provides the basis for social cohesion and a lack of conformity with these moral norms constitutes the central 'strain' in the social system – that is to say, the problem of deviance. The conformity–deviance dimension is a functional problem inherent in socially structured systems of social action, particularly in relation to cultural values. A series of 'structured strains' accentuates the difficulty of conformity. However, these strains do not necessarily imply a theory of social conflict as might be understood by Marx's theory of class struggle or even something fundamental to modern life like Weber's theory of disenchantment. The strains are not a terminal illness but come from adjustment problems as the system develops. The strains derive from the development of social processes rather than anything more inherent. Parsons therefore attacks the Marxist notion of class conflict as nothing more than a 'conflict of interest' that derives from the problem of integration into the reward system (ibid., p. 513). Conflicts are viewed in relation to institutions and strains are the product of changes in the institutional complex. Therefore social cohesion is based on maintaining a dynamic equilibrium, while deviance is seen as a disturbance of the equilibrium of this interactive system. This issue is developed further in the work of Robert Merton.

7. MERTON'S THEORY OF DEVIANCE

Parsons takes up Durkheim's notion of anomie to develop his idea of deviance. Deviant behaviour poses functional problems for the social system and must be counteracted by mechanisms of control. This requires the institutionalisation of a set of role expectations and their corresponding sanctions. Society has varying degrees of institutionalisation and their converse, varying degrees of anomie.

One of the problems with this approach is that it is a rather abstract model. Merton argues that Parsons is wrong to seek a general theory and that rather than 'system-building', social theory should be more 'middle-range'. Rather than seeking a total system, it is necessary to look at social organisation within more inclusive social systems. Concepts need to be more clearly defined and operationalised and applied to empirical research. Whereas Parsons provides a general theory of social integration, relating social consensus to general norms and values, Merton sees social systems in terms of their parts, looking at how they operate in relation to one another. He looks at particular context rather than the whole system and is concerned with the generation of deviance, ambivalence and social conflict. Merton's work on deviance therefore sees itself as a bridge between this empirical work and Parsons's rather abstract functionalism.

Merton looks at the ways different social structures integrate and also conflict with one another. Social structures develop mechanisms that articulate different obligations and values. They also articulate social status based on the allocation of different roles. Individuals stand at the confluence of these different roles and status sets and Merton argues that 'our primary aim is to discover how some *social structures exert a definite pressure upon certain persons in the society to engage in non-conforming rather than conforming conduct*' (Merton 1957: 132). There is an emphasis on cultural structure and the social practices that shape it. Culture is something that imposes on people from the outside and, as with Parsons, is seen as a set of norms governing the behaviour of a social group. But although people's behaviour is routinised, there is a variety of responses. Social disorganisation may come from conflicting values, conflicting interests, conflicting status and social roles, and faulty socialisation and social communication. To control these problems a strong cultural and institutional structure is required in order to secure social consensus while allowing some room for dissent. If there is a breakdown it is because the normal structures are over-whelmed by dissensus.

Merton sees social cohesion in terms of the regulatory capacity of society, while conflict or dissensus is a result of the breakdown of this capacity. This concerns how social structures exert pressure on people so they engage in non-conformity. Social structure and culture produce this deviation. One explanation is that society's overemphasis on material goals or monetary success leads to a breakdown of the regu-latory capacity of society. With people located differently within the opportunity structure, gaps emerge between aspirations and attainment. This breakdown is Merton's way of understanding anomie. This is particularly relevant to North American society and the goal of success. This system fetishises money as a sign of success and blames the worse off rather than the structure for failure.

Merton extends anomie to look at deviant behaviour and the dise-quilibrium between means and ends. If social and cultural structures exert pressure or anomic strain we can try to alleviate this in a number of ways. First, we may choose conformity so that we accept the social goals and the means of achieving them. We thus consent to the cultural and institutional order. Alternatively, we may choose innovation, the assimilation of the goal but not of the institutional norms – that is to say, we may choose illegitimate means to achieve our goals. The third option is ritualism or the abandonment or scaling-down of the goal, focussing on the means or compulsively abiding by institutional norms. Then there is retreatism, which involves a relinquishing of means and goals and can take the form of 'dropping out', such as is the case with outcasts, vagrants and drug addicts. This does not really constitute a renunciation of the supreme value of the success goal whereas the fifth option, rebellion, does seek new and alternative val-ues and means, outside the environmental social structure.

8. COHESION WITHOUT CONSENT, CONFLICT WITHOUT STRUGGLE

Merton's work might be moving towards some sort of theory of social consensus, and away from the overbearing functionalism of Durkheim and Parsons, but this is done in an individualistic way that cannot account for the ways in which exploited groups of people are pacified. The big problem with the whole tradition is that it sees social cohesion in terms of the functional unity of the social system and that issues like conflict, consensus and dissensus become secondary or pathological effects. They tend to be dealt with as problems affecting the smooth functioning of the system that need to be rooted out, or else, in Merton's case, as means by which individuals adapt to their environment.

Still, it might be possible to argue for some theory of social consensus in the work of the functionalists, not least because of the emphasis on morals and cultural norms. Despite the mechanical language, these are not entirely evolutionary theories and even Durkheim is quite aware – indeed he is quite concerned – that there is no guarantee of social progress. Likewise Parsons, while stressing social order, is quite perturbed by the potential for social disorder. Therefore there is a pressing need for the moral regulation of society as a means of achieving order and progress. This moral dimension might be the basis for conceiving of functionalism in terms of social consensus, where people have to conform to others' expectations or common or shared beliefs. But still, it is a very functional type of social consent with little agency involved. It is a process driven by the system and, despite its moral emphasis, deserves to be seen more as social (or systemic) cohesion rather than consent.

One problem is that Durkheim lacks a concept of ideology that is related to particular interests or social institutions. As Lukes says: 'Nowhere did Durkheim consider the role of ideology in maintaining consensus: he never saw the "moral consciousness of societies" as biased, systematically working in favour of the interests of some and against those of others' (Lukes 1973: 133). This relates to a broader issue in Durkheim's work, which is its universalism. With social cohesion and social solidarity treated as universal things, there is a lack of historical grounding. Just as Merton claims that Parsons's work is too abstract and general, so with Durkheim there is a lack of focus on particular groups and their interests. So Durkheim has a strong notion of social cohesion, but he is weak on questions of interests and power. He does not really look at the relation between power and social cohesion. Instead, power is seen as a pathological thing that reflects a lack of social and moral cohesion. In this way, issues of power and domination are transformed into issues about social cohesion and the maintenance of equilibrium.

Instead of developing conceptions of ideology, power and particular interests, Durkheim's functionalism leads him to claim that the development of the division of labour does not necessarily lead to class conflict, but to a new form of social cohesion based on the integration of specialised functions. If there is social conflict, this is a product of deficiencies in the moral coordination of society flowing from the destruction of traditional forms of social integration. If workers feel alienated or oppressed, this is not for economic or class reasons, but is due to an anomic feeling of lack of integration. Durkheim's answer to these problems is not class struggle, but a renewed awareness of our part in an organic totality.

A similar criticism might be levelled at Parsons. The conflict theorists, particularly Dahrendorf, argue that there is too much emphasis on social equilibrium and on how everything has a functional role. Consequently functionalism has been accused of having a conservative tendency to see existing society as functionally justified – indeed, that any inequalities in status, power and wealth are functionally justifiable in that they contribute to the reproduction of the social system. As Alvin Gouldner notes, this is a very 'American' form of conservatism, which tempers loyalty to existing social institutions with individualism.

These theories were developed during a period of stability and economic expansion and reflect this with their emphasis on stability and order. But there were underlying threats in the form of anxieties about the Soviet Union and the dangers posed to social order by rapid economic growth. This explains the strong emphasis on the need for social order and leads Gouldner to comment: 'The new structural vision of Parsons's work, like a leaning tower built of concept piled upon concept, corresponded to a period of social recoalescence that retained an abiding, though latent sense of the powerful potentialities of disorder' (Gouldner 1971: 142).

Durkheim and Parsons *are* concerned with modern society, concerned that it would become disordered and that social conflict might emerge unless it is better regulated. Weber, by contrast, is less fearful of disorder and more concerned about how modern society is becoming disenchanted through the development of instrumental rationality. Marx, meanwhile, viewed the generation of social conflict not as

something pathological, but as the reality of the system. For functionalism the reality is equilibrium, and this leads to a general theory of
social cohesion, but not one of conflict or consent.

Chapter 5

MAX WEBER,
RATIONALISATION AND ELITES

———— ⌒⌐ ————

1. LEADERSHIP AND LEGITIMATION

Unlike his main 'rival' Marx, who places great emphasis on economic mechanisms or the mode of production, Weber sees politics and culture as the main terrain on which conflict, cohesion and consent develop. Weber also lays greater emphasis on the role of social action and he accordingly defines politics as independent leadership in action (Weber 1991: 77). His concept of leadership is central to his overall theory of society and he gives an account of three basic forms of leadership which he derives from his notion of ideal types. This methodology looks at certain features in an abstract or pure form in order to develop a standard by which various historical developments can be assessed. Ideal types are mental constructs that are ideal in the sense that they represent a logical extreme. They deliberately focus on one side of the causal chain. This is used to develop clearly understood general concepts about types of society and types of action. Weber's three notions of leadership are defined as charismatic, traditional and legal–rational domination. These in turn can be said to illustrate the ways in which different forms of society cohere and the different ways in which consensus is achieved. The different powers of leadership, whether political, religious or bureaucratic, each have their basis in forms of legitimacy.

Charisma is the most unpredictable and individualistic type of rule and is thus the least socially cohesive form of leadership. It is based on the rule of some great figure or personality such as a prophet, warrior or political demagogue. Charisma relies on an acceptance of the extraordinary qualities and exceptional powers of the leader. These can be developed through the exercise of magical powers, or through revelations and mystical or symbolic acts. More practically, charismatic leadership must be proved through the achievement of victories that bring success to the community and thus endow the leader with a basis for legitimacy. The ultimate test for charisma, as for many other forms of leadership, is whether or not it brings success or prosperity to the community.

Charisma is an interpersonal form of leadership based on hero worship and personal devotion and loyalty. This loyalty is emotive, and social cohesion is as much psychological as it is social. This personal and emotional type of social cohesion inevitably makes it volatile and unstable. Charisma itself is the source of legitimacy and when charisma wanes, so too does social cohesion. This problem is enhanced by the fact that charismatic leadership is not really rule-bound and is certainly not rational, but depends on creative acts like magical feats, revelations and military triumphs. Lacking in social rules, legitimacy is gained through performative actions by which the leader's reputation is established or enhanced. This inevitably leads to an elitist type of rule based not on the representation or participation of the masses, nor on abstract legal codes or formal rules, but on the direct and personal authority of an individual. Charismatic rule is about leaders and followers or disciples. Legitimacy is based on the trust of the followers or the faith of the believers.

Charisma is the most unstable form or leadership and ultimately it cannot be sustained. Cohesion and consent depend upon established social customs, conventions, norms, practices and structures which are missing from the interpersonal rule of the charismatic personality. It is therefore only a matter of time before consensus breaks down. Or it may be that charismatic leadership evolves into something more enduring, but in this case it ceases to be purely charismatic and assumes the traits of either traditional or bureaucratic rule. The most significant change occurs when charisma becomes routinised. This routinisation may occur in relation to economic developments, or it may be that the personal followers of the leader become officials and set up norms for recruitment to leading positions. Ultimately, this kind of institutionalisation and routinisation is inevitable. However, this does not mean that charismatic leadership is irrelevant. We have noted how Weber's models of leadership are ideal types which represent an extreme case. In actuality, forms of charismatic rule combine, to greater or lesser degrees, with other types of leadership in many societies, including modern ones. And as we shall note later, Weber saw the charismatic personality as a partial solution to the problems of rationalisation and routinisation in his own era.

Traditional forms of leadership may also base themselves on the role of a dominant personality such as a monarch or patriarch. However, they differ from charismatic leadership in that the position of these individuals is dependent on an established order rather than on a dynamic personality. The monarch or religious leader does not rule by virtue of magical powers or personal qualities but through acquired or inherited (hereditary) qualities. Hence, leadership is legitimated by an established tradition or routine. And loyalty is based on a traditional allegiance rather than a personal one.

Traditional leadership therefore depends upon established forms of social conduct. Traditionalism is the belief in the everyday routine as a norm of conduct. Consensus is based on that which has always been and an 'established belief in the sanctity of immemorial traditions' (Weber 1978: 215). Social customs are important as they represent a uniform activity that persists through unreflective social action. Conventions are consensual in that they represent social obligations that do not depend on an apparatus of coercion. Patrimony is the most common form of traditional leadership, based on the established authority of the father, husband or elder or of the lord over the servants, the prince over the subjects. This kind of patrimonial society is based on the extension of the ruler's household. In the household authority derives from the superior strength, practical knowledge and experience of men over women and children. However, cohesion is maintained because the various members of the household are united in dealing with the outside world and because of their communal relation to property and goods.

If this model is extended to society as a whole, with the lord or monarch playing the role of the husband, then cohesion must be maintained through a feeling of common purpose and from the belief that the authority of the leader derives from an established way of doing things. Under the patrimonial variant of traditionalism there is no clear separation of private and public spheres so that rulership is based on personal governance. Rentiers, vassals and servants may be employed as the staff who carry out various social functions. Only later do we get feudal relations based on contractual arrangement. With this feudal form of traditionalism, social consensus is based on a set of obligations and rights. We start to find a separating out of powers and spheres of interest. This model moves away from the personal powers of patrimony towards the kind of social structures and routines associated with the legal–rational model.

Here leadership is based on rules, not rulers. Obedience is not owed to the person but to the order. Emphasis shifts from rulers to organisations. Leadership is established through general rules, regulations and procedures and, as Weber argues, consensus has rational grounds – 'resting on a belief in the legitimacy of enacted rules and the right of those elevated to authority under such rules to issue commands' (ibid., p. 215). It can be seen that this kind of leadership is more instrumentally rational as opposed to the more value-oriented action of traditional and charismatic leadership. Legal–rational society claims technical superiority over the emotive and irrational actions of previous leaderships. This legal–rationality is absolutely necessary in complex societies and it accompanies the growth of industrialisation, the development of the nation state and the modernisation of society. This type of leadership feeds off the general conditions of rationalisation and modernity in society.

Modern leadership is based on a legally established authority. In contrast to the other models, leadership is an impersonal affair and the legitimate right of the power holder to give commands derives from their position of office rather than their personal attributes. Leadership is by virtue of the legality of a social structure based on rationally established rules. The leaders of society are functional superiors or bureaucratic officials, office holders and managers. They rule by virtue of rationally established norms, enactments, decrees, and other rules and regulations. Legitimacy is based on the general belief in the formal correctness of these rules and those who enact them are considered a legitimate authority.

Legal–rational society bases itself on continuous rule-bound conduct. It has specified spheres of jurisdiction involving obligations to perform functions. The source of authority is through delegation or mandate. The organisation of duties follows a hierarchy reinforced by control and supervision, rules and norms. It is characteristic of the legal–rational model that administrative staff are separated from the ownership of the means of production and administration, so that their authority and legitimacy derive solely from their social function and position. This carries over into the realm of politics, which is based not so much on the dominant personality, but on the party apparatus. Modern politics and leadership are formed around the party and its professional staff, administrators and machinery. The need to woo the masses and the importance of direction and discipline mean that real political power rests not so much with the politicians, nor with the active membership of parties, but with those who control the organisation continuously – the party managers (Weber 1991: 103). While legal–rational society is often accompanied by mass democracy, Weber argues that real power is concentrated in the hands of the few.

As we shall see later, Weber considers the main force within legal–rational society to be the bureaucracy. However, this does not mean that democratic politics is entirely worthless. Although Weber saw the impersonal rule of the bureaucracy as an inevitable consequence of the process of the rationalisation of the political, economic and cultural spheres, he did hold out hope that this could be partially offset by the encouragement of charismatic leaders. In what could be said to be a rather elitist view, Weber maintains that modern parliament should not be regarded as an important institution of mass democracy; rather, it is more like a testing ground for selecting charismatic leaders. Political charisma is seen as the only hope of challenging bureaucratic dominance. Unlike the cold, calculating functionary of legal–rational society, the charismatic politician chooses politics as a vocation given that 'genuinely human conduct can be born and nourished from passion alone' (Weber 1991: 115).

Just as Gramsci was concerned to document the crisis of leadership within Italian society, so Weber gives an account of the problems of leadership within German society. His concern is for a country that experienced rapid industrialisation and economic development, but which had been a late political developer and suffered a lack of political consciousness. German politics had been dominated by the giant figure of Bismarck, who left a great gap that no one else was able to fill. The Junkers, as a declining class, could no longer offer a way forwards, but neither the emerging bourgeoisie nor the working class seemed capable of leading the nation either. Although Weber strongly identifies with the bourgeoisie, he questions whether the German bourgeoisie has the maturity to lead the nation.

Like other legal–rational societies Germany had a centralised bureaucracy, but it had neither the institutions nor the level of consciousness capable of providing political leadership and direction. But if this concern of Weber's is legitimate, his solution to the problem is more worrying. For Gramsci, the situation would be posed in terms of the problems of social hegemony and the need to combine leadership and direction with cohesion and consensus. For Weber, this problem is posed in a much more individualistic manner. The solution, it seems, lies with cultivating dynamic and charismatic personalities who are capable of coming forward as political leaders, and who will accept responsibility on the peoples' behalf. As Weber says to Ludendorff: 'In a democracy the people choose a leader in whom they trust. Then the chosen leader says, "Now shut up and obey me." People and party are then no longer free to interfere in his business' (ibid., p. 42).

2. DOMINATION

A clue to Weber's rather authoritarian notion of leadership lies with the fact that his three types of leadership are synonymous with his three types of domination. Domination, in turn, is synonymous with relations of power discipline and obedience.

> By *power* is meant that opportunity existing within a social relationship which permits one to carry out one's own will even against resistance and regardless of the basis on which this opportunity rests.
> By *domination* is meant the opportunity to have a command of a given specified content obeyed by a given group of persons. By 'discipline' will be meant the opportunity to obtain prompt, and automatic obedience in a predictable form from a given group of persons because of their practiced orientation toward a command. (Weber 1993: 117)

For Weber, social cohesion and consent rests on the exercise of power. In fact power might be contrasted with consent in that behind every consensual relation lies the threat of force. At first sight, therefore, it seems that Weber's view of domination is primarily coercive rather than consensual and that social order and stability are maintained through violence and force.

This notion that domination is based on violence is best reflected in Weber's writings on the state. The modern state emerges as it gathers around it the means of administration and the means of violence. We have seen that Weber has a rather pessimistic view of the constraints of legal–rational society. It could be said that all domination involves administration and every administration is domination. Domination is the authoritarian power of command and these commands must be backed up with the threat of violence. Thus 'the state is a human community that (successfully) claims the *monopoly of the legitimate use of physical force* within a given territory' (Weber 1991: 78). Violence is linked with administration in the sense that the state claims the legal right (the sole right) to use force. Every state, Weber claims, is founded on force, but the modern state seeks to legitimate this legally – 'the state is a relation of men dominating men, a relation supported by means of legitimate (i.e. considered to be legitimate) violence' (ibid., p. 78).

So although Weber describes domination as the authoritarian power of command, and although he argues that the state is intimately connected to the use of violence, he does at the same time introduce a consensual element. Commands have to be complied with and obedience is something that must be volunteered. Domination is not simply authority, it is legitimate authority. Legitimation is the motivation that induces subjects to obey the commands of the ruling authority, be it charismatic, traditional or legal–rational. Consequently, domination is regarded as an intersubjective relation because power and domination depend upon compliance. 'Domination does not mean that a superior elementary force asserts itself in one way or another; it refers to a meaningful inter-relationship between those giving orders and those obeying' (Weber 1978: 1378).

Weber is an interpretive sociologist in that he believes that social relations must be analysed in terms of actors' intentions and meanings. The intersubjective relation whereby one subject obeys another requires the sociologist to look into the reasons why this obedience should take place. This means looking at subjectively meaningful reasons for compliance. As Weber says: 'The merely external fact of the order being obeyed is not sufficient to signify domination in our sense; we cannot overlook the meaning of the fact that the command is accepted as a "valid" norm' (ibid., p. 946). It may be that subjects obey out of fear, out of duty or because they feel they will benefit in some way. Or it may be, as Weber's quote implies, that they feel that there is validity in the relation stemming from a set of shared values and beliefs within the community.

In this regard it is useful to compare Weber's notion of the state as based on force and where power is defined in terms of political ends with his notion of the nation which is regarded primarily as a cultural community. The nation and the state combine, of course, and the nation is also regarded as a modern phenomenon that emerges under specific cultural, economic and political conditions. But it depends on long-standing customs, traditions, values and symbols. The people of a nation are brought together through a common history, cultural heritage, language and ethnic origin and common sentiments and feelings. This cultural aspect of social cohesion combines group values with a common political destiny so that 'the significance of the "nation" is usually anchored in the superiority, or at least the irreplaceability, of the culture values that are to be preserved and developed only through the cultivation of the peculiarity of the group' (Weber 1991: 176). This conception is linked, though, to Weber's view that all politics is conflict and struggle and all cultural entities must fight to establish and maintain themselves. The nation implies 'a specific sentiment of solidarity in the face of other groups' (ibid., p. 172). In Weber's own case, this carried over into support for German nationalism and for the imperialist policies of the German state. His reasoning was that in order for a cultural community to develop, it must extend its influence on the world stage. With the modern nation state, cultural heritage and political organisation must be backed up with military power and prestige. It becomes a community of memories, political destiny and common struggles. A strong and assertive German foreign policy would reflect a maturing of national consciousness and political leadership. The relations of domination get transferred to the world stage.

Different types of domination entail differences in the forms of claiming legitimacy and differences in organisation and forms of rule. Some forms of domination will be based on established traditions with servants bound to their superiors through custom, affectual ties, material interests and beliefs. More modern systems of domination will claim legitimacy through their own rules and legal practices. The right of authorities to issue commands is based on a belief in the formal correctness and validity of the rules. Legal–rational domination is based on a set of impersonal relations (as opposed to the personal bonds that characterise traditional and charismatic leadership). Legal domination is based on bureaucratic administrative techniques and this kind of bureaucratic and impersonal legal–rational domination goes hand in hand with the development of modern capitalism, which, according to Weber, bases itself on calculation and prediction. As opposed to value rationality, which is guided by certain fundamental beliefs and principles, modern capitalism and modern bureaucracy tend to embody the instrumental rationality of formal rules, procedures and calculated acts. Western capitalism is 'rationalised on the basis of rigorous calculation, directed with foresight and caution toward the economic success' (Weber 1992: 76). The development of the free spirit of capitalism is best understood as part of the development of rationalism more generally. The different interests of various economic and cultural groups within capitalist society must be reconciled to a belief in the legal–rational order and the legitimacy of the state.

Weber does have a conflict-based theory of history, so domination can be seen in terms of different struggles that occur. His notion of class encompasses those struggles that take place in the market sphere. But this is not an economic theory like Marx's; rather, it is more of a sociology of economic behaviour. The problem is that Weber takes as his model for human behaviour the means–ends rationality of the calculating individual. He therefore sees the key agent within the capitalist system as the rational, calculating and purposeful capitalist entrepreneur rather than the oppressed wage-labourer. His sympathies lie more with the entrepreneur and he advocates a free-market capitalism which he contrasts favourably with the bureaucracy which he sees as crushing the entrepreneurial spirit. Thus, whereas for Marx domination flows from the ownership of the means of production, for Weber the central question is that of control over the means of administration, the state and political power, something that may conflict with the actions of capitalists.

Critics of Weber's model of social action point to two problems – first that it bases itself on rational conduct, second that this conduct is modelled on the actions of individuals. The nature of social action is reduced to the meanings and intentions of an agent, while types of domination and other social relations are reduced to the interactions of such agents. As Paul Hirst has argued, in Weber social relations and institutions are constituted as intersubjective relations where one subject provides the other with the conditions of their action in the form of means, ends and meanings (Hirst 1976: 75). Power is based on influencing others' actions: 'we understand by "power" the chance of a man or of a number of men to realise their own will in a communal action even against the resistance of others who are participating in the action' (Weber 1991: 180). As we shall see later, this presents problems when it comes to analysing how power, domination and consensus operate within society for they tend to be reduced to the relations between individuals or groups. This leaves little room for a structural or institutional account of cohesion and consent, or at least, if there is an account of such things, they tend to be reduced to their intersubjective relations, while domination tends to become merely the relation between leaders and led.

3. LEGAL–RATIONAL SOCIETY, THE MODERN STATE AND ITS LEGITIMACY. CIVIL SOCIETY AND THE DETERMINATION OF SOCIAL STATUS

Whereas for Marx the main historical driving force is the mode of production, for Weber it is the process of rationalisation. Modernity is regarded as the relentless rationalisation of all aspects of society. This rationalisation is bound up with the spread of instrumental reason or means–ends calculation, which comes to dominate the spheres of government, markets, education, law, political parties, trade unions and property. The development of capitalism is therefore seen within the context of wider trends such as the development of rational administration and governance, the advance of technology, and the development of a disciplined labour market. The growth of a capitalist economy does not have the kind of centrality that it does in Marx. Capitalism becomes dominant because it develops within an already existing rational way of life. It is more the case, therefore, that rationalism develops capitalism rather than capitalism being responsible for rationalisation, although the two processes become interlinked.

The rationalisation process brings with it a new level of social cohesiveness. The different social spheres – the economy, state, politics and culture – are all interrelated and interdependent. Within legal–rational society the state is particularly important for the enactment of law, the maintenance of personal protection and public order, defending vested rights, administering social welfare, developing a common culture and protecting the community against outside attack (Weber 1978: 905). The modern state both shapes and is shaped by the rationalisation process, maintaining impersonal legal relations and providing sanction and legitimacy. A crucial relationship exists between the modern economic system and the legal order. The tempo of modern business requires a prompt and predictable legal system which, if necessary, can be backed up with the coercive power of the state: 'Law exists where there is a probability that an order will be upheld by a specific staff of men who will use physical or psychical compulsion with the intention of obtaining conformity with the order, or of inflicting sanctions for the infringement of it' (Weber 1991: 180). In modern society the legal process has become rationalised, centralised and uniform, with the state claiming to be the sole legitimate body. This is what is demanded by the market economy, whose mode of conduct has destroyed the basis for other legal and political centres of power.

Weber regards the market economy as the most impersonal sphere of practical life. Being based on the rational and purposeful pursuit of one's interests, it has a matter-of-factness about it that is alien to fraternal relations. Within modern society it is sadly the case that this rational and purposeful conduct becomes the dominant ethos. Modern capitalist society requires a certain type of personality best suited to purposive–rational activity. This personality must be based on bourgeois values and a 'capitalist spirit' best suited to the economic activities of the marketplace. But whereas many Marxists have argued that social ideas, attitudes and values are determined by social conditions, Weber argues that social conditions can be developed by social attitudes. Most famously, he argues that the purposive-rational conduct of the capitalist market is served by the religious values of Protestantism.

In *The Protestant Ethic and the Spirit of Capitalism* Weber looks at why capitalism developed most successfully in the countries in northern Europe and North America. His conclusion is that in these countries the values and beliefs of the Protestant religion are most conducive to capitalist accumulation. For Weber the relationship between economic activity and religion, ethics and other values and beliefs is most important. In some cases – such as with Hinduism and Confucianism – the religious outlook may be a hindrance to modern capitalist development. Like types of leadership and domination, these religions are based on the inertia of tradition or on irrational (or non-rational) magical beliefs, superstitions and rituals. Protestantism, by contrast, best fits with the spirit of rational economic conduct. Ultimately Protestantism provides an ethical justification, if not for capitalism per se, then for the activities responsible for money-making.

The Protestant ethic is based on puritan asceticism or the belief that self-denial and self-control are the best guarantees of salvation. It also bases itself on the view that it is through everyday worldly activity that we show our devotion to God. This necessarily leads to the adoption of a rational and active worldview. And such a worldview, and such a practical ethic, is best suited to the development of capitalism. It emphasises the importance of hard work, a frugal lifestyle and individual responsibility. It was also single-mindedly directed towards the achievement of economic success (but might allay some of the fears about salvation). The anxiety caused by the question of salvation led to a regulated and responsible lifestyle which in actual fact legitimated profit-making, accumulation, economic specialisation and other activities crucial to the development of a capitalist economy. As Weber says:

> The emphasis on the ascetic importance of a fixed calling provided an ethical justification of the modern specialised division of labour. In a similar way the providential interpretation of profit making justified the activities of the business man ... it has the highest ethical appreciation of the sober, middle-class, self-made man. (Weber 1992: 163)

The development of a Protestant ethic leads to a rationalisation in beliefs and behaviour that best matches the 'spirit of capitalism'. It encourages practical, worldly activity pursued in a practical and rational form. Its ascetic nature encourages hard work and a frugal lifestyle. All this is well matched to the development of a basic capitalist economy and, more generally, a rationalisation of the social environment.

Weber's theory of religion would appear to have both functional and substantive aspects. Functionally religion acts to provide meanings and thus ensure a degree of social cohesion. However, he is also concerned to give weight to the substantive content of religious views. Thus religion, in a general sense, develops consciousness beyond the everyday and provides a basis for individual security and social stability. Previous religions have made use of rituals, magic and tribal practices, but modern religion moves beyond such a plurality of beliefs, advocating one transcendent cosmology. However, the specific content of Protestant religions such as Calvinism leads to a dramatic change in social values and human behaviour. This change is specifically to do with the content of these religions. However, certain unintentional

consequences follow, so that by promoting rational conduct the Protestant ethic accelerates a process of modernisation that eventually
undermines the religious viewpoint. The process of modernisation and
rationalisation demystifies the world and elevates science and technology to new levels of importance. The world becomes more secure
through non-religious knowledge like science and rationality so that
there is less need for religion to provide security, meaning and explanation. Indeed, the rationalisation of the world pushes religion into the
realm of the irrational.

Yet, paradoxically, with rationality comes irrationality. The development of instrumental (as opposed to value) rationalism leads to means
and ends losing their original intent. Thus once the Protestant ethic is
emptied of its religious content, the economic behaviour it motivates
becomes irrational in that it has no clear relation to human needs.
Purposive–rational behaviour turns into its opposite. Profit is pursued
for the sake of profit, accumulation for the sake of accumulation. And
with the erosion of religious powers and other ideologies, meanings
and values a general disenchantment sets in.

What Weber's account of rationalisation does emphasise is that
such a process cannot be reduced to the development of the economic
mode of production but has to take into account the influence of
ideas, values and human practices. Further evidence of this can be
found when examining Weber's account of social stratification. Here
he accepts Marx's stress on the importance of classes, but he also
argues the importance of other social distinctions, such things as
religion, beliefs, traditions, status, honour, occupation and style of life.
Social stratification and differentiation is therefore more than simply
a matter of economic position; it is affected by political, cultural,
ideational, and indeed the most mundane everyday practices.

Therefore the social and the economic orders are not the same,
although Weber agrees that the economic is very influential. He defines
the economic order as the way goods and services are distributed and
used and agrees with Marx that this is largely determined by class.
However, Weber's definition of class determination is slightly different
from Marx's and instead of defining class according to ownership of
the means of production it is defined according to the ownership of
material goods and skills.

'Classes' are groups of people who, from the standpoint of specific interests, have the same economic position. Ownership or non-ownership of material goods or of definite skills constitute the 'class-situation.' 'Status' is a quality of social honour or a lack of it, and is in the main conditioned as well as expressed through a specific style of life. (Weber 1991: 405)

Thus Weber accepts the Marxist view that the class struggle, the economic situation and the relation to material goods determine the 'life chances' that people have, but he differs from Marx in relating class situation to market situation so that a person's fate is determined by their chances in the market. Class therefore becomes the shared interests that a group of individuals may have as a result of their market position, with market position being understood as opportunities for earning income and consuming goods.

Social stratification takes place according to life chances, which means opportunities in relation to such things as employment, income, skills, education, health and living conditions. Class refers to common life chances represented by possession of goods and opportunities for income while, as Weber argues, 'class situation' can be expressed as the 'typical chance for a supply of goods, external living conditions, and personal life experiences' (ibid., p. 181). However, these differences of class are accentuated by differences in status so that '"classes" are stratified according to their relations to the production and acquisition of goods; whereas "status groups" are stratified according to the principles of their consumption of goods as represented by special "styles of life"' (ibid., p. 193). Differences in status involve such things as the level of prestige, honour or social standing attached to different groups. Status groups are communities that are determined not purely on the basis of economic class situation but according to positive or negative estimations of honour and social worth. One group may have a higher status than another due to birth or ethnicity or occupational status and it is on this basis that a group may be rewarded or prohibited in social life. Thus two workers may be of the same class but may have different status because of their different ethnic status, or because of their social background. Status is something that affects market position but which is not reducible to class. Stratification according to status is linked to access to ideational and material goods and opportunities, something that is determined according to the way that social honour is distributed between groups. This would explain distinctions between types of workers, for example between blue-collar and white-collar workers, the latter enjoying a higher social prestige. Within modern societies, where the monopolisation of managerial leadership and decision-making occurs, the middle classes – the intellectuals, civil servants and other white-collar workers – enjoy a high social status that is not reducible to the question of class or economic situation. This is also reflected through lifestyle and patterns of consumption and taste.

These distinctions mean that social cohesion and consensus are not naturally given, but have to be organised in line with the stratification of social groups. In legal–rational societies the middle classes are won over by higher status, material benefits and social prestige. Certain groups of intellectuals enjoy a prominent role as leaders of a cultural community with special access to achievements considered to be 'cultural values'. Wider social consensus may be developed through the cultivation of shared cultural values, for example, through the idea of the nation and the prestige interests that flow from this. However, rather like the process of hegemony, these 'shared interests' actually reflect the position and outlook of certain privileged groups who claim legitimacy through their relationship to the state or through their articulation of the interests of the 'nation' or the 'community'.

Groups may attempt to advance their position though these wider appeals to shared values and interests, but it may be that some form of conflict or struggle is necessary. In this case, groups organise themselves into parties which bring together those people with common aims or interests and direct them towards a common goal. Parties may organise people according to class situation or status or something looser. 'Their action', Weber writes, 'is oriented toward the acquisition of social "power", that is to say, toward influencing a communal action' (ibid., p. 194). These actions are directed towards a goal such as their achievement of personal influence or material standing, usually to secure power for the party's leaders and attain material advantages for its members. They represent an organised form of activity that is bound up with questions of class, status and interests and which presupposes a comprehensive level of socialisation and a political framework of communal action. These parties may well struggle to achieve a level of domination, but Weber makes clear that this is domination within the existing system. Thus struggles may take place over particular interests and values, but a wider social consensus based on social values and an existing political framework is taken as given.

4. ELITISM AND THE RISE OF BUREAUCRACY:
WEBER, MICHELS, PARETO AND MOSCA

Modern society is legal–rational in character and above all else, this is characterised by the rule of a specialist bureaucracy. Bureaucracy is not just a recent phenomenon, as Weber shows in his study of ancient Egypt, but with the modern state it takes on an ever-greater significance. The decisive factor in the rise of bureaucracy is its technical superiority and precision compared with other forms of organisation: 'bureaucratic organisation is technically the most highly developed means of power' (Weber 1991: 332). It offers an almost machine-like efficiency and a technical superiority: 'precision, speed, unambiguity, knowledge of the files, continuity, discretion, unity, strict subordination, reduction of friction and of material and personal costs – these are raised to the optimum point in the strictly bureaucratic administration' (ibid., p. 214).

Bureaucracy is necessitated by the peculiarity of modern culture and its technical and economic basis: 'bureaucracy offers the attitudes demanded by the external apparatus of modern culture' (ibid., p. 216). As everyday life becomes rationalised, bureaucracy takes hold of important aspects of people's personal lives such as their education, their cultural environment and their health and well-being. Bureaucratic rule has a matter-of-fact character based on calculable rules and means–ends rationality. It eliminates all personal, irrational and emotional elements. This brings a new degree of stability and cohesion since, unlike previous forms of domination which rely on more volatile personal and political relations, bureaucracy represents a continuous form of administration carried out by trained professionals who operate 'impartially' according to prescribed rules. The more complex and specialised nature of modern culture demands the personally detached and 'objective' expert. The growing complexity of administrative tasks and expansion of their scope need the technical superiority of those who have training and experience.

The link between bureaucracy and social cohesion derives from complexity. Modern society is characterised by an increasing complexity and an increasing need for specialisation and competence. That Weber (and the elite theorists) explores this link between bureaucracy and social complexity indicates a belief that bureaucracy is important for the maintenance of social cohesion. In a modern society, it is the bureaucracy that is responsible for coordinating different processes and regulating various different aspects of the social system. But if social complexity gives the bureaucracy this special function, it also gives it the basis for developing its own power and its own interests based on its specialised role.

Weber writes that modern officialdom concerns fixed and official jurisdictional areas that are ordered by rules, laws and administrative regulations. Duties are distributed in a fixed and official way, as is the authority to give commands. These duties are fulfilled by those who have the appropriate qualifications and authority operates through the bureaucratic structures in a hierarchical way. In this hierarchy officials are selected according to merit and expertise and they are trained to fulfil a particular function. For Weber a vitally important aspect of this type of bureaucracy is the separation of the office holder from the means of administration. This makes the bureaucrat dependent on their office and makes them fully identify with their position. It 'functionalises' human beings by shaping their psychology. They become devoted, not to people, but to an organisation. Their position within the organisation gives them the security of a salary and various other rewards and privileges. Because the bureaucratic organisation has a career structure, office-holding is looked upon as more than just a job; it becomes a vocation. The bureaucrat strives to improve their rank within the organisation and thereby enhance their salary, status and social esteem.

Bureaucracy is related to social control, discipline, specialisation and expertise. It becomes a form of domination whereby 'the bureaucratic structure goes hand in hand with the concentration of the material means of management in the hands of the master' (Weber 1991: 221). In fact it becomes the main disciplinary force in society, clearly defining the roles, functions and allocations given to those within and without the bureaucratic organisations. The masses become dependent on its functioning, as may be seen from the operation of the institutions of the modern state – the health and welfare systems, the educational establishment, the political parties and trade unions and other such bodies. Weber refers to the more-or-less permanent character of the bureaucratic machine when he writes:

Once it is fully established, bureaucracy is among those social structures which are the hardest to destroy. Bureaucracy is *the* means of carrying 'community action' over into rationally ordered 'societal action'. Therefore, as an instrument for 'societalising' relations of power, bureaucracy has been and is a power instrument of the first order – for the one who controls the bureaucratic apparatus. (Ibid., p. 228)

This explains Weber's pessimistic stance in relation to mass democracy, for bureaucracy inevitably accompanies it. Modern mass democracy requires the large-scale organisation of political institutions and parties, yet the democratic ideals inevitably come into conflict with these bureaucratic tendencies. Ultimately it is not the politicians but the bureaucrats (or the politician–bureaucrats) who run the country. Those who are in overall control are those who control the means of organisation. In fact, not only do routine changes in government not make much difference to the structure of society, but more drastic changes such as those advocated by the socialists would make little difference either. Revolution would not remove bureaucracy; it would merely take it over.

Michels

Weber's writings on bureaucracy are comparable to those of his friend Robert Michels, who is best known for his 'iron law of oligarchy', which states that the development of complex social organisations always leads to oligarchy and bureaucracy. For Weber the democratic ideal can never be achieved, mass democracy will always become the rule of a minority over a majority. Socialism, despite its claims, would lead to the same thing since bureaucracy is an inherent modern condition. For Weber and Michels alike, the complexity of modern society means that democracy leads to oligarchy and the dictatorship of the administrator.

Michels, like Weber, looks at how the bureaucracy develops its own interests based on its social position, the security offered by employment, and the opportunities to increase power or status. This increasing tendency for bureaucracy to advance its own interests, and the bureaucratic framework within which political life operates, means that it becomes impossible to advance a radical agenda for social change. Democracy always leads to oligarchy; this is an inherent feature of modern political representation. Government develops a life of its own. The fundamental aim of political struggle is power and political ideology is always sacrificed to political expediency. Degeneration is inherent in modern democracies.

Social stability is guaranteed by the development of a complex state bureaucracy. In developing this bureaucracy the modern state gets itself a large number of defenders who will support the state by defending their own interests in it. The state assembles for itself a numerous collection of officials and functionaries who will defend it because their interests depend upon it. This goes not just for permanent position holders but also for political leaders, who end up becoming bureaucratic officials of the party or state. According to Michels:

> History seems to teach us that no popular movement, however energetic and vigorous, is capable of producing profound and permanent changes in the social organism of the civilised world. The preponderant elements of the movement; the men who lead and nourish it, end by undergoing a gradual detachment from the masses, and are attracted within the orbit of the 'political class'. (Michels 1915: 408)

Therefore, writers like Marx are wrong to believe that social equality and justice can be achieved. Although Marx was right to stress the importance of the economy, it is also necessary to examine human individuals, political struggles and the nature of organisation. All these contribute to oligarchy and undermine socialist or even more basic democratic aspirations.

Michels is usually bracketed with the Italian elite theorists Gaetano Mosca and Vilfredo Pareto because he sees the rule of a minority over a majority as an inherent feature of human history. In his view it is the general incompetence of the masses that provides the basis for justifying elite rule. In modern society this is encouraged by the complex division of labour which requires and creates specialisation and expertise and which thereby provides the basis for authority. Democracy is transformed into government by those best suited to govern – in effect, this is government by a political aristocracy which represents the most mature leaders of society. Unfortunately, though:

> The apathy of the masses and their need for guidance has as its counterpart in the leaders a natural greed for power. Thus the

development of the democratic oligarchy is accelerated by the general characteristic of human nature. What was initiated by the need for organisation, administration and strategy is completed by psychological determinism. (Ibid., p. 217)

So Michels combines with his theory of organisation a psychology of leaders and led, of aristocracies and masses. It is a rather pessimistic psychology at that, based on the assumption that the great majority are incapable of political maturity while the minority have a tendency towards self-interest and corruption. This psychological element is a strong feature of Michels' iron law of oligarchy, which attributes to the leaders the psychological characteristics of greed and deviousness and which views the masses as apathetic followers who are easily led and swayed by rhetoric.

However, the iron law of oligarchy is also based on historical experience, taking as it does the situation in Germany at the time of the First World War and looking in particular at the conduct of the leaders of the German Social Democratic Party (SPD). In this party Michels witnessed the victory of the bureaucracy over the democratic structures and the socialist ideals. As the war approached, the party, he claims, sold its internationalist soul and, compelled by the instinct for self-preservation, became patriotic. At the same time the war accelerated the oligarchical character of the party leadership, not just in the SPD, but in all parties.

From these experiences Michels drew some more general conclusions about political parties and political organisation. The iron law of oligarchy is about the tendency for political parties to become oligarchic, however democratic they may claim to be. They fall under the domination of a professional leadership. The original goals of the movement are replaced by more instrumental goals, most notably that of preserving the organisation itself. Like other forms of bureaucracy, the political machine develops its own interests.

The two factors that lead to oligarchy are the psychological tendencies of the leaders and masses and the requirements of organisation itself. The oligarchic and bureaucratic tendency of party organisation is a matter of practical and technical necessity. 'It is organisation which gives birth to the domination of the elected over the electors, of the mandatories over the mandators, of the delegates over the delegators. Who says organisation says oligarchy' (ibid., p. 418). Democracy requires organisation and organisation requires leadership and these combined spell the end for democracy. The current democratic form of political government veils the tendency towards aristocracy, yet it is within the structure of party organisation that the tendency towards oligarchy is strongest.

Michels' more general historical point is that government is always by aristocracy and that in modern party life the aristocracy presents itself in democratic guise: 'On the one hand we have aristocracy in a democratic form, and on the other democracy with an aristocratic content' (ibid., p. 13). The masses consent to the modern form of government, believing it to be democratic and idealistic, but in reality they are hoodwinked by the modern form of an age-old phenomenon. All government is the organisation of a minority whose aim is to impose on the rest of society a particular order. History shows us that although one dominant class replaces another, oligarchic rule is always maintained. And as soon as one set of political leaders have achieved their ends and overthrown the old tyranny they undergo their own transformation and become like the old tyrants so that 'the revolutionaries of today become the reactionaries of tomorrow' (ibid., p. 195). History, as Marx had claimed, is indeed a continual series of class struggles, but these conflicts invariably culminate in the creation of new oligarchies which undergo fusion with the old. While Marx's theory radiates optimism, it is hard to avoid the impression that Michels suffers from pessimism and cynicism, especially in his general claims about inherent historical tendencies:

> When democracies have gained a certain stage of development, they undergo a gradual transformation, adopting the aristocratic spirit, and in many cases also the aristocratic forms, against which at the outset they struggled so fiercely. Now new accusers arise to denounce the traitors; after an era of glorious combat and of inglorious power, they end by fusing with the old dominant class; whereupon once more they are in their turn attacked by fresh opponents who appeal to the name of democracy. It is probable that this cruel game will continue without end. (Ibid., p. 425)

But it is possible to end on a more slightly more optimistic and practical note. Michels admits that his work on political parties overstates the rigidity of his iron law. In fact the iron law of oligarchy is comparable to Weber's ideal types; it is a deliberately one-sided account that aims at encouraging a frank examination of the oligarchic dangers to democracy in order to spur us to try and confront these dangers and minimise their risk even if they cannot be altogether avoided. It is true that 'the mass will never rule except *in abstracto*', but then, 'the question we have to discuss is not whether ideal democracy is realisable, but rather to what point and in what degree democracy is desirable, possible and realisable at a given moment' (ibid., p. 419). In this sense Michels shares Weber's concern with the practical consequences of democracy and he sees it as something that is worth struggling over.

Pareto

If Michels is concerned about democracy, Vilfredo Pareto is entirely dismissive of it. There is no such thing as a political system where the people express their will; politics is not made by the many but by the few. Even more than Michels, Pareto emphasises psychological characteristics: the minority that rules does so by virtue of its superior moral and intellectual qualities. However, these qualities do not remain stable but decline and this, essentially, is Pareto's theory of social change. This leads Pareto to make his famous claim that: 'aristocracies do not last. Whatever be the reason, it is incontestable that, after a certain time, they disappear. History is a graveyard of aristocracies' (Pareto 1976: 249).

All societies can be divided into a governing elite and governed majority irrespective of what type of social system exists. Social change is to be understood in terms of conflicts between rival elites which may end in the replacement of one with another. But only the form of governing class differs, not the essence. Within modern society, even if it claims to be based on mass democracy, oligarchy still prevails. The distribution of wealth and resources differs little between societies, as this relates not to the ideals of the system of government but to the distribution of the psychological and physiological characteristics of human beings.

Pareto's theory of the circulation of elites is based on these psychological characteristics. The ruling elites begin to decline in quality and lose their vigour. The ranks of the ruling class are then replenished with those who, rising from the lower orders, exhibit superior qualities. Genuine social transformations do not really occur, what happens is simply the replacement of one elite with another. The composition of elites may change but the basic structure of society remains the same.

Pareto's theories reject the Enlightenment project in that they deny that rational conduct and ideas can bring about social progress. As Irving Zeitlin argues, whereas for Weber a process of rationalisation is embodied in the main institutions of modern society, for Pareto society is to be understood in terms of people's psychological characteristics, and in particular, their essentially non-rational and unchanging attitudes and behaviour (or what Pareto calls residues). Whereas Weber's theory of society is institutional, Pareto's is more psychologistic. Institutional conduct is to be understood as an expression of basic psychological characteristics, which for Zeitlin rules out the significance of cultural or economic factors and leaves little room for comprehending the social conditions that facilitate or impede rational action (Zeitlin 1981: 171, 192).

Pareto's theory of social equilibrium sees society in terms of a number of interacting particles and interdependent forces which combine together but are in a constant movement of equilibrium. Pareto calls these 'internal forces' or human inclinations, attitudes, interests and beliefs. Different social strata are made up of different combinations of these elements, leading to different physical, intellectual and moral characteristics. If Pareto's theory of equilibrium represents a theory of social cohesion, then this is based on an unpromising combination of pychologism and atomism.

However, owing to the influence of Machiavelli, there is a considerable amount of emphasis on coercion and consent. As Pareto writes:

> There is everywhere a governing class, not large in membership, which maintains itself in power partly by force and partly by consent of the governed, who are very numerous. Between one governing class and another the difference lies mainly in regard to substance, in the ratio of force to consent, and, in regard to form, in the ways by which force is used and consent procured. (1976: 267)

Differences in the balance between force and consent come from differences in proportions of sentiments and interests. Sentiments and residues are a kind of social version of human nature. Residues are like instincts, but they are not reducible to them, as they are both innate and socially acquired. They comprise human sentiments or states of mind, impulses and attitudes and they form the basis for the non-rational beliefs and conduct that we discussed earlier. The non-rational is the main form of human action, based as it is on residues rather than reason.

The art of government is to manipulate consent by taking advantage of sentiments and residues among the masses. Legislation can only work by influencing these and appealing to the masses. Governments may combine force and consent, but the proportions and means used will vary among different leaderships. The more effective ones will appeal to the masses' interests and sentiments and utilise the residues. Force should not be used against these residues; rather, as Pareto cynically suggests, people should be governed by their own prejudices.

Residues and derivations (the rationalisations which are advanced by social forces to justify their actions) are central to Pareto's theory of how elites rule through force and consent. The notion of derivations is perhaps the closest we get to an elaborated theory of social consent since they represent the reasonings that groups use to justify and legitimate their actions. However, the social aspect of this theory is still secondary to the more psychological emphasis on human residues. Although justifications (derivations) may vary, the basic residues of human behaviour remain constant. Among Pareto's six categories of residues, two main classes stand out. Class 1 represents the instinct for combination and class 2 refers to the persistence of aggregates. This latter, being the tendency to preservation, is conservative. It relies on traditions and is authoritarian and bureaucratic. It bases itself more on physical force rather than persuasion, although it may appeal to established ways of life such as religious sentiments.

Class 1 or the instinct for combination is, by contrast, innovative and based on guile, skill, flair and imagination. However, Pareto also gives this class a negative aspect so that its members are guided by self-interest and a cunning that lacks scruples. Class 1 elites circulate more rapidly, producing constant innovation, but also leaving themselves open to being overthrown by force. Therefore governments are based on various combinations of these two classes and, in Machiavellian fashion, Pareto calls those who use force 'lions' and those who use guile 'foxes'. Lions are always necessary because force is said to be the foundation of all social organisation. But in modern democracies art and guile become more significant, as it is necessary to appeal to people's sentiments. This creates a more stable situation, for 'it is much more difficult to seize power from a governing class which shrewdly knows how to employ cunning, fraud and corruption' (ibid., p. 258). Those best equipped for government are those who have most energy and imagination, but who use them to undermine and outmanoeuvre their opponents: 'To prevent or resist violence, the governing class may use guile, cunning, fraud and corruption – in short, government passes from the lions to the foxes' (ibid., p. 257).

In fact, Pareto's theory of the circulation of elites points to the fact that there is a constant shift in the balance between class 1 and class 2 and that the rise and fall of aristocracies is due to these altering proportions. This is consistent with the view that elites are not stable blocs, but are more like hegemonic constructions with a small group leading and directing, so that 'the governing class is not homogeneous; it has within itself a governing authority – a more exclusive class or a leader or a power-group – which exercises control in effect and practice' (ibid., p. 268). There is also a distinction between the wider social elite – various intellectuals, entrepreneurs, artists and other leaders in civil society – and a narrower governing elite which exercises its rule. This governing elite is the main factor that determines the nature of each society and it determines the particular balance between force and consent.

Another similarity between this theory and that of hegemonic blocs lies with Pareto's description of the way that governing elites attempt to assimilate some subaltern groups:

> Dominant peoples sometimes endeavour to assimilate their sub-
> ject peoples. Success in achieving this assimilation is certainly the
> best way of ensuring their power. But often they fail because they
> seek to change residues violently instead of making use of existing
> residues. (Ibid., p. 267)

A ruling group should therefore take account of the sentiments and interests that exist within the subject group and should attempt to articulate its own interests through them. A cunning group will be successful if it can make use of existing attitudes and manipulate them for its own ends. A successful ruling group would therefore relate to the feelings of the people, albeit in a manipulative and cynical way. This occurs at different levels so that some groups may be assimilated, others won over to some degree, while others may still require the threat of force. Ultimately, for Pareto

> persuasion is but a means for procuring force. No one has ever persuaded all the members of a society without exception; to ensure success only a selection of the individuals in a society need to be persuaded . . . it is by force that social institutions are established, and it is by force that they are maintained. (Ibid., p. 136)

We can see that there is some agreement with Marx's theory of history in that Pareto claims that 'the struggle of some individuals to appropriate the wealth produced by others is the great factor dominating all human history' (ibid., p. 117). This basic assumption is contained in Pareto's theory of spoilation – that there is always a class of people who live off the goods of others. But whereas for Marx this gives rise to conflict that drives history forward and culminates in a better society, for Pareto this history is a cyclical process which only ever leads to new combinations of forces, new means for achieving consent, and new ways of maintaining power. This is consistent with Pareto's view that derivations (rationalisations and justifications) may vary from one society to another, but that residues (instincts) are relatively invariant (being more psychological than historical). Spoilation, as one of these invariants, is a general feature of all elites as greed and manipulation are considered to be universal human characteristics. This indicates the negative impact of psychology on Pareto. He allows for a theory of social consent, but it is a very one-sided account based on the assumption that consent is won through fraud and deception. Other groups may be brought on board, but in such a way that they are deceived and manipulated. In fact for Pareto, the most significant aspect of modern society is that 'there seems to be a very close correlation between "democratic" evolution and increasing use of that method of governing which resorts to artifice and clique-politics as opposed to the method which has recourse to force' (ibid., p. 261). And although force is now less direct, the modern democratic state plays an increasingly totalitarian role in social and private life.

Mosca

Unlike Pareto, who ended up giving his support to Mussolini, Gaetano Mosca is less dismissive of liberal democracy. As with other elite theorists he believes that all societies contain two basic groups, a class that rules and a class that is ruled, and that, 'the first class, always the less numerous, performs all political functions, monopolises power and enjoys the advantages that power brings, whereas the second, the more numerous class, is directed and controlled by the first' (Mosca 1939: 50). The control, however, may vary, being sometimes legal, sometimes arbitrary and violent. Given this choice, Mosca prefers legality and favours consensus over violence. Hence liberal democracy is a greatly preferable option as it plays a fundamental role in managing social consensus. Likewise political parties, even if we accept the criticisms provided by Michels, play an important consensual role in organising support for ideas, even if these are the ideas of a minority. Liberal democracy legitimates rules through social values and institutions and this, though it does represent the exercise of power by the few, is far preferable to the totalitarian or authoritarian alternative.

There is a familiar psychological element to Mosca's claim that existence of a ruling class is a permanent feature of society. The ruling class has superior moral and intellectual qualities by which it gains its social advantage. Society is divided into social groups on the basis of beliefs, passions, sentiments and habits as well as more social interests like religion, nationality and ethnicity. Conflicts take place over wealth, power and prestige, and history is a constant battle for pre-eminence. All history, he claims, has been like this, and we have no reason for believing that it will ever be anything else. However, despite this psychological element, Mosca gives a more sociological account of social change than Pareto. Social relations are of importance in maintaining the equilibrium of society. Mosca is aware of the need to defend democratic structures and parliaments, and more generally, liberal society, against the totalitarian impulse of new social forces. His book *The Ruling Class* ends by urging people to unite in the conviction that they have many common interests to safeguard, that they are bound together by the fabric of intellectual, sentimental and economic relations and that they have psychological and cultural affinities. The ruling class must rid itself of its prejudices and realise its responsibilities, change its psychological attitude, raise its level of political competence and understanding, and go beyond its immediate interests: 'It must become aware that it is a ruling class, and so gain a clear conception of its rights and duties' (ibid., p. 493).

Given that history is made by dominant groups, the actual positions of these groups becomes an important issue:

> The whole history of civilised mankind comes down to a conflict between the tendency of dominant elements to monopolise polit-ical power and transmit possession of it by inheritance, and the tendency toward a dislocation of old forces and an insurgence of new forces; and this conflict produces an unending ferment of endosmosis and exosmosis between the upper classes and certain portions of the lower. (Ibid., p. 65)

Like Pareto, Mosca argues that aristocracies that cannot defend themselves adequately from idleness decline rapidly, and that subal-tern groups become the new masters. Within the lower classes a 'directing minority' emerges which acts like a class within a class and which may find itself in the position of challenging for power. A more farsighted ruling class will try to incorporate such a group, although this may weaken the homogeneity of the ruling group.

The ruling class monopolises political power and rules over the majority on the basis that it is better organised and is composed of superior individuals. It is not homogeneous and may contain within it various strata, whether these be different aristocracies or co-opted subaltern groups. Nevertheless, elites tend to display a greater cohe-sion and consensus among their members. Because a ruling class is a minority it can reach a higher level of mutual understanding and therefore 'the domination of an organised minority, obeying a single impulse, over the unorganised majority is inevitable ... A hundred men acting uniformly in concert, with a common understanding, will triumph over a thousand men who are not in accord' (ibid., p. 53). The ruled can still bring pressure to bear on the ruling class, but they lack its organisation and cohesion. There is no way that the masses can play a full role in political life, and this, unfortunately, undermines the idea of mass democracy. Mass participation in elections is counteracted by the more significant question of the division of labour and the fact that specialisation and expertise have been carried to extremes in modern societies. So although the masses have the vote, the specialists have the power.

This relates back to the issue of rationalisation and bureaucracy, which are distinguishing features of modern society. Bureaucracy is inherent in the nature of the modern representative system and the specialised functions of government. When everyone has the right to vote a clique detaches itself from the middle classes and tries to seek leverage in the instincts and appetites of the more populous classes. Though the bureaucracy is legally open to all classes, in practice it will be drawn from a stratum of the middle classes which has the right educational and family background. The middle class is distinguished from the labouring classes by its scientific and literary education, its manners and habits and its economic status (Mosca's definition is comparable to Weber's), and this layer is ideally suited to the bureaucratic state. These layers become entrenched, officialdom is the key aspect of the modern ruling class.

The elites who come to power in modern states represent the most significant sections of those societies – government officials, captains of industry, managers, intellectuals and, perhaps, sections of the liberal aristocracy. Mosca favours the last two groups because they are more capable of playing an independent role – intellectuals stand between the ruling class and the workers, while the liberal aristocracy carries with it a more benevolent social attitude and is more detached from the rigours of modern economic life. These leading groups must then try to forge a unity and win the support of the masses:

> Ruling classes do not justify their power exclusively by de facto possession of it, but try to find a moral and legal basis for it, representing it as the logical and necessary consequence of doctrines and beliefs that are generally recognised and accepted. (Ibid., p. 70)

Mosca's notion of the political formula describes this important consensual aspect of elite rule. It tries to provide a universal moral basis and develop common values, sentiments and beliefs. This political formula is the ideology the rulers use to justify their position. Although it is based on the particular beliefs and sentiments of the dominant group, it uses the universal human need for moral principles to get these across. Again we may compare these aspects of elite theory with Gramsci's theory of hegemony and the fact that the ruling group must seek to gain social consent and stabilise its rule by making it acceptable to the masses.

All these theories provide an alternative to Marx's idea of a classless society. Elites, it is argued, are a natural phenomenon common to all types of society. They all reject the Marxist emphasis on the primacy of economics and argue that the ruling class is the product of social, political and psychological factors. For Weber rule by a minority is an inherent condition of social organisation, while for Pareto and other elite theorists it is an inherent condition of humans themselves. But the rather simplistic and schematic distinction between elites and masses has proved strong reactions. As Tom Bottomore says:

> They insist strongly upon an absolute distinction between rulers and ruled, which they present as a scientific law, but they reconcile democracy with this state of affairs by defining it as competition between elites. They accept and justify the division of society into classes, but endeavour to make this division more palatable by describing the upper classes as elites, and by suggesting that elites are composed of the most able individuals, regardless of their social origins. (1966: 148)

Some, for instance C. Wright Mills, have drawn on elite theory to present a more critical view of society. In *The Power Elite* he examines the different political, military and business leaders in the USA. Like elite theorists he believes that Marx's focus on the economically dominant class is too simplistic and that it is necessary to look at how the ruling elite is drawn from a variety of different social spheres. Unlike these theorists, Mills stresses the importance of institutional factors in determining elites as opposed to moral or psychological characteristics. Mills would agree with the other elite theorists and Weber that the size and complexity of administrative tasks within modern society means that a specialist bureaucracy is inevitable. The people are separated from the means of administration and from technology and knowledge. Modern society is characterised by the tension between democracy and bureaucracy. The democratic procedures that claim to empower the masses actually give increased significance to the bureaucratic and legal apparatus and those who operate within them. Formal democracy is rather empty; these elites are the real rulers of society. But whereas Pareto and Mosca accept this situation, Mills uses elite theory to criticise society from a broadly Marxist perspective.

But critics, such as Paul Hirst (1976: 88), have argued that elite theorists, and also Weber, ignore the question of why the masses comply. Their methodology remains too psychologistic or individualist and they fail to adequately theorise the objective social conditions that institutionalise consensus. The elite theorists see the relationship between rulers and ruled in terms of psychological characteristics, while Weber tends to see social relations in terms of the interaction between subjects:

> The term 'social relationship' will be used to designate the situation where two or more persons are engaged in conduct wherein each takes account of the behaviour of the other in a meaningful way and is therefore oriented in these terms. (Weber 1993: 63)

Such an approach cannot do justice to the sources of power – the institutions, structures and apparatuses that manufacture social control. They tend to define legitimacy from the point of view of rulers rather than the ruled and the masses play only a small role in determining how legitimacy is maintained. Their concern is with rulers rather than the ruled, hence they tend to focus on the rule of the rulers at the expense of the consent of the masses, which is rather taken for granted. Hirst argues that Weber does not question the basis of legitimacy, but rather, he tends to take legitimacy at face value while Wolfgang Mommsen (1974) comments that for Weber legitimacy is little more than an equivalent of the stability of the political system.

5. MODERNITY AND THE IRON CAGE

Karl Löwith argues that Weber shares with Marx a preoccupation with the cultural significance and consequences of modern Western capitalism and its alienating tendencies. Where they differ is that Weber focuses almost entirely on the individual. While Marx looks to collective political struggle, Weber's concern is with individual freedom and autonomy. Both Marx and Weber see modern capitalism as an irresistible force that imposes itself on the actions of human subjects. But for Weber the real issue is not the plight of the proletariat but the plight of the individual, who is overwhelmed by the process of rationalisation. Whereas Marx sees rationalisation as stemming from modern economic production, Weber sees it as a more general feature of modern society. The technical complexity of society, rather than its particular class character, gives rise to modern bureaucracy. Consequently, Weber is concerned not with the fate of the class struggle, but with the struggle to preserve liberal values and individual freedoms. For Marx the key question is the ownership of the means of production. For Weber the key question is the control of managerial positions. Therefore, because bureaucracy and rationalisation are inevitable features of modern society, the Marxist solution to social divisions would only make bureaucratic control worse. Socialism would also base itself on bureaucratic administration and political management, and would therefore merely develop the dominant features of the capitalist system – it would continue in the economic realm what is already happening in the political sphere. Weber condemned the Bolshevik revolution as one that was led by intellectuals who had achieved command over the workers, and he described it as a military dictatorship like any other.

Marx saw alienation as the product of class society and capitalist relations of production and, consequently, saw a way out of this through collective struggle. Weber, however, because he sees bureaucracy and rationalisation as inevitable, is more pessimistic and writes that 'the fate of our times is characterised by rationalisation and intellectualisation and, above all, by the"disenchantment of the world"' (Weber 1991: 155). Modernity comes to signify a loss of meaning, a fragmentation of social life and a lack of social unity. The ever-increasing power of instrumental reason leads to the retreat of cultural and religious values into the private sphere and the disenchantment of politics. Rationalised forms of instrumental action impose themselves on the individual and exert a kind of disciplinary power that regulates the lives of human beings and imposes an abstract and meaningless form of social conduct. The rationalisation of modern society represents an iron cage that imprisons the individual.

This is reflected in Weber's political views, where he expresses his growing anxiety about liberal society and future of democracy. Democracy, he argues, is an ideal that is only possible in small societies. Under conditions of mass democracy it has become simply a means for choosing efficient leaders and parliament should be regarded as a sort of testing ground – a forum for public debate and a way of getting popular support. Weber's notion of domination is comparable to the ideas of the elite theorists because it seems to exclude the idea of popular rule. The democratic process allows people the chance to select a leader, but not much more. The people certainly do not rule themselves. The best hope for the people lies in the election of a charismatic leader and here we find the influence of Nietzsche on Weber's thought. The only hope of escaping the rationalisation of society is through the creative powers of a leading individual. Hope lies with the *übermensch*, the superhuman personality. But this rather elitist view of the political process becomes more sinister when we remember that Weber also believes in the need for a powerful national state, and argues that the German nation must assert itself through strong leadership and an imperialist policy.

Weber defines legitimation as acceptance of a leader who is deemed worthy of obedience. This in turn is influenced by the Nietzschean belief in the spontaneous charismatic personality and by the social Darwinist idea that history is the struggle between human beings. As J. G. Merquior has argued, these Nietzschean influences tend to overwhelm Weber's discussion of social power and downplay the historical conditions that give rise to episodic eruptions of charisma (Merquior 1980: 208). Social change derives from the value-oriented actions of individuals and groups so that the main hope for historical change is the power of charisma. Emphasis is on the superiority of certain individuals who have the necessary 'will to power'. As the world becomes increasingly disenchanted, individuals are thrown back on themselves and forced to construct their own meanings and context. The self-sufficient individual becomes the only true and real social entity. The essence of human freedom is the capacity to choose ends and the nature of social action is determined by the relation of the subject to its own meanings and intentions. But Weber makes two assumptions about the individual which then dominate his theory of society. One is that human beings are essentially rational and goal-driven, the other that freedom is part of the human essence. Because Weber's social model is based on the individual, these drives tend to define the character of society itself. Thus the problem of rationalisation within society derives from the assumption that human beings are essentially goal-driven. In effect Weber's theory of the rationalisation of society is itself dependent upon rationalist assumptions about the nature of the individual.

Weber does stress the importance of legitimation, which provides subordinate subjects with subjectively meaningful reasons to obey. Dominance implies an amount of compliance and legitimacy exists when a form of domination is recognised as worthy of obedience. The problem with this is that social relations and institutions become constituted as intersubjective relations where one subject provides the other with the conditions of their action in the form of means, ends and meanings. Social cohesion may well derive from the process of rationalisation and consensus may well be an important aspect of domination, but because Weber uses the individual as his model, questions remain about just how 'social' his theory of cohesion and consent can be.

Chapter 6

CULTURE AND COMMUNICATION IN THE FRANKFURT SCHOOL

―――⊃⊂――――

1. LATE CAPITALISM AND THE ORIGINS OF THE FRANKFURT SCHOOL

We have seen that Weber is concerned with the rationalisation of society, the dominance of instrumental reason, the growth of bureau-cratisation and ever more efficient forms of social domination and control. In Weber's work social cohesion becomes monolithic and alienating. Marx's optimistic view of historical progress may have some truth at the material level, but is clearly untrue for the spheres of cultural and spiritual life. Despite his anti-Marxism, Weber's views were highly influential in Marxist circles. In particular Weber was an influence on his friend, the Hungarian Marxist philosopher and politi-cian, György Lukács. In turn, Lukács's ideas were influential among the diverse body of scholars who, due to their institutional affiliation, became known as the Frankfurt School.

Weber's theory of rationalisation is combined with Marx's theories of alienation and commodity fetishism. According to Marx, commodities take on the appearance of independent things and they assume a rational all-embracing character that conceals the real basis of society – the relation between people. Influenced by Weber, Lukács sees the process as going deep into the very psychology of human beings:

The transformation of the commodity relation into a thing of 'ghostly objectivity' cannot therefore content itself with the reduction of all objects for the gratification of human needs to commodities. It stamps its imprint upon the whole consciousness of man . . . This rationalisation of the world appears to be complete,

128

it seems to penetrate the very depths of man's physical and psychic nature. (Lukács 1971: 100–1)

Reification is like the 'thingification' of social relations and it would seem that Lukács shares Weber's misery about the all-encompassing nature of rationalisation. But whereas Weber retreated into despair, Lukács, as a Marxist, must try to find a way out of the iron cage. How can we develop a 'true' consciousness in a reified world? The answer lies in the Hegelian dialectics of history. The proletariat is given a unique historical role. The emancipation of society depends upon it acquiring self-consciousness and self-understanding, which simultaneously means an understanding of society as a whole:

> The dialectical method as the true historical method was reserved for the class which was able to discover within itself on the basis of its life-experience the identical subject–object, the subject of action; the 'we' of the genesis: namely the proletariat . . . The self-understanding of the proletariat is therefore simultaneously the objective understanding of the nature of society. When the proletariat furthers its own class aims it simultaneously achieves the conscious realisation of the – objective – aims of society. (Ibid., pp. 148–9)

The proletariat represents the universal class, both the subject and object of history. The fate of the revolution, and hence of society, is determined by the maturity of the working class. Lukács stresses the importance of the unity of theory and practice and, just in case his theory of proletarian self-consciousness runs into difficulties, he guarantees this through the role of the Communist Party, which is said to be 'the bearer of the class consciousness of the proletariat and the conscience of its historical vocation' (ibid., p. 41).

There is no such luxury for the Frankfurt school theorists Theodor W. Adorno and Max Horkheimer. They not only share Weber's pessimism, but in some ways extend and generalise it. Rationalisation covers the whole totality, especially the cultural sphere, and this makes the overthrow of society impossible. Despite claiming allegiance to Marxism, the Frankfurt school move away from the main emancipatory ideas of Marx, and in particular rejects the idea of a revolutionary subject.

The Frankfurt school theorists draw on both Marx and Weber, as can be seen in their notion of 'late capitalism'. They side with Marx in stressing the importance of capitalism, whereas Weber tends to see the development of capitalism as secondary to the more general development of rationalism. But the term 'late' pays homage to Weber's ideas on modernity, the dominant political trends, the role of the state, the growth of bureaucracy and the prevalence of instrumental reason. In this sense, the capitalism that Adorno and Horkheimer are concerned with is quite different to the capitalist society described by Marx.

In 'Late Capitalism or Industrial Society?' Adorno asks whether the world is now so dominated by technology that social relations have lost their significance. Even if Marxist theories like the falling rate of profit are not untrue, the capitalist system has proved resilient enough to indefinitely postpone the anticipated collapse. Class conflict is also in decline since technological progress allows the system to produce enough consumer goods to mollify the masses. Marx's economic theory was supposed to provide the basis for understanding class conflict. But his theoretical analysis corresponds closely to the liberal stage of capitalist development, a very different world to the one discussed by Adorno. With mass production, mass consumption, monopolisation, rationalisation, bureaucratisation, militarisation, totalitarianism and the growth of the culture industry, the world has become a different place and the identity of the revolutionary subject is no longer clear.

Whereas Marx believed that social cohesion came from the economic system, Adorno agrees with Weber on the importance of political command. The economy now functions through political domination. Social relations are concerned not only with production but also with administration. Production and distribution are collectively administered with the state acting like a 'general capitalist'. This makes political domination more important in determining social cohesion. Humans are still dominated by the economic process, but this now takes the political form of totalitarian state management. State intervention into the economy is not, as liberals might argue, a secondary interference, but is now essential to the functioning and cohesion of the capitalist system. The state plays a commanding role so that 'the telos of state intervention is direct political domination independent of market mechanisms' (Adorno 1987: 245).

Late capitalism therefore represents the integration of the economic and the political. Production, administration and distribution reach into every sphere of social and material life, including, importantly, the cultural sphere. As with Weber, this is seen as true for every industrial and bureaucratic society, including the Soviet Union, where the desire for economic progress brought about a dictatorial and austere administration. Thus the immiseration of the masses does take place, but not as Marx predicted. Rather, the immiseration of the masses is intellectual rather than material. The masses are confined to a state of immaturity. Unable to control their own lives and to develop a critical consciousness, they instead experience the world as blind fate, as myth (ibid., p. 237). As Adorno and Horkheimer argue:

> The over-maturity of society lives by the immaturity of the dominated. The more complicated and precise the social, economic, and scientific apparatus with whose service the production system has long harmonised the body, the more impoverished the experiences which it can offer. (1986: 36)

Unlike Marx, therefore, reification is not just an economic phenomenon, but has important cultural, political and epistemological dimensions affecting our very ways of thinking and knowing: 'Through the countless agencies of mass production and its culture the conventionalised modes of behaviour are impressed on the individual as the only natural, respectable, and rational ones' (ibid., p. 28).

The early Frankfurt theorists see monopoly capitalism as bringing about increasing domination and centralisation and they examine these effects in the cultural sphere, looking, for example, at the way in which technological developments debase mass culture. However, this is contested by Walter Benjamin, who is more loosely connected with the school and who argues that technology has a revolutionary potential that, for the first time, can bring art to the masses. The 'age of mechanical reproduction' destroys the elitist aura of art and undermines the influence of tradition. The 'mechanical reproduction of art changes the reaction of the masses toward art . . . The progressive reaction is characterised by the direct, intimate fusion of visual and emotional enjoyment with the orientation of the expert' (Benjamin 1973: 236). In contrast to other Frankfurt theorists Benjamin regards mass culture as having a radical potential, particularly new forms such as cinema.

Herbert Marcuse also differs somewhat from Adorno and Horkheimer in holding out more hope for a radical transformation of society. However, as we shall see, he finds his revolutionary agents not among the traditional working class, but among the outsiders and outcasts. This nevertheless shares the pessimistic view that the great mass of people has been incorporated into the system, and that political and cultural domination is all-pervasive. In order to explain such pessimism, it is necessary to take into account the fact that the early Frankfurt theorists were writing at a time of crisis and defeat. The members of the school were, after all, forced into exile in order to escape the dangers of fascist Germany. The fascist state, the product of a particular period, tends to be seen by the Frankfurt theorists as representing the general direction of late capitalist society. Fascism and war were products of monopoly capitalism, bureaucratisation and administration, and the spread of technological rationalisation. Their experience in exile in the United States led Adorno and Horkheimer to believe that this process was not confined to the openly fascist or Stalinist states, but was a general historical trend.

A debate took place within the Frankfurt school over the nature of fascism. Whereas Franz Neumann's important study *Behemoth* (1966) tends to concentrate on political, legal and economic institutions, Horkheimer's focus is on social psychology, mass culture and the spread of irrationalism. Here the influence of Freud's psychoanalysis is strong. The totalitarian leaders are powerful because they are able to project the image of a father figure. This appeals to the narcissistic ego, which remains in an infantile state. The narcissistic personality undermines social relations between people and personal and emotional attachments. Individualisation begins to disappear and a rational and coherent ego identity is lost. The weak human ego allows for social consensus to be achieved by psychological manipulation. This allows for the dominance of authoritarian political personalities, but it also allows for the kind of manipulation carried out by what is termed the culture industry. The culture industry appeals to our weakened emotions and it steps in to gratify human needs. It takes advantage of the erosion of our individual autonomy and integrates individuals into the social system. The culture industry encounters very little resistance. Social consensus is almost total. And we are left wondering, like Weber, whether enlightened individuals can ever escape the iron cage.

2. ENLIGHTENMENT

For Marx, alienation is a product of class society and capitalist relations of production, but for Adorno and Horkheimer our estrangement runs deeper than this. It is a product not of a particular class society, but of society in general, or more particularly, of the dialectic between society and nature. The more society comes to dominate nature, the more it becomes alienated from itself. As Horkheimer puts it: 'The history of man's efforts to subjugate nature is also the history of man's subjugation by man' (1987: 105).

This, then, is the dialectic of enlightenment. As humanity tries to free itself from nature and bring nature under its control, so, at the same time it degrades itself and destroys its own basis. In *Dialectic of Enlightenment* Adorno and Horkheimer write:

> As soon as man discards his awareness that he himself is nature, all the aims for which he keeps himself alive – social progress, the intensification of all his material and spiritual powers, even consciousness itself – are nullified . . . Man's domination over himself, which grounds his selfhood, is almost always the destruction of the subject in whose service it is undertaken . . . (1986: 54)

Society's domination of nature becomes 'internalised' so that it becomes domination over our own nature. All nature, including our own nature, becomes mere material, emptied of all purpose. Nature becomes a mere tool of humanity, something to be dominated, but humanity itself, though this process, loses sight of itself. Our attitude towards nature and towards each other and ourselves becomes merely instrumental. And, as with Weber, we are dominated by instrumentality in the form of reason. Enlightenment thinking represents the attempt to create a unified scientific order, but because society is striving to control nature, reason loses its critical faculty.

The dialectic of enlightenment leads to self-destruction and alienation from nature and ourselves. It is about cultural decline due to the rise of scientific rationality and instrumental reason. It is about the way that developments in science and technology, coupled with the advancement of capitalism, lead to new, bureaucratic and totalitarian forms of domination and control. These differ widely, from reason itself, through to social institutions and practices. Cohesion and consensus are maintained through the technocratic–bureaucratic functioning of different social institutions – institutions like the family, the state and the culture industry. The early critical theorists agreed with Weber against Marx that rather than opening up the possibility of a classless order, society was becoming ever more integrated, and its structures ever more impenetrable. Technology and rationality are abstract forces that shape society beyond human control while instrumental values take over and undermine personal freedom. However, Adorno and Horkheimer argue that Weber is wrong to see the development of instrumental reason as the main driving force of modern society. They argue that this must be seen in the context of the development of capitalism or, more precisely, late capitalism. Weber cherishes a false belief in the free market, an ideal appropriate to the liberal phase of capitalist development, but now undermined by the domination of monopoly capital. The 'rationality' of the free market is increasingly subordinated to the irrationality of political domination. Weber is right to stress the trend towards bureaucracy and other forms of legal–rational domination, but these in turn must be seen in the context of the development of late capitalism or the drive to achieve political domination over the economy.

Late capitalist society suppresses social heterogeneity and treats individuals as exchangeable things. Social cohesion has become a repressive force and modern society has become so organised and impenetrable that all forms of critical consciousness have been marginalised. The culture industry operates to monopolise public opinion and minimise our critical awareness. Fetishisation is so developed that it paralyses our ability to imagine the world differently from the way that it appears. This mental condition has become a real material force (Adorno 1987: 241). Such a position is close to Marx's theory of commodity fetishism, but it is also similar to Weber's theory of the disenchantment of the world. Adorno and Horkheimer clearly combine the two ideas when they write: 'With the extension of the bourgeois commodity economy, the dark horizon of myth is illuminated by the sun of calculating reason, beneath whose cold rays the seed of the new barbarism grows to fruition' (1986: 32).

The Enlightenment aimed at liberating us from fear. It brought about the disenchantment of the world by dissolving myths and superstition so that 'the spirit of enlightenment replaced the fire and the rack by the stigma it attached to all irrationality' (ibid., p. 31). However, the dialectic of enlightenment is such that it brings in new forms of domination. The modern world is seemingly disenchanted, but in fact this reinforces reification: 'Myth turns into enlightenment, and nature into mere objectivity. Men pay for the increase in their power with alienation from that over which they exercise their power' (ibid., p. 9). The anti-authoritarian impulse of the Enlightenment turns into its opposite. This again is similar to Weber's theory of rationalisation, where reason kills myth only to become a new form of domination that undermines the original goal of liberation and enlightenment. But the Frankfurt theory places more emphasis on the relation between Enlightenment thought and the dominant mode of production, although even here, Adorno and Horkheimer's argument reminds us of Weber's theory of bureaucratisation:

> On the one hand the growth of economic productivity furnishes the conditions for a world of greater justice; on the other hand it allows the technical apparatus and the social groups which administer it a disproportionate superiority to the rest of the population. The individual is wholly devalued in relation to the economic powers, which at the same time press the control of society over nature to hitherto unsuspected heights. (Ibid., p. xiv)

It can be seen in the rise of the technical and bureaucratic apparatus and in forms of political domination that become increasingly totalitarian. This is related to the development of late capitalism and in particular the growth of monopoly capitalism, which demands an increasingly political form of domination. This domination becomes so overpowering that it filters through to every level of society, every institution and indeed our very ways of thinking.

Enlightenment thinking extinguishes the traces of its own self-consciousness. Thought loses its element of self-reflection and becomes alienated, reified and ritualised. Reason becomes formalised and lacks the ability to make critical judgement or comment on the desirability of any goal. As Horkheimer says, the Enlightenment philosophers attacked religion in the name of reason but they killed not the church, but metaphysics, the objective concept and hence reason itself. With the American and French revolutions reason becomes harnessed to social process, but becomes a social instrument. As a result, meaning is supplanted by social function (Horkheimer 1987: 22). Horkheimer's view is similar to Weber's in its claim that bourgeois thought begins with the struggle against the authority of tradition, replaces it with reason as the legitimate source of right and truth, but ends with the deification of naked authority (Horkheimer 1972: 72). He further echoes Weber's views on religion and asceticism when he writes:

> Ever since Calvinism sanctified man's calling in the world, poverty, contrary to the accepted notion, has in practice been a taint to be washed away only by toil. The same process that freed each man from slavery and serfdom, and returned him to himself, also broke him into two parts, the private and the social, and burdened the private with a mortgage. Life outside the office and shop was appointed to refresh a man's strength for office and shop; it was thus a mere appendage, a kind of tail to the comet of labour, measured, like labour, by time, and termed 'free time'. (Ibid., p. 275)

Late capitalism represents the subordination of reason to commerce and industry, while critical and reflective thought is transformed into instrumental reason. Justice, equality, happiness and tolerance, all of which are supposed to be inherent in or sanctioned by reason, have lost their intellectual roots. Yet this is something that is willingly given up in the name of progress. The history of civilisation is the introversion of sacrifice, the history of renunciation.

3. THE CULTURE INDUSTRY

The culture industry is founded on the alliance of late capitalism and instrumental reason and the concept emphasises the cultural aspect of domination. It plays a role similar to ideology in securing consensus within late capitalist society. This consensus is deep and underlying; it is not merely superstructural or instrumental but is rooted in the foundations of social life. The status of the culture industry is rather contradictory. On the one hand, Adorno and Horkheimer see it as deep rooted and all-pervasive; on the other, they see it as a rather shallow and complacent industry. It makes no real attempt to disguise its false or manipulative aspect; indeed, it celebrates its commodified and commercialised form. It is not deep or profound, it simply claims that things are the way they are. The ideology of late capitalism is transparent.

Late capitalism encourages standardisation and conformity and the development of culture is no different to any other branch of industry. Films, music and other entertainments are mass produced to a standard formula so that all culture becomes more or less identical. Commercialisation brings about the fusion of culture and entertainment. Culture is measured by its exchange value. Not only does social rating become the new measure of artistic status, but this is openly celebrated by the industry:

> No object has an inherent value; it is valuable only to the extent that it can be exchanged. The use value of art, its mode of being, is treated as a fetish; and the fetish, the work's social rating (misinterpreted as its artistic status) becomes its use value – the only quality which is enjoyed. (Adorno and Horkheimer 1986: 158)

So Marx's notion of commodity production and fetishism is extended to cultural production. Not only are cultural products marketable and interchangeable like any other product, but this situation is promoted as an ideology. Films are measured in terms of their box-office success, records by their position in the charts, and this becomes the main means for differentiating products, given their standardised character. The culture industry holds a monopoly over what is to be produced and promoted, and this in turn becomes a form of social control and means of eliminating dissent and originality:

> Under monopoly all mass culture is identical, and the lines of its artificial framework begin to show through. The people at the top are no longer so interested in concealing monopoly: as its violence becomes more open, so its power grows. Movies and radio need no longer pretend to be art. The truth that they are just business is made into an ideology in order to justify the rubbish they deliberately produce. (Ibid., p. 121)

Under monopoly capitalism the cultural product loses its innovation and uniqueness. However, although cultural goods are standardised, an attempt is made to create the illusion of choice through a pseudo-individualisation. Small differences of detail such as the style of a film star's hair create the illusion of distinctiveness. With the standardisation of the industry these small differences of features become significant. The industry relies on a stereotyped portrayal of the world. It reinforces certain images and types of behaviour, but attempts to disguise this through its pseudo-individualisation. The stereotypes of the culture industry encourage pathological forms of collectivity. People prefer what is familiar to them. Thus any distinctiveness must be contained within a general standardised form that satisfies our psychological disposition. As with more naked forms of advertising, the culture industry ensures that there is no longer any need for us to think for ourselves. The public is catered for by a hierarchy of mass-produced items, with different mass products produced for different social groups. Consumers are statistics for research organisations. Anticipating Foucault, Adorno and Horkheimer write of the importance of cataloguing and classifying, which brings the cultural consumer into the sphere of administration.

Here Adorno and Horkheimer's views are close to Foucault's notion of social cohesion through organised practices and disciplines: 'The stronger the positions of the culture industry become, the more summarily it can deal with consumers' needs, producing them, controlling them, disciplining them, and even withdrawing amusement' (ibid., p. 144). We consent to the demands of the culture industry because of our need for gratification – a need that is denied to us in our everyday life.

> Pleasure always means not to think about anything, to forget suffering even where it is shown. Basically it is helplessness. It is flight; not as is asserted, flight from a wretched reality, but from the last remaining thought of resistance. The liberation which amusement promises is freedom from thought and from negation. (Ibid., p. 144)

The price we pay is the loss of our freedom of imagination. The pleasure we receive is at the expense of our critical faculties. Real life becomes indistinguishable from the movies, and the movies, as a passive product, leave little room for reflection or imagination. Therefore, the process of standardisation should not just be seen as a product of mass production, but contains an important psychological element. Standardisation is also about stereotyping and controlling our imagination and organising our experiences. In particular, it is about imitation and mimicry. The culture industry gains its consent through the psychological methods of repetition and recognition.

This is clearly similar to the method of commercial advertising with which the culture industry merges. Adorno and Horkheimer write that 'the assembly-line character of the culture industry, the synthetic, planned method of turning out its products . . . is very suited to advertising' (ibid., p. 163). The product is interchangeable, detachable and repeatable. The cultural product is like a propaganda slogan with 'the easy yet catchy, the skilful yet simple; the object is to overpower the customer' (ibid., p. 163). Products are made easy to digest so that they fit in with the intensive demands of modern society, 'occupying men's senses from the time they leave the factory in the evening to the time they clock in again the next morning with matter that bears the impress of the labour process they themselves have to sustain throughout the day' (ibid., p. 131). The products of the culture industry also play a pacifying role: 'It [the culture industry] comforts all with the thought that a tough, genuine human fate is still possible' (ibid., p. 151). As with Marx's theory of religion, the culture industry stands in for the missing human ties and relations. Morality is now to be found in the heroes and villains of children's books. Tragic film becomes an institution for moral improvement.

The connection between culture and everyday life debases culture and turns it into a mere effect of the social order. The inferior work of art relies on imitation and with the culture industry 'this imitation finally becomes absolute. Having ceased to be anything but style, it reveals the latter's secret: obedience to the social hierarchy' (ibid., p. 131). Even more dismissively Adorno and Horkheimer write: 'By craftily sanctioning the demand for rubbish it inaugurates total harmony' (ibid., p. 134). The products of the culture industry should therefore be seen as a form of ideology that helps maintain social cohesion. Its product lacks spontaneity, is reified and artificial, it is 'stylised barbarism', but it is at least a more subtle form of enslavement and gaining acceptance for domination. For Adorno and Horkheimer compare the culture industry to fascism. Both make an appeal to the emotions and impulses and we submit ourselves to them because of our psychological needs. But the war ended with the triumph of the American culture industry rather than the less subtle psychological domination of the fascist dictatorship.

4. CRITICAL THEORY AND NEGATIVE DIALECTICS

The cohesion of modern society has been shifted to the institutions of the cultural sphere, which provide us with our reasoning, morality and world-outlooks. These relate to deeper psychological needs which the culture industry skilfully manipulates. It fills the gap between modern economic activity and moral, ethical and cultural life. In this way the culture industry acts as an ideological binding that ties together different aspects of the cultural system. It also provides consent to this system, getting us to acquiesce in the production and consumption of cultural commodities. The commodification of the cultural sphere and the debasement of artistic values is hardly hidden. Indeed, it might be said that these values are openly promoted as selling points. The culture industry is very open about its shallow, commercial values, which are marketed to the general public like anything else. However, it is important to see that the culture industry is not just a clever ploy by the ruling class. It has deeper material and intellectual roots that relate to the effects of the development of monopoly capitalism, which con-stitutes the whole way of modern social life. This does leave us with a rather miserable situation. Cohesion and consent seem overpowering, late capitalism seems irreversible. The working class seems entirely pacified and assimilated into the economic and cultural order. We are left wondering which way out?

Adorno and Horkheimer argue that late capitalism is dominated by identity thinking, which is the belief that things are as they are or, to put it another way, it is the inability to see things differently to how they appear in their immediacy. The products of the culture industry lack any kind of speculative element and rely on the endless repetition and reproduction of what is. The culture industry makes no real attempt to conceal this situation, but relies on unapologetic straightforward legitimation. This carries over into the theoretical or philosophical sphere. Fredric Jameson likens this to fetishism and makes the point that for Adorno identity thinking is in fact another expression of exchange relations: 'His achievement then was to have powerfully generalised, in richer detail than any other thinker of the Marxist or dialectical tradition, the resonance and implications of the doctrine of exchange value for the higher reaches of philosophy' (Jameson 1990: 26). We can see how the then dominant idea of positivism cele-brates the existence of that which is, and takes social reality at imme-diate face value. It does not register contradictions, and refuses to see the social as a process of development and change. Positivism claims that philosophy is merely concerned with the classification and formalisation of scientific methods, while modern science is reduced to statements about facts. Positivism is fetishism in theory. Its rigid concepts presuppose the reification of life in general and our perception in particular (Horkheimer 1987: 81). The fact is like an abstract object of exchange. The fact-form, like the commodity-form, is a reification.

Critical reflection must be able to see through these facts and recognise them as historical products. Against identity thinking, the critical theorists put forward an immanent ideology critique. The aim is to show that what exists does not have to be as it is, that things are not given, that things are contradictory and that possible alternatives exist. Dialectical theory questions the immediacy of empirical facts by seeking out the underlying structural conditions and social processes: 'The task of cognition does not consist in mere apprehension, classification and calculation, but in the determinate negation of each immediacy' (Adorno and Horkheimer 1986: 27). That the struggle against reification takes place in the realm of theory comes as no surprise. Adorno and Horkheimer follow Weber in giving (instrumental) reason a prominent role in the constitution of social life. They reject the class-struggle politics of Marxism in favour of philosophy and aesthetics. The working class is fully integrated into the structures of capitalist society and its consciousness is too atomised, reified and passive to offer any hope of liberation.

Looking for a possible escape from total despair Horkheimer ultimately turns to religion as the only way to preserve the idea of a better world. Adorno, the more brilliant theorist, develops his dialectical critique of philosophy in his classic work *Negative Dialectics*. As Joan Alway notes (1995: 51–2), because Horkheimer saw Marxism as a moral theory he was more affected by its collapse and he turned to religion as an alternative faith. Adorno did not share this disillusionment because he never had such a faith. He viewed Marxism more as a method of analysis, and so he was more able to continue his critical project.

Adorno's philosophical–aesthetic approach leads him to see the work of the 'authentic artist' as the only path to liberation. The ideology of enlightenment does not entirely act as a dominating force. Liberal ideas become part of the self-understanding but in a debased form. However, they do contain some speculative content and are therefore open to question. Likewise the consciousness is partially aware of the role of the culture industry. Therefore, like Weber, Adorno turns his focus to the bourgeois individual and the educated middle classes as the focus for resistance. He comes to the view that political action should not be about overthrowing the bourgeois order, but about protecting bourgeois freedoms and preserving individual liberty. This view clearly lacks any collective emancipatory vision. What unites the Frankfurt theorists is the belief that social cohesion is based on the domination of the system over the lives of individuals. Adorno and Weber, when faced with the Iron Cage, turn to the isolated bourgeois individual as the last hope.

5. ONE-DIMENSIONAL SOCIETY

If Adorno and Horkheimer give up on the revolutionary subject, what hope is there for the other main critical theorist of this period, Herbert Marcuse, whose work *One-Dimensional Man* is very much a popularised version of *Dialectic of Enlightenment*? We find Marcuse arguing a similar line to Adorno and Horkheimer when he claims that the working class has been so integrated into capitalist society that it no longer has a revolutionary potential. However, Marcuse does maintain hope of revolutionary change, only he turns from the working class to the outcasts, outsiders, rebels and intellectuals, who, he believes, have not been integrated and who represent the most radical consciousness. This led to Marcuse becoming a darling of the radical student movement, a strange position indeed considering the accusations of intellectual elitism and passivity levelled against the other members of the school.

Marcuse echoes the theme of *Dialectic of Enlightenment* when he writes of the 'totalitarian universe of technological rationality as the latest transmutation of the idea of Reason' (1966: 123). Modern society is dialectical, it represents both opportunity and repression. Advanced industrial civilisation contains a 'terrifying harmony of freedom and oppression, productivity and destruction, growth and regression' (ibid., p. 124). Marcuse also agrees with the view that this complex situation stems from society's control over nature so that 'history is the negation of Nature. What is only natural is overcome and recreated by the power of Reason' (ibid., p. 236). Our relationship with nature becomes instrumental and this instrumental reason becomes the dominant force within society. This takes the form of totalitarian political control and administrative bureaucratisation. The world becomes the stuff of

total administration. Society sustains itself because alongside this domination it offers continued material development and progress, but this
is achieved at a high political and personal price: 'The productivity
and growth potential of this system stabilise the society and contain
technical progress within the framework of domination. Technological
rationality has become political rationality' (ibid., p. xvi). Social cohesion can be expressed as 'a comfortable, smooth, reasonable, democratic
unfreedom [that] prevails in advanced industrial civilisation, a token of
technical progress' (ibid., p. 1). This leaves the majority of people on
the side of that which is rather than what ought to be. Social cohesion
is very powerful: 'the political machine, the corporate machine, the
cultural and educational machine which has welded blessing and curse
into one rational whole. The whole has become too big, its cohesion
too strong, its functioning too efficient' (Marcuse 1969: 13).

Marcuse, like other members of the Frankfurt school, rejects the
Marxist view that society is beset with economic crises. In fact late
capitalism is able to overcome these tensions by means of a more
regulated form of economic activity and an increased amount of state
intervention and political domination. This material stability forms
the basis for a new social consensus. Imitating Hegel, Marcuse writes:
'The Happy Consciousness – the belief that the real is rational and
that the system delivers the goods – reflects the new conformism
which is a facet of technological rationality translated into social
behaviour' (1966: 84). Individual happiness is founded on the provision
of abundant material goods. This is a consequence of the development
of the productive apparatus, but the price paid is the domination of this
apparatus, which shapes people's needs and desires and turns them
into compliant individuals:

> In this society, the productive apparatus tends to become totali-
> tarian to the extent to which it determines not only the socially
> needed occupations, skills and attitudes, but also individual needs
> and aspirations. It thus obliterates the opposition between the
> private and public existence, between individual and social needs.
> Technology serves to institute new, more effective, and more
> pleasant forms of social control and social cohesion. (Ibid., p. xv)

It is here that Marcuse makes an interesting contribution to the
arguments of critical theory, for he examines how the domination of

the system becomes internalised and how these processes shape the development of the individual. As with the other critical theorists, his view of the human individual is rather pessimistic, as is indicated by the term 'one-dimensional man'. Marcuse argues that the development of modern society has obliterated our mental faculties. The goods and services that people buy control their needs and petrify their faculties. We are satisfied by the provision of material goods, but we do not realise that our desires and needs have been shaped for us and that we have lost our critical and reflexive understanding. Material life becomes soulless: 'The ideology of today lies in that production and consumption reproduce and justify domination ... The individual pays by sacrificing his time, his consciousness, his dreams; civilisation pays by sacrificing its own promises of liberty, justice and peace for all' (Marcuse 1969: 80).

Technical power has taken over the system and eliminated conflict from social life. The capitalist system is stabilised and social change is contained. The ever-greater mechanisation of labour both sustains exploitation and modifies the attitude of the exploited. Its effects on the individual are exhausting and stupefying. The growth of technical power turns the individual into an automaton.

In fact social cohesion and individual integration are so far advanced that the fundamental (and antagonistic) class basis of society has been irreparably altered. In the one-dimensional society the working class and the bourgeoisie are no longer dominant social forces:

> The capitalist development has altered the structure and function of these two classes in such a way that they no longer appear to be agents of historical transformation. An overriding interest in the preservation of the institutional status quo unites the former antagonists in the most advanced areas of contemporary society. (Marcuse 1966: xii–xiii)

The working class as Marx conceived it is no longer the majority of the population and it no longer seeks to change the system. The working class is no longer revolutionary in a subjective sense. It sees its interests as within the system and it has neither the consciousness nor the need for a revolution. It may be a class 'in itself' but it is not a class 'of itself'. In any case, the new majority within society are the specialists, technicians and white-collar workers who are a product of the development of the state, political domination and the bureaucratisation of society. Late industrial society increases the number of parasitic and alienated functionaries who lack any sense of social solidarity or class consciousness.

Consequently, 'the struggle for the solution has outgrown the traditional forms. The totalitarian tendencies of the one-dimensional society render the traditional ways and means of protest ineffective' (ibid., p. 256). Therefore Marcuse shifts agency from the economic to the political. Revolutionary agents are not defined according to economic conditions, but according to political forms of oppression. In the totally integrated society they are the ones on the margins. They are the outsiders and outcasts, the underprivileged and the intellectuals, all those who carry with them an extra awareness, who have not been totally integrated into society. Marcuse makes a particular play for the student movement, the black movement, Third World liberation struggles, the hippies and those engaged in moral and sexual rebellion. These groups, he believes, are concerned with more than just narrow economic or political issues; their outlook is concerned with the system as a whole. The traditional working class is part of the passive majority which needs to be rescued by this active minority, who act as potential catalysts of rebellion.

In his earlier Hegelian–Marxist work Marcuse sees our fundamental essence as constituted through labour. But his critique of instrumental reason develops in the direction of psychology, sexuality and repression of the instincts. This is further developed in his social–psychoanalytic work *Eros and Civilization*, where he writes: 'Even at the beginning of Western civilization, long before this principle was institutionalized, reason was defined as an instrument of constraint, of instinctual suppression; the domain of the instincts, sensuousness, was considered eternally hostile and detrimental to reason' (Marcuse 1969: 132). Whereas Marxism emphasises the alienation of labour, Marcuse is now concerned with how social cohesion is maintained through the repression of erotic and aesthetic needs and impulses.

According to Freud, human history is the history of repression. Culture constrains our societal and biological existence and controls our instincts. History becomes that of the denial of pleasure and civilised morality is the morality of repressed instincts. Marcuse sees this in terms of the transformation of the pleasure principle into the reality principle, which is based on renunciation and restraint. The individual realises that the gratification of their needs is impossible and that unrestrained pleasure comes into conflict with our natural and human environment. The reality principle modifies our behaviour: immediate satisfaction becomes delayed satisfaction; pleasure is restrained; joy, play, receptiveness and the absence of repression are replaced with work, productiveness and security (ibid., p. 30). The main function of the ego is to control the instinctual impulses of the id; it is the mediator between the id and the external world and it acts to minimise conflicts with reality. The conflict between the ego and the id indicates the contradiction between the individual and society and the struggle against or conformity with repressive forces and objective reason. Thus the reality principle sustains the organism in the external world. However, the reality principle is not purely a psychological process. It is embodied in social institutions and has to be reproduced in social life. The dominance of the reality principle over the pleasure principle is never complete and has to be socially secured (ibid., p. 32). In this sense civilisation can still be seen as organised and institution-alised domination. Consensus is not simply a psychological matter, but relates to the reproduction of social life. Subjection brings with it certain rewards: 'What started as subjection by force soon became "voluntary servitude", collaboration in reproducing a society which made servitude increasingly rewarding and palatable' (ibid., p. 12).

Marcuse asks why it is that revolutions have never fully succeeded. We might answer that to a large extent this is because of deep-rooted social cohesion and a consensus that reaches right down to our basic psychology. But Marcuse suggests that there is a series of moments when the struggle against domination might have succeeded, but that revolutionary movements always seem to contain an element of self-defeat. Marcuse looks to a psychological explanation – it is the development of the guilt feeling that prohibits and constrains our actions and holds back social change. Civilisation develops through the repressive control of the instincts. Progress is accompanied by an increasing sense of guilt. And the rationalisation of power brings with it the guilt of rebellion.

6. HABERMAS: CONSENSUS, THE PUBLIC SPHERE AND LEGITIMATION CRISIS

Jürgen Habermas aims to overcome the pessimism of his German predecessors Adorno, Horkheimer, Weber and Nietzsche and sees his task as recovering the positive aspects of modernity. Habermas believes that if he can rehabilitate the concept of reason and extend it beyond Weber's restricted understanding of instrumentality, then we can complete the unfinished project of modernity. To do this Habermas turns away from the subject–object paradigm towards the activities of intersubjective communities. In particular, he looks at the intersubjective foundations of consensus to be found in the public sphere, the life world and the structures of communication and discourse. This project might also be contrasted with the Marxist one, so that while Marx tends to see history and society in terms of the mode of production, Habermas shifts attention to forms of language and communication as the main basis for social cohesion, integration and emancipation. Here the aim is to examine the structures of mutual understanding. This places much more emphasis on the role of consensus formation within society. Such a theme is already being developed in his early work *The Structural Transformation of the Public Sphere.*

Habermas conceives of the public sphere as that realm which mediates between civil society and the state, it is the realm of social life where public opinion is formed. It concerns matters of public interest or social concern. These matters are given legitimacy as critical discussion of public issues is institutionally facilitated. In this sphere citizens debate their common affairs. Consensus is grounded in the intersubjective understanding of interests and needs. Public discourses are developed and debated and this dialogue develops as a practical discourse that evaluates the validity of social and political norms of action.

The public sphere developed as power shifted from the aristocracy to the new bourgeoisie. Eighteenth-century Europe saw the growth of public participation in political life, a widening concept of citizenship, increasing demands for representative government and constitutional and legal freedoms. Accompanying this was the development of new social, cultural and political discourses and new bodies such as literary societies, cafés, public lectures, journals and newspapers. This was a particular phase in history, that of early bourgeois society, where private individuals became increasingly concerned with the government of society. The new bourgeoisie saw itself as the reasoning public, as those charged with fighting absolutism and defending the public interest. Such contestation threw up new legitimating ideologies and universalistic doctrines.

Paradoxically (and here Habermas echoes Adorno, Horkheimer and Weber's views on the development of rationality), the growth of capitalism, while initially developing the public sphere, eventually undermines it. The development of capitalism leads to the decline of the classical liberal public sphere, as it undermines the legitimacy of its institutions and erodes its independence. The radical discussion typical of the early bourgeois era is undermined by the process of rationalisation and commercialisation. The independence of the public sphere is lost when private institutions increasingly assume public power, and when the state begins to penetrate public realm. State and civil society become increasingly entwined and the distinction between public and private realms becomes blurred: 'This dialectic of a progressive "societalisation" of the state simultaneously with an increasing "staification" of society gradually destroyed the basis of the bourgeois public sphere – the separation of state and society' (Habermas 1989: 142). The new sphere that emerges is neither private nor public, but is a pseudo-public sphere reflecting the interpenetration of state and society.

Under the liberal model of the public sphere, rational debate and consensus is still limited to a small elite with a shared social, cultural and educational background. But the growth of mass democracy, rather than developing and expanding the public sphere, has in fact had the opposite effect. Here Habermas returns to the concerns of the early Frankfurt theorists – the impact of the culture industry, the manipulation of public opinion, the role of the mass media, the bureaucratisation of social and private life, and the instrumental actions of the state. Ideologically, it is not so much 'false ideas' but the domination of 'technocratic consciousness' that undermines the emancipatory potential of the public sphere. The justification of social life is no longer related to normative action in the public sphere, but takes on an instrumental, means–ends character.

The structural transformation of the public sphere raises the question of the relation between the state and civil society, and it is certainly true that the critical function of the public sphere is undermined by state intervention. But private ownership offers no protection against this intrusion:

> According to the liberal model of the public sphere, the institutions
> of the public engaged in rational–critical debate were protected
> from interference by public authority by virtue of their being in the

hands of private people. To the extent that they were commercialised and underwent economic, technological, and organisational concentration, however, they have turned during the last hundred years into complexes of societal power, so that precisely their remaining in private hands in many ways threatened the critical functions of publicist institutions. (Ibid., p. 188)

This transformation takes place due to the development of electronic mass media, advertising and the entertainment industry, the growth of information, and bureaucratic centralisation. The media may have a greater range and effectiveness, but is more closely tied to the realm of commodity exchange. Rational debate is replaced with cultural consumption. Consumer culture exerts the ideological function of gaining conformity to existing conditions. Two crosscutting processes occur – the communicative generation of legitimate power and the manipulative deployment of media power – to promote mass loyalty, consumer demand and compliance with systemic imperatives. The rise of the mass media and mass politics indicates how the critical aspect of the public sphere turns into the manipulation of the public. As channels of communication become more regulated and access to public communication more selective, the public arena is infiltrated by power relations. The media and political parties develop accordingly:

The institutions of social–convivial interchange, which secured the coherence of the public making use of its reason, lost their power or utterly collapsed; the development toward a commercialised mass circulation press had its parallel in the reorganisation of the parties run by dignitaries on a mass basis. (Ibid., pp. 202–3)

Like Michels, Habermas argues that parties are linked to the bureaucratisation of society. They are bureaucratic apparatuses aimed at mobilising the public and manipulating public opinion. They do not aim to stimulate debate in the public sphere; rather, they are concerned with ideological integration. The politics of the plebiscite replaces genuine political discourse and political leaders seek public acclamation. With the development of the social–welfare state, political participation is further eroded as the bureaucratic apparatus takes on the role of a distributor and administrator.

Habermas's views on consensus formation in the public sphere have generated widespread interest but have been subject to a number of criticisms. The main criticisms are that his theory is too generalised and idealises the bourgeois model, that it does not pay enough attention to agency and that it takes social cohesion and consensus for granted. Habermas's generalised model tends to idealise the early bourgeois public sphere and thereby ignores possible alternative public spheres. In particular, it neglects the importance of the plebeian public sphere, which emerged alongside but in opposition to the bourgeois one, and which developed different institutions such as trade unions and different values such as solidarity rather than individual interest. Such a sphere is analysed in the work of E. P. Thompson and Raymond Williams, who excavate this often neglected tradition and venerate its culture, customs and discourses. Similarly, in excluding the household from the public sphere, Habermas neglects the main site of gender relations and his model has been criticised by feminists.

Habermas's model is too universalistic and fails to account for such a plurality of interests. It is also too rationalised in that it tends to take the consensus of the public sphere for granted, ignoring the possible irreconcilability of competing positions. The bourgeois public sphere is not a universal realm and public debate is engaged in by only a small social elite. Alternatives to this elite may exist outside the bounds of the public sphere. The public sphere should not just be about consensus and political will formation. It is also shaped by conflict, while consensus is itself a complex construction that takes place in a concrete, structured environment. It seems that what is lacking here is a concept like hegemony that is able to look at how the public sphere is constantly contested, and how public positions have to be constructed and struggled for. Likewise a concept of hegemony would be useful in bringing in a stronger agential aspect. In emphasising systemic distortions, Habermas underplays agency and it is not surprising that he has been criticised for not paying enough attention to such things as social movements, gender, class and other struggles in the public sphere.

However, the themes of *The Structural Transformation of the Public Sphere* were developed in Habermas's later work. First, this is an early example of Habermas's appeal to a communicatively grounded rationality. Second, Habermas's idealisation of the public sphere has a deliberate aspect to it – he is constructing an ideal type model by which to judge historically developed deformations, something that prefigures his notion of the distortion of the ideal speech situation. Finally, his discussion of the consequences of increased state intervention and the undermining of the public sphere leads to his next major work on what he calls the legitimation crisis.

In terms reminiscent of Weber's theories of legitimation and domination he writes: 'The legitimacy of an order of domination is measured against the *belief* in its legitimacy on the part of those subject to the domination' (Habermas 1991: 199). We can see here that Habermas follows Weber and the early Frankfurt theorists in equating legitimation with a system of domination. The social system has become more integrated and cohesive in the sense that the economy, the state and the cultural sphere become more integrated. Like the early Frankfurt theorists Habermas sees how capitalism has developed a state-regulated market in an effort to overcome crisis tendencies while also using cultural means to manipulate mass consciousness. Habermas's theory also has some similarities to the approach of the regulation school that we encountered in the chapter on Gramsci (indeed, this is developed in the work of third-generation critical theorists such as Claus Offe). The state comes to intervene in the public sphere, but it also intervenes into the economic sphere to safeguard capital accumulation. In this way, the state aims to control the tendencies towards economic crisis through increased intervention and regulation. The state plays the leading role in the maintenance of the cohesion of the socio-economic system.

However, this comes at a price. It may be that the state can better control the economic sphere, but this closer relation also means that the crisis of the economy may be transferred to other spheres of social and political life. Because the economic system has forfeited its functional autonomy in relation to the state, crisis manifestations become a social issue affecting a range of social spheres. This means a transformation and displacement of inherent contradictions in one system onto another. The measures taken by the state to avoid economic crisis may precipitate a crisis of rationality and legitimacy in the political and socio-cultural system. Habermas calls this potential problem a legitimation crisis, which can only be contained for as long as economic growth is achieved:

> The political system requires an input of mass loyalty that is as diffuse as possible. The output consists in sovereignty-executed

administrative decisions. Output crises have the form of a *ratio-nality crisis* in which the administrative system does not succeed in reconciling and fulfilling the imperatives received from the economic system. Input crises have the form of a *legitimation crisis*; the legitimising system does not succeed in maintaining the requisite level of mass loyalty while the steering imperatives taken over from the economic system are carried through. (Habermas 1988: 46)

The problem faced is that 'the state apparatus must fulfil its tasks in the economic system under the limiting condition that mass loyalty be simultaneously secured within the framework of a formal democracy and in accord with ruling universalistic value systems' (ibid., p. 58). As well as the possibility that economic crisis may be shifted onto the political system, there is also a problematic relation between the state and the private sphere. The increasing intervention of the state into the private realm may alter patterns of motivation formation, and lead to a motivation crisis. This may be linked to the process of rationalisation and the loss of meaning in social life.

Indeed, Habermas identifies four potential threats to social cohesion and consensus concerned with the economy, rationality, legitimation and motivation. These occur when:

- the economic system does not produce the requisite quantity of consumable values;
- the administrative system does not produce the requisite quantity of rational decisions;
- the legitimation system does not produce the requisite quantity of generalised motivations;
- the socio-cultural system does not generate the requisite quantity of action-motivating meaning.

(Ibid., p. 49)

Crises in social systems are produced by structurally inherent system imperatives that are incompatible and cannot be integrated. Crises come from what Habermas calls unresolved steering problems. It is argued that 'on the basis of a class compromise, the administrative system gains a limited planning capacity, which can be used, within the framework of a formally democratic procurement of legitimation, for purposes of reactive crisis avoidance' (ibid., p. 61). Indeed, threats towards legitimacy can be averted if the state can credibly present itself – for example as a social welfare state – and intercept the dysfunctional side-effects of the economic process. But if it cannot do this then manifestations of disequilibrium are unavoidable and a steering crisis emerges whereby the credibility of the state is called into question. The state may act as a factor of social cohesion, but if a crisis in the economic sphere undermines this role, then a crisis of legitimacy spreads across a range of political, cultural, public and private domains.

7. HABERMAS: SYSTEM AND LIFEWORLD

Habermas looks at the development of modern society in terms of crises of legitimacy, loss of meaning and lack of social solidarity. In this sense, Habermas shares the concerns of Weber and the critical theorists but he sees their critique of instrumental reason as one-sided and limited to the confines of a philosophy of consciousness that emphasises the alienation of the individual. It is possible to escape such a negative evaluation of modernity if we move away from the subject–object model and see society as based on mutual agreement within an intersubjectively constituted context. The basis for such an approach lies in an examination of communicative interaction.

Habermas distinguishes four different types of action. The first type of action is teleological, goal-oriented or means–ends rationality. The second is normatively regulated, based on values, norms and agreed behaviour. The third type is dramaturgical, concerned with the presentation of the self in everyday life. Finally, there is communicative action, where actors seek to reach understanding. The trouble with Weber's account of modernity is that his study of rationalisation focuses only on the purposive–instrumental or goal-oriented aspect of reason. This indeed helps to explain some of the problems raised in *Legitimation Crisis* and *The Structural Transformation of the Public Sphere* where rationalisation and the overextension of the instrumentalism of economic life leads to the impoverishment of culture and the depoliticisation of the public sphere. But Weber's one-sided focus on instrumental reason means that he mistakenly sees the problems caused by the expansion of the capitalist economy as those characteristic of rationality generally.

A somewhat similar accusation is made against Marx, who,

Habermas believes, also reduces social life to instrumental action by focusing on the economic sphere and thereby ignoring the processes of communicative interaction. It is in this latter sphere that Habermas believes we can retrieve more progressive and emancipatory theories of modernity and rationality. It is through communicative interaction and the process of reaching understanding that we are bound together. Our ability to communicate has a universal basis and Habermas grounds his idea of reason in the universal structures of communicative understanding and competence. These structures are dialogical and mutual, they are where we integrate the contents of the symbolic world through communicative action, discussion, negotiation and agreement. The stress is now on reciprocity, cooperation and mutual understanding.

We come to reach understanding through the intersubjective recognition of criticisable validity claims. This moves the focus away from narrow instrumentalism: 'As soon as we conceive of knowledge as communicatively mediated, rationality is assessed in terms of the capacity of responsible participants in interaction to orientate themselves in relation to validity claims geared to intersubjective recognition' (Habermas 1987b: 314). The intersubjective recognition of validity claims means that we reach understanding through the cooperative negotiation of common definitions of the situation. Thus discursive communication implies consensual rationality and, in order for communication to be possible at all, these communicative forms of reason are necessarily prior to any instrumental or strategic ones. In other words, communicative rationality is a necessary condition for meaningful social life. It is universal and transcendental in the sense that it is necessarily presupposed by forms of social activity.

Habermas's transcendental position invokes the notion of an ideal speech situation in which a rationally motivated consensus or agreement is achieved. The ideal speech situation presupposes rationality, justice and freedom and therefore, like Weberian or Kantian ideal types, it acts as a measure against which historical forms of communicative distortion can be understood. Habermas's theory of universal pragmatics aims at disclosing the universals of dialogue that people must acquire if they are to participate in a speech situation. Speakers raise universal validity claims and the ideal speech situation provides the rational basis by which we test the truth or validity of these claims.

As well as providing the basis for mutual understanding, communicative action is also responsible for social integration and socialisation:

> Under the functional aspect of *mutual understanding,* communica-
> tive action serves to transmit and renew cultural knowledge;
> under the aspect of *coordinating action,* it serves social integration
> and the establishment of solidarity; finally, under the aspect of
> *socialisation,* communicative action serves the formation of per-
> sonal identities. (Habermas 1987a: 137)

Social integration is concerned with mutual obligations and legiti-
mately ordered interpersonal relations. The process of socialisation
secures personal identity and social competence. However, and this
will be now explored through the system–lifeworld distinction, the
erosion of the communicative sphere by the market and administrative
system leads to the kinds of problems identified in Habermas's earlier
works. The corresponding failure of these processes are the loss of
meaning, the crisis of legitimacy, the lack of social solidarity and
psychopathologies.

What is made explicit in our communicative action is our shared,
historically structured lifeworld. It represents a set of background resources that make human interaction and communication meaningful:

> It both forms a *context* and furnishes *resources* for the process of
> mutual understanding. The lifeworld forms a horizon and at the
> same time offers a store of things taken for granted in the given
> culture from which communicative participants draw consensual
> interpretive patterns in their efforts at interpretation. The soli-
> darities of groups integrated by values and the competences of
> socialised individuals belong, as do culturally ingrained back-
> ground assumptions, to the components of the lifeworld.
> (Habermas 1987b: 298)

The lifeworld reproduces itself to the extent that it fulfils the previously mentioned functions of promoting mutual understanding,
social coordination, social integration and socialisation. It is therefore
necessary to see the lifeworld as simultaneously the reproduced
outcome of and necessary condition for communicative action:

> Communicative action not only depends upon cultural knowledge,
> legitimate orders, and competences developed through socialisa-
> tion; it not only feeds off the resources of the lifeworld; it is itself

the medium through which the symbolic structures of the lifeworld are reproduced. (Habermas 1987a: 255)

The symbolic aspect of the lifeworld is its important feature. It
represents a background of shared meanings that makes ordinary
symbolic interaction possible. This background contains the social
institutions, normative structures and social practices that are responsible for the reproduction of society. The purpose of Habermas's *Theory
of Communicative Action* is to show that 'the symbolic structures of the
lifeworld are reproduced by communicative action [and that this]
points the way now to a fruitful analysis of the *interconnections between
culture, society and personality*' (ibid., p. 222). The lifeworld provides a set
of background understandings that gives coherence to our social actions
and forms the horizon within which communicative actions are always
already moving. Since subjects always come to an understanding
within the horizon of a lifeworld, this is both historical in that it is
'defined by cultural tradition, legitimate orders and socialised individuals [where] performances draw upon and advance consensus' (ibid.,
p. 182) and transcendental in that

> the lifeword is, so to speak, the transcendental site where speaker
> and hearer meet, where they can reciprocally raise claims that
> their utterances fit the world (objective, social, or subjective), and
> where they can criticise and confirm those validity claims, settle
> their disagreements, and arrive at agreements. (Ibid., p. 126)

The lifeworld is transcendental in that it represents the background
conditions present in all societies based on the fact that communication is an intrinsic aspect of all human conduct. But how the lifeworld
is elaborated is a historical matter. The lifeworld is both the basic
condition for the evolutionary development of society and the product
of it. Although the historical aspect of Habermas's work is weak and
tends to suffer from the priority given to transcendental conditions, it
is possible to find some general historical points about the evolution
of society. We have already examined Habermas's discussion of the
historical erosion of the public sphere. In his later work we can find a
discussion of the process of modernity, the increasing differentiation of
value spheres in society and the development of historical worldviews.

The lifeworld is concerned with cultural reproduction, social integration, the stabilisation of group identity, solidarity, socialisation and the development of competences. Worldviews are closely related in that they

> are constitutive not only for processes of reaching understanding but for the social integration and the socialisation of individuals as well. They function in the formation and stabilisation of identities, supplying individuals with a core of basic concepts and assumptions. (Habermas 1984: 64)

Worldviews are the means by which social identities are secured and therefore play an important part in cohering social groups. They are cultural interpretive systems that reflect the background knowledge of social groups. If the lifeworld represents the general set of background conditions, then worldviews represent a more conscious and historical framework operating against this background. They bring together the personal, the cultural and the political, shaping group identity and interests and also legitimating political systems:

> Worldviews have the function, among others, of legitimating political leadership. They offer a potential for grounding that can be used to justify a political order or the institutional framework of a society in general. They thus lend support to the moral authority or validity of basic norms. (Habermas 1987a: 56)

However, all this is done within a broader evolutionary framework. Cultural modernity is the process of creating a rational worldview and differentiating three cultural value spheres – those of science and knowledge, morality and law, and aesthetics. Here Habermas is closely following Weber as well as echoing Kant's three critiques. These three spheres of validity – science, morality and art – each have their own distinct truth claims, validity and authenticity which are, respectively, cognitive–instrumental, moral–practical and aesthetic–expressive.

But whereas Weber is unsure about this process, believing it to lead to the dominance of technical rationality, Habermas sees this separation as progressive in that it rids society of dogma, mysticism and religion and allows each value sphere to develop its own characteristics. If

Weber is right about the impoverishment of modern society, then this is not the result of separate value spheres, but is due to the elitist separation of expert cultures from everyday life. The matter of the differentiation of value spheres and the dominance of instrumental rationality raises a deeper problem about the imbalance between the lifeworld and the system. Weber is wrong to see the problem in terms of purposive rationality alone; rather, the growth of bureaucracy and loss of meaning are a consequence of the uncoupling of the system and lifeworld and a process of colonisation:

> Because Weber's action theory is too narrowly gauged, he is unable to see in money and power the media which, *by substituting for language*, make possible the differentiation of subsystems of purposive–rational action. It is these media, and not directly the purposive–rational actions themselves, that need to be institutionally and motivationally anchored in the lifeworld. (Habermas 1984: 342)

The system–lifeworld distinction replaces the Marxist notion of base and superstructure so that instead of a model of economic base and cultural, political and ideological superstructure, we have a model based on systemic functioning and communicative interaction. This emphasises the fact that societies reproduce themselves both materially and symbolically. If Marx's error is to overemphasise the productive paradigm of labour, then Habermas makes the distinction between labour and interaction so that labour belongs to the system and is purposive–rational, instrumental and strategic, while interaction belongs to the lifeworld and involves communicative action, consensual norms and mutual understanding. The system requires the integration of diverse activities in accordance with adaptive goals of the market economy and the political–administrative system. The problem is that systemic integration needs to be institutionalised and anchored in the lifeworld, requiring laws and institutions. The danger here is that of the system overextending itself so that the lifeworld is subject to colonisation by economy and state, power and bureaucracy. The dominance of instrumental reason is indicative of this process of colonisation.

So the theme of legitimation crisis is now developed within a new framework of system–lifeworld disjuncture. The legitimation crisis is now represented by the colonisation of the lifeworld by the system and, in particular, the steering media of power and money. It may be that citizens are rewarded with a more efficient market that provides consumer affluence and a more developed and coordinated state system that is able to provide such things as education and welfare. But the price to be paid is a loss of individual autonomy and a lack of genuine social consensus. As the system is uncoupled from the life-world, spheres of action are taken over by power and money and no longer integrated into the process of mutual understanding and con-sensus formation. The problem of modern capitalism is the selective process of rationalisation and the technical and instrumental use of reason. But, versus the pessimism of Weber, this particular development of rationalisation is only one of a number of possibilities. The colonisa-tion of the lifeworld represents domination and control by instrumental rather than communicative rationality. The problem is not rationality generally, but the domination of technical rationality over communica-tive rationality. The solution is to redress the imbalance.

By maintaining this distinction between different spheres of rationality, Habermas attempts to avoid the pessimism of the early Frankfurt school while maintaining their insights on domination and reification. These are now seen in the context of the colonisation of the lifeworld by the more instrumental system, where the supposed sub-systems of economy and state become dominant over the reproduction of the lifeworld. By contrast, Habermas argues that 'Horkheimer and Adorno detach the concept [of reification] not only from the special historical context of the rise of the capitalist economic system but from the dimension of inter-human relations altogether . . .' (ibid., p. 379). Habermas seeks to return to interhuman relations to find an optimistic solution to the problem of modernity.

Rationalisation has a positive aspect in that it rids society of dogma, mysticism and religion and opens up the possibility of critical debate and discussion. It also requires political power to be legitimated and provides the basis for rational consensus. Whereas legitimacy in Weber is in reference to itself, Habermas argues that legitimacy is possible only in so far as the production and application of legal norms are conducted in the moral–practical sense of institutionalised procedural rationality. In other words, legitimacy draws on the morally binding force of intersubjective norms.

Habermas's theory is important to theories of social cohesion and consensus in that it focuses on the problem of consensus within a framework of communicative rationality and mutual understanding. It also holds a theory of social cohesion based on the relation between the system and the lifeworld. Habermas studies mass democracy from the point of view of the democratic procedures of political will formation. But he recognises the tensions that exist between capitalist and democratic processes, between opposed forms of societal integration. Political parties are in the position of having to appeal both to the masses and to capitalist interests. Such a tension also affects a range of social bodies. The welfare system is the clearest example of an institution torn between the spheres of system and lifeworld, which attempts to deal with the worst effects of the capitalist system while still being responsible to its demands.

Habermas optimistically believes that there is an inherent human interest in emancipation. This he defines as communication without distortion or domination. Through this focus politics shifts from the sphere of production to the lifeworld. He looks to such activities as democratic debate, protest, civil-rights campaigning, identity politics, lifestyle politics and any activities that show resistance to the colonisation of the lifeworld. His aim is not to overthrow the system but to safeguard it and protect the public spheres of communication and identity. In keeping with this perspective, Habermas, like other critical theorists, looks not to any one privileged agent, but to many diverse actors. His focus is not on the economy but on culture, the aesthetic, the psychological and the lifeworld. Marx's ideal of a free society of producers is replaced with the idea of a fully rationalised lifeworld.

This may be a more optimistic project, but does it work? Big questions remain about the viability of Habermas's theory. His is an attempt to provide a normative foundation for critical theory based on open and equal discussion and consensus. But maybe Habermas's account contains too much consensus. As Rick Roderick notes, the process of reaching mutual understanding is given so much emphasis that misunderstanding is somehow derivative; there is an assumption that understanding is prior to misunderstanding (Roderick 1986: 159). Against a correspondence theory, Habermas advocates a consensus theory of truth. But how do we test validity claims, how do we choose theories, how is agreement reached?

The focus on normative foundations leads to a harmonious account of capitalist social relations that underplays the problems of state and economy. Because these normative foundations are seen as transcendental and universal rather than historical and specific, Habermas's theory of social consensus turns us away from an analysis of concrete social and political forms. Instead of engaging in concrete historical analysis, Habermas looks for general human conditions. It is in giving this general account of human societies that Habermas's assumptions become problematic. In contrast to an approach such as Gramsci's theory of hegemony, social consensus is not seen as something that is a product of a complex historical struggle involving multiple actors with varying interests and beliefs. Habermas's account cannot adequately explain variations in consciousness or interest. His transcendental approach overemphasises rationality and there is an absence of the sensuous or non-rational. Because his theory is inter-subjective, no account is given of how social agents interact with objective social structures. In short, Habermas's evolutionary account of human communicative capacity is transcendental at the expense of being historical. By contrast, the next chapter will turn to Foucault for an attempt at a less general, more historical account of the development of different types of rationality and consensus.

Chapter 7

MICHEL FOUCAULT:
DISCOURSE, POWER AND REGULATION

―――○○――――

1. KNOWLEDGE AND DISCOURSE

The approach of Michel Foucault differs sharply from that of many of the other theorists covered so far. It is true that he strongly identifies with the earlier generation of the Frankfurt school and shares with Weber a concern with domination and techniques of discipline as well as a liking for Nietzsche, but Foucault's approach is explicitly in opposition to many of the key themes of the other writers. He is strongly opposed to those models that place emphasis on the actions of the subject and consequently rejects the kind of subject–object distinction found in many of the other writers. His writing is greatly concerned with the exercise of power, but not only does he distance power relations from the actions of subjects, but he also opposes those theories (in fact all those we have covered so far) that focus on centralised power relations and institutions such as the state. Like the other theorists he does have a theory of domination, but, as we shall see, he opposes the idea of top-down power invested in sovereignty. Foucault might also be said to reject the model of legitimation and consensus that has been a major theme of previous chapters, but in dealing with such things as social practices, discourses and disciplinary power, Foucault develops an alternative way of dealing with cohesion. As Barry Smart says of Foucault's notion of hegemony:

Hegemony contributes to or constitutes a form of social cohesion not through force or coercion, nor necessarily through consent, but most effectively by way of practices, techniques, and methods which infiltrate minds and bodies, cultural practices which cultivate behaviours and beliefs, tastes, desires, and needs as seemingly

162

naturally occurring qualities and properties embodied in the psychic and physical reality (or 'truth') of the human subject. (Smart 1986: 160)

A distinction must be made between Foucault's early, middle and late works. Indeed, in the late works there is something of a turn to the subject or at least the self. However, the early works are heavily influenced by an antihumanist structuralism which is employed in the studies of madness and illness and theoretically elaborated in *The Order of Things* and *The Archaeology of Knowledge*. These works attempt to study social history according to changes in discourse. The concept of discourse becomes an overarching category that explains the cohesion and unity of social practices. And we find in Foucault's first book, *Madness and Civilization*, an attempt to apply this notion of discourse and shifts in discourse to the history of madness.

The foundation of the Hôpital Général in Paris is identified by Foucault as a decisive event. With it begins the period of the great exclusion, of which Foucault asks: 'What, then, was the reality represented by this entire population which almost overnight found itself shut up, excluded more severely than the lepers?' (Foucault 1971: 45). The Hôpital Général contained 6,000 people, one per cent of the population, and through its power of segregation 'provided a new homeland for madness'. Such a shift in sensibility was great indeed. A sensibility that isolated and confined large sections of the population, that gave the community the ethical power of segregation and ejected into another world those who were no longer deemed compatible. To explain this we need to go beyond the question of madness and look at the complex social unity of other issues – a new sensibility to poverty and unemployment, new reactions to economic problems, a new ethic of work, the joining of moral obligation and civil law. In short, a new unity of bourgeois society.

Madness becomes an issue because it threatens the foundations of this new bourgeois order. The ambivalence towards madness in medieval society is transformed into a matter of great public concern. The Middle Ages gave madness a place in the hierarchy of vices, but in the Renaissance it comes to the fore as a major issue of social concern:

Madness was thus torn from that imaginary freedom which still allowed it to flourish on the Renaissance horizon. Not so long ago, it had floundered about in broad daylight: in *King Lear*, in *Don Quixote*. But in less than a half-century, it had been sequestered and, in the fortress of confinement, bound to Reason, to the rules of morality and to their monotonous nights. (Ibid., p. 64)

In the Age of Enlightenment there emerges a sharp separation between sanity and insanity. The medieval dialogue with madness gives way to its separation and silencing. This requires new powers to be invested in institutions such as the Hôpital Général. But these powers are not simply repressive in the narrow sense of the term. This is about the construction of a new social unity or cohesion based on a new moral, ethical and rational discourse. The directors of the Hôpital are invested with a moral charge and ethical duty. They have the power of authority, direction, administration, jurisdiction, correction and punishment. Thus 'morality castigates by means of administrative enforcement. For the first time, institutions of morality are established in which an astonishing synthesis of moral obligation and civil law is effected' (ibid., p. 60).

What was happening to the insane is really only part of a wider issue – the construction and maintenance of the discourse of reason and, consequently, the guarding against the subterranean danger of unreason. In a 'rational' social order, madness represents a kind of freedom, something that is outside that order, a radical other that is both in the social world and beyond it. But in the classical period that we have described, madness ceased to be the sign of another world and became instead the manifestation of non-being. The process of confinement attempted to suppress this non-being and make it nothingness. For Foucault, social cohesion is dependent upon exclusion.

However, the discourse of the classical age was to give way to that of the modern age. At a most basic level, it is not feasible to lock up so many people. Often it was simply the poor who were locked up and treated as insane and this inevitably had an effect on the labour market. The process of confinement was linked to the classical belief that the mad person's body was the visible and solid presence of the problem. Now, in the modern period, there was a shift in emphasis from the body to the soul. The collapse of the classical discourse led to the emergence of new domains of psychology and morality and new ideas and practices concerned with diseases of the nerves. This shift is reflected in the birth of the asylum. But this is not simply an institutional development; it represents a deeper discursive shift in that the asylum is associated with the new science of mental disease. This science is based on a system of observation and classification, surveillance and judgement. The judgemental aspect is of a moral as well as a physical nature. The treatment of madness shifts away from physical constraint towards self-constraint. The new discourse places emphasis on the recognition of guilt and a new notion of responsibility. Self-awareness is now linked to shame, reinforced by perpetual judgement. The truth and cure of madness is located in the moral sphere and the asylum becomes 'a religious domain without religion, a domain of pure morality, of ethical uniformity' (ibid., p. 257).

In Foucault's next work the birth of the asylum becomes the birth of the clinic. Again, the point is to show how new social institutions and practices are bound up with the emergence of new social discourses – in this instance, the emergence of a new medical discourse. Foucault charts the process by which the medical discourse is transformed from the classical idea of a pathological essence independent of its manifestations to the modern focus on the body, or that which is visible. This visibility is linked to spatiality and a new arrangement of the discrete elements of corporal space. The appearance of the clinic is related to these reorganisations of discourse, from 'what is wrong with you?' to 'where does it hurt?' (Foucault 1976: xviii). The birth of the clinic does not necessarily represent scientific progress, but instead indicates this shift in medical discourse with its new emphasis on the visibility of the body. This idea of visibility links to Foucault's notion of the gaze, which is that which 'establishes the individual in his irreducible quality. And it thus becomes possible to organise a rational language around it' (ibid., p. xiv). The gaze not only sees, but touches and hears. Illness is projected onto a plane of absolute visibility. The gaze determines the entire field of possible knowledge.

This is no longer the gaze of just anyone, but that of a suitably qualified doctor, backed up by an institution that gives the doctor the power of decision and intervention. This makes the gaze calculating with the 'formation of the clinical method . . . bound up with the emergence of the doctor's gaze into the field of signs and symptoms' (ibid., p. 91). The symptom becomes a sign and the gaze takes the form of a medical examination. There occurs a transformation from classificatory medicine to an anatomical medicine of symptoms. This 'is nothing more than a syntactical reorganisation of disease in which the limits of the visible and invisible follow a new pattern' (ibid., p. 195). Language is opened up to a new domain of the visible and expressible, there is a new subservience to experience, a new truth in the discursive space of the body, the corpse (autopsy), and the interior revealed.

Eighteenth-century medicine was concerned much more with health whereas nineteenth-century medicine was regulated more in accordance with normality and in relation to a standard of functioning. The cohesion of these approaches is provided through discourse while the institution of the clinic is crucial to the maintenance of that discourse: 'The clinic figures, then, as a structure that is essential to the scientific coherence and also to the social utility and political purity of the new medical organisation' (ibid., p. 70). It can be seen, therefore, that because of Foucault's structuralist influences, social cohesion takes the form of discursive cohesion. In fact discourse is presented as extremely cohesive and almost total in its scope and power. In keeping with this structuralism, the subject is seen as a secondary effect of discourse and social practices. History is not a process with a subject, but is in fact a series of shifts in discursive paradigms. The notion of paradigm is important, for history is not, as Enlightenment rationality would have it, a process of logical progression, but a process that involves the breakdown and displacement of discourses and their associated social practices and institutions.

In *The Order of Things* Foucault tries to show how 'rationality' is dependent on a discursive framework that determines what it is or is not possible to say, and what counts as truth or knowledge. In structuralist and archaeological fashion, this work is concerned with uncovering the laws, regulations and rules of formation of systems of thought. In place of progress and continuity we find the idea of 'epistemic breaks' in relatively autonomous knowledge and discourse. The epistemic break represents the replacement of one discursive paradigm by another. The Renaissance, the classical age and the modern age are described as three distinct epistemes, or three distinct structures of representation, forming a cohesive unity:

> By *episteme*, we mean, in fact, the total set of relations that unite, at a given period, the discursive practices that give rise to epistemological figures, sciences, and possibly formalised systems . . . The episteme is not a form of knowledge (*connaissance*) or type of rationality . . . it is the totality of relations that can be discovered,

for a given period, between the sciences when one analyses them at the level of discursive regularities. (Foucault 1989: 191)

The episteme is a structure of knowledge which determines the way the world is experienced or seen. It is described as a 'positive unconscious of knowledge'. The classical episteme was organised so that representation was at its centre. This involves the idea of universal measurement and classification. Language is seen as transparent and unproblematic in the way it performs its function of representation. There is a coherence in the classical episteme between the theory of representation, the theory of language, the theory of a natural order and theories of wealth and value. In the classical age, the attempt at a universal method, the system of classification and the process of representation mirror the order of things in the world. The totality of the classical episteme is the relation to a knowledge of order and it contains a mathesis as a science of calculable order and a genesis as the constitution of orders on the basis of an empirical series where everything is present and in its proper place.

The episteme is a constantly moving set of articulations, shifts and coincidences; one is established only to give rise to others. The classical view of the world was later undermined by a profound historicity that invaded it. In particular, whereas the classical episteme had no place for the human subject, in the modern episteme this now becomes central. In place of universal classification, certainty, and the infinity of God's cosmology, there emerges a new humanist paradigm, an anthropological episteme founded on human finitude through which history unfolds. The human subject is now trapped within language, life and labour and knowledge becomes finite. Historicity has been introduced into the realm of human beings. The new human sciences and disciplines like political economy stress the importance of human labour. The nineteenth century brings with it a new kind of reasoning that throws into question the form of truth and the form of being and this is again related to the question of representation:

The end of Classical thought – and of the *episteme* that made general grammar, natural history, and the science of wealth possible – will coincide with the decline of representation, or rather with the emancipation of language, of the living being, and of need, with regard to representation. (Foucault 1974: 209)

By moving away from direct representation, the visible relates to the invisible, the deeper cause, the buried depth in that 'language began to fold in upon itself, to acquire its own particular density, to deploy a history, an objectivity, and laws of its own' (ibid., p. 296). These ideas might be related to the account of medical knowledge given earlier. The visible body indicates the deeper invisible cause. There is a new focus on the body, on its physicality, indeed on its finitude. There is a new attitude towards death, which is no longer seen as a point at which time stops, but is part of an uneven process of degeneration. The human body is now real and tangible:

> At the foundation of all the empirical positivities, and of every-
> thing that can indicate itself as a concrete limitation of man's
> existence, we discover a finitude – which is in a sense the same: it
> is marked by the spatiality of the body, the yawning of desire, and
> the time of language . . . an analytic of finitude, in which man's
> being will be able to provide a foundation in their own positivity
> for all those forms that indicate to him that he is not infinite.
> (Ibid., p. 315)

Foucault calls his method an archaeology. The approach of archae-ology is not to focus on the history of ideas, but to examine the conditions under which the subject is constituted as an object of knowledge – as we have seen, for example, in the histories of madness and medicine. In these studies the archaeological approach aims to show how it is that the patient's body becomes the object of scientific and medical examination. Because he rejects the humanist emphasis on conscious intent (itself the product of the modern episteme), the archaeological method is deployed to uncover the unconsciousness that eludes the consciousness of actors. *Savoir*, or 'knowledge in general', is the underlying condition of possibility for everyday forms of *connaissance*. Foucault's archaeology looks at the rules of formation of a group of statements; the a-priori set of rules that allows discourse to function.

In *The Archaeology of Knowledge* the notion of the episteme is replaced with the concept of the archive, which refers to the general conditions of possibility that make knowledge possible in any given period. It is not so much a condition for the validity of statements but a condition for their reality. Discursive relations are not interior to discourse, not simply that which connects words to each other, but they are not exterior either. Discursive relations offer discourse objects of which it can speak; they determine what discourse must establish in order to speak of this or that object. Foucault calls this system a discursive formation:

> Whenever one can describe, between a number of statements, such a system of dispersion, whenever, between objects, types of statement, concepts, or thematic choices, one can define a regularity (an order, correlations, positions and functionings, transformations), we will say . . . we are dealing with a *discursive formation* . . . The rules of formation are conditions of existence (but also of coexistence, maintenance, modification, and disappearance) in a given discursive division. (Foucault 1989: 38)

A discursive practice is 'a body of anonymous, historical rules, always determined in the time and space that have defined a given period, and for a given social, economic, geographical, or linguistic area, the conditions of operation of the enunciative function' (ibid., p. 117). The social–institutional field only becomes meaningful once articulated within a discursive formation. We can see that this, like Foucault's previous work, shows all the influences of structuralism. In Foucault's early work the unity and cohesion of the social is provided first by discourse, then by the episteme and now by the discursive formation. Because structuralism is opposed to humanism, there is little room for agency within this system. It is not the individual that gives discourse meaning but the discursive formation that provides an array of subject positions that individuals occupy. Foucault leaves very little room, therefore, for agency. So little room, in fact, that it is impossible to speak of social consent or consensus. Agents simply do not have this option; they are the more or less passive constructs of discourse. Their needs, wants, ideas, values and actions are entirely the product of the dominant discourse. This does not mean, however, that social cohesion is entirely guaranteed. Although discourses provide cohesion, the discursive system is always open to change. Foucault is willing to speak of discontinuities, ruptures and gaps and the replacement of one exhausted episteme or discursive formation by another. But these changes are the product of structural breakdowns and crises, not the result of human actions. It is only in Foucault's middle period that an extremely limited and one-sided account of human action emerges.

2. POWER AND DISCIPLINE

The above comments notwithstanding, there is already some shift present in *The Archaeology of Knowledge* away from high structuralism towards the view that social unity is secured by more than just discourse. Institutions and practices are no longer included within discourse: 'Archaeology also reveals relations between discursive formations and non-discursive domains (institutions, political events, economic practices and processes)' (Foucault 1989: 162). We might say, therefore, that there is a shift in this middle period from an emphasis on discourse to an emphasis on practice and then again to the effects of power. Discourse is no longer seen as autonomous or total in its scope and power. There emerges a new understanding of non-discursive relations as constitutive of discursive possibility. There is an analysis of social institutions and practices coupled with a renewed emphasis on the body. In the works on punishment and sexuality there is an emphasis on the strategies, techniques and disciplines that power exercises on the body.

Whereas works like *The Order of Things* present the rather structuralist view that discourse is the all important factor that brings order and cohesion to the social system, the later works place an emphasis on multiplicity and the dispersion of knowledge and power. This allows more room to explain continuities and change, and it seems that it is not the case that the episteme or discursive formation reflects the sovereign unity of a period, but that there is a more disparate system of interacting discursive and non-discursive practices. This signifies a shift in Foucault's methodology – a transition from an archaeology to a Nietzsche-inspired genealogy that welcomes in the more diverse, more fragmented and less unified aspects of society. Foucault's work opposes grand historical systems and modernist notions of lineal development and progress, and tries to disrupt the security of our knowledge, through highlighting the plurality, discontinuity and fragility of historical forms. Foucault shows how subjects are constructed by knowledge and power, but he does this through a new emphasis on disciplinary power. But as Foucault's emphasis shifts towards relations of power, there is also a move away from the previous emphasis on structure with the result that power is no longer regarded as centralised, or even as unified by a particular hegemonic discourse, but in fact is more dispersed. Indeed, as the modern body becomes fragmented, so too does the dispersion of power relations in society.

Consequently, *Discipline and Punish* examines the shift from central-ised and overt repression and punishment to more covert and dispersed forms of authority, surveillance and judgement. The book opens with the spectacular execution of Damiens the regicide, which highlights the way in which public executions would serve to emphasise the power of the sovereign over wrongdoers. Public execution functions to visibly restore the power of sovereignty; it is a ritual showing 'the physical strength of the sovereign beating down upon the body of his adversary and mastering it' (Foucault 1979: 49). This 'theatre of pain' shows the vengeance of the sovereign and serves as a warning aimed at striking fear into the public. However, later there is a shift from the notion of revenge to the idea of appropriate punishment. Crime is no longer regarded as a direct attack on the sovereign, but is seen as a threat to wider society and to social norms. Punishment, therefore, is a response to the wrong done to the community. It is now less about overt repression, more about getting the subject to conform to norms of social behaviour and thought, sets of standards and values. The aim is to restore the 'criminal' or 'deviant' to their place in society. Instead of revenge, punishment becomes a process of curing or educating. Foucault sees this process as one of training the body in that the body is caught up in a system of constraints, privations, obligations and prohibitions. Punishment is now a procedure for reforming the subject.

This, then, is the disciplinary society. Social cohesion is based on the conformity to social norms and on the correction of deviants through a combination of coercion and persuasion. The aim is the production of what Foucault calls 'docile bodies'. So there is a shift from the society of the spectacle to a society based on judgement and surveillance.

That these changes occurred was not necessarily because a more humane approach to punishment emerged, as is the customary humanist explanation. It had more to do with the need for a more accurate, efficient, controllable, calculable system. The old feudal society approached punishment in a most spectacular but dysfunctional way, personified by the bungled efforts to inflict pain on the body of Damiens. As a capitalist society replaced the feudal one, the new system of accumulation had to be matched with a new regulation of social life and the development of a system of education, correction and disciplinary power. So the system of punishment was reorganised to meet new needs and to make it more effective. The reform movement was less concerned with making punishment more humane as with setting up a new 'economy' of punishment, to make it more regular, effective and constant. As Foucault writes, the aim was 'not to punish less, but to punish better; to punish with an attenuated severity perhaps, but in order to punish with more universality and necessity; to insert the power to punish more deeply into the social body' (ibid., p. 84). Punishment is seen as a political tactic and Foucault claims that the aim of his work is 'to study the metamorphosis of punitive methods on the basis of a political technology of the body' (ibid., p. 24). This is not a biological but a socio-historical conception of the body as a political field invested with power relations. It is connected to a whole range of discourses, practices, institutions and social bodies. This technology of power forms the basis of both the humanisation of the penal system and the human sciences. Crime is regarded as a social injury and penal laws seek recompense for the harm done. There emerges a taxonomy of crimes and their appropriate penalties.

Discipline and Punishment may in some senses be regarded as a rather pessimistic and negative work, as it challenges the idea that modern society is necessarily more enlightened or humane, arguing instead that it is characterised chiefly by different methods, techniques and strategies of discipline. But Foucault's aim is not to concentrate on repressive effects alone and he tries to make the case that punishment is a complex social function that also has positive, enabling effects. Foucault introduces the idea of the *dispositif* or apparatus of power that consists of institutions, laws, scientific practices, statements, administrative decisions and regulations that aim at securing a dominant strategic function. These functions are not simply repressive, they are also crucial to the formation of the modern person. But again, as with the previous works, the subject has little control over this process and most of the language of *Discipline and Punish* concerns acts of exclusion, repression, correction and control.

The agents of this society combine the functions of normality and surveillance: 'The judges of normality are present everywhere. We are in the society of the teacher-judge, the doctor-judge, the educator-judge, the "social-worker"-judge; it is on them that the universal reign of the normative is based' (ibid., p. 304). The examination is another particularly important procedure of observation and supervision combined with normalising judgement. It forms part of the process whereby the individual is constituted as the effect and object of knowledge and it combines hierarchical surveillance with normalising judgement and classification. So discipline is achieved through surveillance, delegation of supervision, hierarchic observation, normalising judgment and examination. Such processes of normalisation are related to social cohesion in the sense of imposing homogeneity and uniformity of thought, action and behaviour.

If there is a strong normative element to this system of control, then there is also a strong spatial component. Part of the disciplinary strategy involves techniques of segregation, the control of activities through careful scheduling and enforcement of regular behaviour. Examples of these techniques would be the use of exercises and tactics designed to create orderly bodies. This links to ideas of military discipline, but also to other institutions, in particular to the methods used in prisons. Although the subtitle of the book clearly indicates that the prison is going to be a major focus, it should be stressed that the prison is seen by Foucault as society in microcosm and that it is only the purest form of techniques that spread well beyond its confines: 'The prison must be the microcosm of a perfect society in which individuals are isolated in their moral existence, but in which they come together in a strict hierarchical framework' (ibid., p. 238).

The prison controls the spatial–temporal body and represents an apparatus intended to render criminals docile and useful. The prison uses measures of repression and punishment, but it also sets itself the task of educating the prisoner in the interests of society. It uses a specialist staff that has the moral qualities and technical abilities appropriate to this educative function. Imprisonment must be accompanied by supervision and assistance with the aim of rehabilitating the prisoner and returning to society a 'normalised' civilian. If we combine the spatial confinement of the prison with the normative function of the gaze, we arrive at Foucault's well-known use of Bentham's Panopticon. This centralised vantage point subjects the inmates to the possibility of permanent surveillance and produces in the inmate a permanent, conscious visibility. This is important in 'normalising' the behaviour of the inmate, for it is not direct coercion but rather the fear of observation that forces the inmate to impose self-discipline and regulate their behaviour. Punishment has moved from the body to the mind, from the overtly physical to the more covert psychology of surveillance. The Panopticon also acts as a site where knowledge is produced, recorded and classified. It is a laboratory where training and correction take place, a privileged place for experimenting on people, for analysing these experiments and the changes they produce. The point of *Discipline and Punish*, then, is to indicate the emergence of the disciplinary society and its strategy of permanent, exhaustive, omnipresent surveillance.

Barry Smart has argued that Foucault's analysis of the operation and effects of techniques of power and their associated regimes of truth provides the basis on which we are to understand how forms of social cohesion are constituted (Smart 1986: 170). But it seems from the above that despite Foucault's claims to present power and discipline in a positive way, social cohesion and normative consensus would appear to be based on repressive forms of regulation and control. This also seems to be the case with sexuality, although again Foucault is at pains to stress that, despite the popular perception of Victorian repression:

> We are dealing not nearly so much with a negative mechanism of exclusion as with the operation of a subtle network of discourses, special knowledges, pleasures and powers. At issue is not a movement bent on pushing rude sex back into some obscure and inaccessible region, but on the contrary, a process that spreads it over the surface of things and bodies, arouses it, draws it out and bids it speak, implants it in reality and enjoins it to tell the truth: an entire glittering sexual array, reflected in a myriad of discourses, the obstination of powers, and the interplay of knowledge and pleasure. (Foucault 1981: 72)

In the first volume of *The History of Sexuality* Foucault shows how from the eighteenth century there emerges a new desire to talk about sex, and to tie this discourse to rationality as well as to morality. Those who talked about sex wanted to analyse and classify it: 'Sex was not something one simply judged; it was a thing one administered. It was in the nature of a public potential; it called for management procedures; it had to be taken charge of by analytical discourses' (ibid., p. 24). So sexual discourse was linked to administration and science, while those who talked about sex claimed to do so from a neutral, scientific viewpoint. Sex became a public issue around which a wide range of discourses arose. Contrary to the view that the Victorians imposed a silence on sexual matters, there emerges a new set of discourses and a new way of talking about sex. The Victorians talked about sex ad infinitum while exploiting it as a secret.

Of course administration and classification were linked to a normative discourse. The nineteenth century set out to talk about the 'truth of sex' as something universal and uniform. The purpose of classification was to set a standard by which deviations from the sexual norm could be judged. Foucault argues that sex was now situated at the intersection between scientific discourse and the religious technique of confession. Sexuality becomes a pathological field calling for therapeutic or normalising intervention. Hence sexuality is linked to Foucault's other main themes – medicalisation, deviancy and mental illness. As *The Birth of the Clinic* attempted to show, the body produces a field of knowledge so that sexuality can constitute an object of scientific study. The issue of sexuality should be seen as related to wider consciousness of the body, political technologies of life, and the discipline and regulation, administration and government of people and populations. Foucault uses the term 'bio-power' to describe these issues that concern the wider social body – the questions concerning population, public health, birth control and marriage. These issues all relate to the development of a capitalist society and processes of industrialisation and urbanisation.

The discourse around sex brings a sort of cohesion to a series of problems. It makes it possible to group together in some sort of unity different anatomical elements, biological functions, sensations and pleasures, as well as social issues such as reproduction and birth control. Foucault considers the repressive issues associated with the Victorian treatment of sex, and the way that sex is used to discipline and control social behaviour. This can be seen with the treatment of deviants and Foucault discusses the 'hysterisation' of those women considered to be 'saturated with sexuality', the 'pedagogisation' of children's sexuality and the socialisation of procreative behaviour. *The History of Sexuality* looks at attempts to legitimate the heterosexual couple as the norm by pathologising 'perverse pleasure' and 'sexual irregularity'. The nineteenth century sees the construction of a working-class sexuality. For a long time the question of the sexuality of the masses had been avoided, but now the need to form a labour force demands a more open discussion of working-class sex. The working class previously did not have a body; now it is constituted in terms of a labour force and must therefore be subject to discipline, regulation, surveillance and administration. Sex emerges as a tool for disciplining the population, harnessing and intensifying the distribution of forces, establishing an economy of energies. Bio-power is subtle and all-encompassing with its strategies of control, routinising of conduct, surveillance and normalising judgement.

Foucault argues that it is not the case that the bourgeoisie was trying just to repress sexuality and use it as a tool of social control. The development of technologies of sex allowed for the constitution of the body and sexuality. But, like *Discipline and Punish*, it still seems as though the majority of emphasis is on repression and the fact that the Victorians used sexuality to impose social control – to regulate it, confine it, censor it and establish restrictive rules of propriety and decency. This raises the issue of the exercise of power:

> Sexuality must not be thought of as a kind of natural given which power tries to hold in check, or as an obscure domain which knowledge tries gradually to uncover. It is the name that can be given to a historical construct . . . a great surface network in which the stimulation of bodies, the intensification of pleasures, the incitement to discourse, the formation of special knowledges, the strengthening of controls and resistances, are linked to one another, in accordance with a few major strategies of knowledge and power. (Foucault 1981: 106)

Sexuality is bound up with power relations and forms a terrain on which power operates. In turn, power is not a fixed thing, but a strategic relation; it has no fixed origin or centre, but is dispersed across the social realm. This view also suggests a new, more complex understanding of discourse that attempts to correct the one-sided view of the early works. Foucault writes that 'we must not imagine a world of discourse divided between accepted discourse and excluded discourse, or between the dominant discourse and the dominated one; but as a multiplicity of discursive elements that can come into play in various strategies' (ibid., p. 100). Discourse no longer has a central unifying point, but becomes a terrain for the exercise of power. Power, in turn, is exercised from numerous points. It is not something that is acquired, seized or shared but is dispersed across different social relations. Power is not exterior to such things as economic processes, knowledge relations and sexuality, but is immanent in them.

For this reason, Foucault rejects the Marxist view that there are always underlying relations of power – like economic conditions or class relations – that are already given. Foucault argues that the political conditions themselves are the very ground on which the subject, domains of knowledge and truth relations are formed. This is because power and knowledge are bound together. It is not that one acts upon the other, but that 'power and knowledge directly imply one another; that there is no power relation without the correlative constitution of a field of knowledge, nor any knowledge that does not presuppose and constitute at the same time power relations' (Foucault 1979: 27). The notion of ideology must necessarily be abandoned, for it is no longer the case that ideas are distorted by power relations, economic relations or class relations but rather, power and knowledge always act together so that the 'effects of truth are produced within discourses that, in themselves, are neither true nor false' (Foucault 2001: 119).

Because Foucault takes the view that power is not is not a fixed property that belongs to or is controlled by someone or something, he also rejects the traditional view of power as sovereignty – something we shall explore further in the next section on governmentality. Sovereignty implies a top-down, unified notion of power that is exercised from a central point – the sovereign or the state. Foucault rejects this notion in favour of the view that in a modern society, power is multiple, strategic and dispersed:'Power has its principle not so much in a person as in a certain concerted distribution of bodies, surfaces, lights, gazes; in an arrangement whose internal mechanisms produce the relation in which individuals are caught up' (Foucault 1979: 202).

This view comes across in Foucault's writing on discipline, where he shows how control of bodies has moved out of the hands of the sovereign, and indeed out of the hands of any one particular institution or central body:

'Discipline' may be identified neither with an institution nor with an apparatus; it is a type of power, a modality for its exercise, comprising a whole set of instruments, techniques, procedures, levels of application, targets; it is a 'physics' or an 'anatomy' of power, a technology. (Ibid., p. 215)

Discipline becomes the new form of domination, economically and politically more discreet and efficient than sovereign power. It deploys new techniques for controlling an expanding population and encourages individuals to discipline themselves and show self-control. The human body is at the centre of power struggles, and the way in which disciplinary techniques act upon the body indicates a micro-physics of power:

> The study of this micro-physics presupposes that the power exercised on the body is conceived not as a property, but as a strategy, that its effects of domination are attributed not to 'appropriation', but to dispositions, manoeuvres, tactics, techniques, functionings ... In short this power is exercised rather than possessed; it is not the 'privilege', acquired or preserved, of the dominant class, but the overall effect of its strategic positions. (Ibid., p. 26)

Again, it is stressed that this is a power that operates through bodies, not upon them. This is captured by the notion of capillary power that operates from below and runs through people rather than being imposed from above. As Foucault says: 'Power comes from below; that is, there is no binary and all-encompassing opposition between rulers and ruled' (Foucault 1981: 94). Power is exercised rather than possessed. It comes from neither states, nor classes, nor individuals, and although it is intentional, it is not subjective: 'There is no power that is exercised without a series of aims and objectives. But this does not mean that it results from the choice or decision of an individual subject' (ibid., p. 95).

Foucault focuses on the strategies and techniques that interrelate with forms of knowledge and the regulation of the body. The exercise of power is accompanied by the production of apparatuses of knowledge. Foucault emphasises that power is not fixed or given but has to be continually reasserted and that domination is far-reaching but never fully stable. The social is a terrain of continual strategic interaction and struggle and it is argued that where there is power there is opposition: 'Where there is power, there is resistance, and yet, or rather consequently, this resistance is never in a position of exteriority in relation to power' (ibid., p. 95). The trouble is that by denying this exteriority – by denying the importance of classes or the state or underlying economic relations – it is never clear exactly what power is exercised for, nor what resistance is exercised against. And despite the insistence that resistance and struggle occur, it could be argued that power still seems to be overly effective in achieving conformity and regulation. There seems to be little space for difference, dissention, subculture or alternative strategies. Foucault's work does introduce the idea of social norms and meaningful agreement, but only in the context of routinised behaviour, and making disciplinary modes of power appear natural. The emphasis remains on an overly repressive form of social cohesion that is not normative in the sense of genuine norms and social dialogue. Still Foucault's work shows signs of an overly structuralist and functionalist account of social cohesion and control.

3. GOVERNMENTALITY AND THE SELF

For Foucault, power is about instrumental techniques of regulation that control the actions of people and make them act one way rather than another. In this sense there are similarities with Weber and the Frankfurt school, although Foucault tries to avoid their more general focus on the exercise of power and looks at the way power is applied to specific situations. This can be seen in Foucault's theory of governmentality, which rejects a general view of the modern state and sees it not as a unified apparatus, but as a network of different institutions and practices. Power operates not from a single source but through a set of procedures and techniques. Foucault's studies move from centralised forms of power to the local and regional level. He is concerned not with the possession of power but with its exercise, application and effects, and how it circulates through the social body. Instead of looking at how groups or institutions exercise power, Foucault looks at the processes by which subjects are constituted as the effects of power. His study of governmentality proceeds from the micro level, where power is a part of our everyday routines and practices. These are appropriated by macro powers and interests – such as the state or the ruling class – but this view reverses the traditional understanding that power is top-down. These methods are not invented by the ruling groups; rather, they utilise what already exists, adopting, adapting and developing them for their own purposes.

It might be said, then, that Foucault is opposed to a statist conception of the state – that is, he is opposed to the view that the state is a central institution that imposes its power from above. For Foucault the state is not a single unified body but a composite reality connected to a wider and more dispersed range of powers that operate through networks rather than some centralised institution. His concept of governmentality expresses how the state adopts a wide range of different techniques. These are not all immanent in the state; rather, the state adopts and utilises a set of already existing power networks:

> The state is superstructural in relation to a whole series of power networks that invest the body, sexuality, the family, kinship, knowledge, technology, and so forth . . . this metapower with its prohibitions can only take hold and secure its footing where it is rooted in a whole series of multiple and indefinite power relations that supply the necessary basis for the great negative forms of power. (Foucault 2001: 123)

Power, then, is not reducible to an institution or a structure, but resides in a complex network of strategic relations. With this as our starting point it is then possible to examine the 'strategies in which [power relations] take effect, whose general design or institutional crystallisation is embodied in the state apparatus, in the formulation of the law, in the various social hegemonies' (Foucault 1981: 92–3). But it must be stressed that power does not begin or end with the state, the state is only one aspect of power relations, described by Foucault as secondary or superstructural. The power relations that are concerned with governing the social body go beyond the limitations of the state and are to be found across a much wider strategic field.

> [Power] must not be sought in the primary existence of a central point, in a unique source of sovereignty from which secondary and descendent forms would emanate; it is the moving substrate of force relations which, by virtue of their inequality, constantly engender states of power, but the latter are always local and unstable . . . Power is everywhere; not because it embraces everything, but because it comes from everywhere. (Ibid., p. 93)

Governmentality is bound up with the new, more sophisticated methods of discipline and regulation based on observation, calculation and administration. We have seen how Foucault links sovereign power to spectacular, ritualistic, visible and violent repression whereas modern governmentality is based on techniques of normalisation, regulation and control of bodies. This shift corresponds to big demographic and economic changes. New techniques are required for controlling an expanding population and dealing with questions of wealth, health and labour. Population emerges as the new object of government, which attempts to develop the individual's capacity for self-regulation and subjects their conduct to instrumental control. Foucault does see how these methods relate to changes in the mode of production, but disciplinary power is regarded not as a secondary effect of these developments but as something that has equal status.

The traditional view of power is that it is seen as legitimate if it is based on consent. Foucault moves away from consent in that it implies subjectivity. That is to say that consensus implies consciousness and agreement. Foucault's notion of disciplinary regulation can be seen as an alternative to the idea of consensual agreement, although we have noted that this raises problems about Foucault's lack of agency. It would seem that disciplinary power is responsible for social cohesion without having to rely on achieving consent. Foucault's critique of the notion of consent is also bound up with his rejection of the sovereignty model that focuses its attention on the role of the state. Sovereignty, for Foucault, is too narrow a concept and it is necessary to distinguish it from the mechanisms of governmentality, which are much wider. Governmentality is about the regulation of conduct using various technical means and encouraging individuals to regulate themselves. In presenting this alternative model, Foucault distinguishes between the practical rationality of government and the normative basis of sovereignty.

With the theory of governmentality the focus is not on the power of the sovereign or the state, but on the condition of the population which is the subject and object of government. Historical forces act not over but through the social body. The theory of governmentality goes beyond the limits of state power by looking at the network of institutions, practices, procedures and techniques. Government is the rational application of technical means for the regulation of conduct. An example of Foucault's expanded concept of governmentality is his notion of pastoral power. This concept describes the modern concern with the governance of populations and their welfare. Pastoral power implies responsibility for the welfare and constant care of the flock. The police, rather than simply being a repressive force, are an important agent of pastoral power, as are those responsible for the improvement of life, health and wealth. This shift in governmentality is connected to the emergence of new problems – population and birth, security and protection and political economy. The organs of pastoral power are the police, philanthropic organisations, medical institutions and state organisations.

Rejection of the traditional model of state and sovereignty also implies rejection of the kind of domination/dominated schema that we have found in the writings of the other authors we have covered. Domination is the hegemonic effect of a multiplicity of micro powers. This allows for the possibility of multiple resistances. Relations of power are everywhere, but they are not necessarily stable. Foucault moves from his earlier view of domination where disciplinary power appears to be total. He now argues that power is relational and strategic and wherever there is power there is resistance. The theory of governmentality broadens the category of power so that it goes beyond violence, domination and control. Force and consent are more subtle, requiring the strategic interplay of different powers. In this less monolithic account of power, techniques of domination are balanced with techniques of the self. Foucault is placing more emphasis on practical self-consciousness, critical self-awareness and reflexivity. His late works start to move away from the more negative view of power with its one-sided focus on the institutional basis of power. There is a shift in focus towards power in relation to the subject. There is an interplay between power and freedom as individuals struggle against imposed identities.

There is a need to break from the view of power as juridical and negative. Power should not just see it in terms of law, prohibition and sovereignty. This is a reductionist approach that ignores the positive effects of power. Power should be seen as a productive and enabling force. Foucault argues:

> If power were never anything but repressive, if it never did anything but to say no, do you really think one would be brought to obey it? What makes power hold good, what makes it accepted, is simply the fact that it doesn't only weigh on us as a force that says no; it also traverses and produces things, it induces pleasure, forms knowledge, produces discourse. It needs to be considered as a productive network that runs through the instance whose function is repression. (Foucault 2001: 120)

This allows more space for the self. Power may constrain individuals but it also constitutes the conditions of possibility for their freedom. Power is not just an objectifying force (producing docile bodies) but is also a source of subjectivity, providing a basis on which opposition and resistance can develop. Politically this means an ethics of the self. Foucault makes a third shift in his final works in order to analyse the subject and 'the games of truth by which man proposes to think his own nature' (Foucault 1985: 7). But what are the games of truth by which people come to see themselves as desiring individuals? Unfortunately Foucault's examples are largely limited to antiquity, although clearly the aim is to contrast these attitudes with modern attitudes.

For the Greeks, the three major techniques of the self were dietetics, economics and erotics. In economics and dietetics the voluntary moderation of the male was based on his relation to himself. Erotics constitutes a domain of ethical practice based on pleasurable acts in an agonistic field of forces. The Greeks did not have a notion of homosexuality as we know it and they did not see love for one's own sex and love for the other sex as opposites. Foucault's study of classical antiquity aims to show that the reflection on pleasures was not so much concerned with a codification of acts or a hermeneutics of the subject but a stylisation of attitudes and an aesthetics of existence (ibid., p. 92). The relations between restraint and excess, activity and passivity were of great importance. Regimen is the art of living, a way of forming oneself into a subject, a strategy involving the body, equipping the individual for a rational mode of behaviour. It is about the active stylisation of bodily existence. The self-mastery and superiority one exercised over the self was closely connected to the authority one exercised in the household and over one's wife. But changes in matrimonial practices brought about more reciprocity and equality. The issue was no longer mastery over others; the dominion of oneself is now manifested more through obligations to others.

Sadly, Foucault did not complete his history of sexuality so we can only speculate about the direction his work was going in. Although his work turns back to Greece and Rome, it is possible to see Foucault's aim of revealing the changing relationship between sexuality and the self. The discourse of sexuality produces the truth of the sexual body, but also there is a role for subjectivity in the constitution of the self. Just how much power the self can have is a matter of debate, and just how this newly found subjectivity fits into the subject-producing worlds of discourse and discipline is an issue for endless debate.

4. FOUCAULT AND FEMINISM

Foucault's work has had a big influence on feminist debates despite having very little to say on feminism itself. The importance of Foucault's work lies in its rejection of the idea of an innate sexuality, implying that gender, and even the body itself, is a social construct. Both are the product of historically specific social relations and are bound up with processes of power, control and regulation. So Foucault rejects any essentialist or biologistic readings of the body that attempt to 'naturalise' it. The body is a social and cultural product and femininity has to be inscribed into the body – in particular, this is related to the operation of power on and through the body. Foucault's approach to sexuality and the body offers an alternative not only to the mechanical model presented by mainstream, male-dominated science, but also to the kind of biological essentialism present in radical feminist discourse. Foucauldian feminists are offered a critical history that challenges the assumptions of both dominant and oppositional discourses, and a radical politics based on the notion of difference.

Still, there are two sides to this debate. Could it be that the laudable anti-essentialism gives way to hopeless relativism? For the sympathetic Judith Butler this relativism (contingency) and politics of difference is important. She takes up Foucault's emphasis on the body as a surface on which gender identity is created and argues that the task of genealogy is to reveal that what seems natural is really based on contingent power relations. The more critical Kate Soper argues that Foucault's position goes too far and that its questioning of what is 'natural' becomes too anti-naturalist. After all the body is a physical entity irrespective of how it is culturally articulated, so instead of rejecting the natural, it is necessary to look at the relation between the 'natural' and the 'normal' (Soper 1993: 33).

Nevertheless, that such a debate is possible is testimony to the radical shift Foucault makes in switching focus from the subject to the body. By paying attention to the body, Foucault is challenging the traditional Enlightenment approach that bases itself on the rational subject. The Enlightenment's emphasis on the rational subject is achieved through the repression, exclusion and marginalisation of bodily expressions, desires and emotions. Control of the body is achieved through its 'naturalisation', a process that denies the fact that the body is in fact the product of struggle and confrontation. Likewise, human sexuality is 'naturalised' and Foucault's task is to show how this naturalisation is achieved and how it relates to issues of power/knowledge and regimes of truth. The naturalisation of sex performs an important regulatory function. As Lois McNay notes, it brings together a number of disparate biological functions and bodily pleasures, it provides the regulatory notion of a 'natural' sexuality, and it presents sexuality as an unruly force which needs to be controlled, whereas it is in fact the very product of the exercise of power (McNay 1992: 29). This can be seen, for example, in Foucault's account of the hysterisation of female sexuality and the need to regulate and control 'unnatural' female desires.

A feminist account can certainly show how this repression of sexuality and construction of female behaviour is linked to a hierarchical social order. But can Foucault's account of power show how men (or certain social groups) benefit from this process? Why is this so and where does male power come from? Ironically, Foucualt's account of sexuality itself reflects this male bias, as it focuses primarily on the construction and experience of male sexuality. Furthermore, Foucault's account of sexuality suffers, like many of his ideas, from being very abstract. He fails to look at concrete examples of gendered discursive techniques and how they act upon and regulate the body. And as far as the female body is concerned, he still has a tendency to see power as centralised and repressive and moving in only one direction despite his new emphasis on heterogeneity and resistance. As McNay complains:

> Thus whereas feminists have recognised the need to show that women are more than passive victims of domination through the rediscovery and re-evaluation of their experiences and history, Foucault's understanding of individuals as docile bodies has the effect of pushing women back into this position of passivity and silence. (Ibid., p. 47)

McNay's point seems valid for there appears to be a tension in Foucault's later work. What interests feminists is the way Foucault supposedly shifts from the idea of centralised domination and repression to bio-power and technologies of the self. The emphasis in these late works is on the production of the self, and the way in which subjectification gives a degree of self-determination. The advantage of Foucault's late works should be that they move away from the view that power is negative and totalising. But he still sees the exercise of subjectivity more in terms of discipline and control rather than agency. It may be that he gives room to resistance, but Foucault does not locate where this might take place. Soper's criticism is that this work fails to link the bio-political to the socio-economic (Soper 1993: 35), while McNay argues that Foucault's aesthetic approach to practices of the self does not allow for differences of priority, or why society may impose some practices more than others (McNay 1992: 82). To start to address this it would be necessary to look beyond the exercise of power and make some claims about where this power comes from in the first place.

Innovative though Foucault's approach is, it leaves unresolved many questions that feminists are still attempting to grapple with. The differences between Foucault's ideas and traditional feminist discourse are again revealed by the notions of oppression and liberation. By shifting away from the conventional view of power as something that is possessed, Foucault moves away from the idea of the oppressor and oppressed. Everyone is caught up in power, no one owns or controls it. It is difficult, then, to conceive of the points at which resistance will occur or of the agents who will carry it out. Foucault, and many of those feminists influenced by his account of the dispersal of power, is opposed to the idea that there is any single revolutionary subject and even to the idea of centralised resistance. This is seen as continuing the process of a dominant hegemony, at best leading simply to new power/knowledge relations and new hierarchies. Those who oppose such a view argue that Foucault's idea of resistance becomes too marginal and individualistic, unable to offer a radical alternative. One such feminist, Linda Alcoff, argues that we do need the idea of a counter-hegemony to fight power and that even if hegemony implies authority and centralisation, this is a necessary strategy:

> The solution to the problems that Foucault sees with regard to hegemonic power/knowledge systems is not to restrict ourselves to the local sphere but to formulate a more inclusive discourse than traditional liberalism and to develop a political practice that maintains the maximum local autonomy possible. (Alcoff 1990: 86)

What of women's liberation? Foucault's emphasis on small-scale resistance can be related to his refusal to take a normative stance and outline the basis on which liberation is to be achieved. The idea of 'liberation' would imply the kind of totalising discourse that Foucault rejects. But then, is liberation really the key question? Foucault's argument in his last works is that power is not so much about the repression of sexuality as about creating the forms that sexuality takes. If this is the case, then what exactly is it that women should be liberated from? Here we find that Foucauldian feminism might just be becoming postfeminism.

5. TOWARDS POSTMODERNISM

It can be seen that Foucault's legacy is much debated and that some, such as Judith Butler, push Foucault in a postmodernist direction, so it seems right to end this study with an assessment of Foucault in the light of current trends towards postmodernist thinking. It would seem that Foucault's work meets the postmodernist criteria of rejecting the idea of scientific rationality, rejecting a unitary notion of progress and a providing a critique of representation and truth claims. Certainly Foucault is a poststructuralist, moving away from an emphasis on underlying structures (and rejecting his earlier notion of structures of ideas, or epistemes) and concentrating instead on the interplay of diverse power relations. But it is debatable whether Foucault should be considered a postmodernist, for this would constitute a rejection of any attempt to give an explanation of social life, including his own rich accounts of the operation of power.

Certainly Foucault rejects the idea of historical progress and many of the ideas of the Enlightenment. His work tries to show that history is not a singular or unitary process, but contains many diverse and competing elements. Foucault follows Nietzsche in showing history to be a constant process of struggle and his genealogical method attempts to highlight the plurality, discontinuity and fragility of historical forms. History is not determined by essential forces, but is a contingent affair comprising multiple relations and forces, complex material conditions and competing social discourses.

Like Adorno and Horkheimer and even Weber, Foucault questions the Enlightenment and its claims to progress. But whereas Weber and the early Frankfurt school focus on the disenchantment of society and the problems with the general conditions of rationality, Foucault examines specific rationalities and their effects in different fields including madness, medicine, crime and sexuality. Whereas Adorno, Horkheimer and Weber emphasise domination and see it as irreversible, Foucault claims that domination is contestable and that wherever there is power there is resistance, although it must be said that the precise nature of this resistance is never adequately addressed.

Foucault and Habermas locked horns over the question of modernity and Foucault rejects the Enlightenment link between morality and universal rationality. He opposes Habermas's view of communicative rationality and normatively reached consensus. He sees this story of consensus as sinister, as an imposition of uniformity and an effacement of difference. Foucault sees Habermas's defence of modernity and universal reason as a defence of the modern order at the expense of radical alternatives.

Habermas's defence of modernity follows others who are also influenced by the Marxist tradition. Foucault is critical of the way that Marxism seeks to justify modernity and its idea of historical progress. Many commentators have pointed out how Marx's work seems to admire the progressive role of the bourgeoisie and the need for continued economic growth and development (the productive forces being seen as the 'motor of history'). Foucault claims that 'at the deepest level of Western knowledge Marxism introduced no real discontinuity'(1974: 261), that it found its place quite comfortably in the new dominant order, and that 'Marxism exists in nineteenth-century thought like a fish in water: that is, it is unable to breathe anywhere else'(ibid., p. 262). Yet Foucault later praises Marx for initiating a decentring of anthropological humanism by looking beyond the discursive structure to the historical analysis of the relations of production, economic determinations and class struggle – and in this sense Marx deserves to be considered as a radical alongside Nietzsche and Freud (Foucault 1989: 13).

Whereas modernity tends to see itself in opposition to the past, Foucault attempts to make sense of the past, not to pass judgement on it. In fact he tries to show that there was a certain coherence to the past. For example, in *Discipline and Punish*, Foucault is at pains to show that the punishment of Damiens was not irrational but in fact a carefully constructed and regulated social procedure designed to produce effects on the criminal and to give a public display of the power of the monarch, thus producing fear among the masses. In showing this, Foucault is able to demonstrate that the present system is not noticeably different to those past regimes that it so readily denounces, that it does not have a unique claim to legitimacy and that modern society, like past regimes, is also finite and susceptible to change. Foucault follows a Nietzschean genealogy that attempts to undermine the claims of the present through a comparison with a past it tries to dismiss.

By arguing that there is coherence and reason to these societies, Foucault would seem to reject the irrationalist strand of postmodernism. For even if he does question reason, he does not reject it altogether, but is concerned with its claims, limitations and historical context. Postmodernism goes further, so, for example, Jean-François Lyotard's notion of language games argues that there is a collapse of all 'grand narratives' and we are left with a fluid reality made up of incommensurable language games each with its own immanent criteria of rationality. Consensus is replaced with 'dissensus' and we have no basis on which to judge any of these discourses. The return to the notion of social discourses is symptomatic of postmodernism, as is reflected in Jean Baudrillard's claim that reality is largely linguistic or symbolic. Foucault's early work argued that discourses were unifying and cohesive, whereas for postmodernism discourses are multiple and fragmented. Of course Foucault influences postmodernism with his own shift towards a diverse and pluralistic social world. But the big difference is that Foucault's shift emphasises various material practices, not just discursive ones. For all its faults, Foucault's study of these diverse practices is useful and insightful. Postmodernism, on the other hand, provides no useful insights and in fact denounces any attempt to do so.

Foucault's method deserves to be considered alongside Jacques Derrida's form of deconstruction. Its aim is to critically analyse different discourses, including those that attempt to explain history and society. His archaeology opposes itself to a 'total history'

> that seeks to reconstitute the overall form of a civilisation, the principle – material or spiritual – of a society, the significance common to all the phenomena of a period, the law that accounts for their cohesion – what is called metaphorically the 'face' of a period. (Foucault 1989: 9)

This appeals to a postmodernist feminism, or even to a postfeminism of the sort found in Julia Kristeva which opposes totalising discourses, including those found in liberation strategies. Feminism, it is argued, should be based on an assertion of difference and a rejection of the dominant 'phallogocentric' tradition. In attempting to unravel the claims of dominant discourses and to expose their motives, Foucault is providing a useful service. Like deconstruction, his approach is critical and reflexive, trying to take its distance from modernist ideology in order to expose the political interests that lie behind dominant discourses.

Now that we have moved on to questions of method, it does seem, though, that Foucault's work opens the door to relativism. It is argued that the production of knowledge is bound up with historical regimes of power that produce or sustain it. Foucault is against generalised truth claims, arguing that the effects of truth are produced within discourse, epistemes or apparatuses of power. This is certainly relativist in the sense that truth is internal to regimes of knowledge and further, that these knowledge systems are bound up with strategies of domination. There is no 'truth', only 'truths'. So truth is related to the Nietzschean struggle or will to power, the interplay between truth and power and between theory and practice. Instead of seeking the 'truth', Foucault is looking for the link between reason and domination.

If it is difficult to speak of an absolute 'truth', then it is also difficult to speak of 'falsity', hence Foucault avoids the notion of ideology, as it presupposes some truth against which this mystification can be compared. There is a danger also that the theory of ideology sees the subject as the source of ideas. Instead of ideology, Foucault has a conception of discourse that is non-subjective and embodies both material and symbolic relations as well, of course, as power relations. In arguing that discourse provides social cohesion, it could be thought that Foucault is embracing an idealist position. But for Foucault discourse is seen as a material relation that interacts with non-discursive practices. In some ways Foucault's notion of discourse is better than the concept of ideology in that it gives a clearer explanation of how material and ideational forces are bound together. But in other ways it lacks the Marxist understanding that ideology is produced by dominant social structures, and thus it might be claimed that Foucault's concept of discourse is confined to a shallower surface role as compared to the Marxist view that ideology is bound up with underlying social relations.

Because Foucault is a poststructuralist, he tends to avoid the question of underlying social structures, concentrating instead on the network of power–knowledge relations operating at the level of their exercise. Keen to overcome the structuralist tendencies of his earlier work, Foucault aims to rid his work of all forms of determinism, including what he sees as support for underlying structures and essential social relations. This explains his criticism of Marxism and its reliance on 'external' categories of power like class and mode of production. For Foucault power becomes pluralistic, operating at all levels of society and is immanent in (rather than external to) knowledge and discourse. Foucault sees power also as a strategic technique, which is why he develops a concept of hegemony. However, the deployment of this concept is somewhat different to, say, Gramsci's, in that it has less to do with social consent and is more about the strategic deployment of power. On sexuality Foucault writes that 'the nineteenth century witnessed a deployment of sexuality, starting from a hegemonic centre. Eventually the entire social body was provided with a "sexual body", although this was accomplished in different ways and using different tools' (Foucault 1981: 127).

This more restricted understanding of hegemony can also be found in the work of Ernesto Laclau and Chantal Mouffe, whose book *Hegemony and Socialist Strategy* is influenced by Foucault, Gramsci and Derrida. They take up Foucault's concept of a discursive formation and argue that this contains contingent elements that hegemony acts upon and articulates. Taking a position that is more postmodernist and idealist than Foucault's, they reject his distinction between discursive and non-discursive practices (Laclau and Mouffe 1985: 107). Laclau and Mouffe reject the idea that there are any interests – be they based on class, gender, economics or whatever – prior to their articulation in discourse. Their work embraces 'the openness and indeterminacy of the social, which gives a primacy and founding character to negativity and antagonism, and assures the existence of articulatory and hegemonic practices' (ibid., pp. 144–5). If Foucault does lead to postmodernism, then this is what we get – all social elements are fluid, there are no social relations, everything is contained within discourse, and hegemony acts as an articulator of discursive formations.

Similarly, nowhere in Foucault's work do we find out where power comes from. Like Laclau and Mouffe the hegemonic moment or exercise of power is everything. Instead of looking at where power comes from, Foucault is concerned only with its exercise and effects. He does not link power to a particular class, nor even to the state. It is claimed that power is not something that is imposed upon us, but is something that runs through us. Such a position is criticised by Nicos Poulantzas, who argues that Foucault fails to give power a material foundation or grounding. He asks, if power has no clear material foundation, why should there be resistance and on what basis? 'In the absence of a foundation for resistances, power is in the end essentialised and absolutised' (Poulantzas 1978b: 150).

Poulantzas argues the standard Marxist view that power derives from the division of labour. At least by making such an identification, he holds out the possibility of escape. By contrast Foucault scatters power among microstructures and underestimates the significance of the state and the importance of class struggle. In Foucault the state is reduced to the process of normalisation and imposition of homogeneity. It becomes a site for technologies of power, but has little power in its own right.

Poulantzas also argues that Foucault's view of power focuses on violence but ignores the matter of consent. We have seen that this is so because consent implies a relation between subjects whereas Foucault is more concerned with the formation of subjects. As Barry Smart argues, 'Foucault does not so much neglect the question of consent as attend to a fundamental precondition, namely analysis of the particular modes by which human beings become subjects' (1983: 107). But what happens to the subjects after they have been formed? Are they created to be consensual, or must consensus be continually reasserted? Poulantzas argues that consent must be explained by other processes as well as normalisation, 'for if those disciplines were enough to account for submission, *how could they admit the existence of struggles?*' (Poulantzas 1978b: 79). He continues:'In point of fact, there has to be organised physical violence for the very reason that there has to be consent' (ibid., p. 79).

If there are problems with consent, Lois McNay argues that Foucault's theory of power cannot provide a satisfactory account of social cohesion. She argues that there is an unresolved tension between Foucault's idea that social relations are fragmented and contestable and his view of a totally administered society. She wonders how such diffuse forms of struggle can develop into relatively permanent and enduring hierarchies of power (McNay 1994: 111). A more general criticism of Foucault's ontology of power is provided by Thomas McCarthy, who argues that Foucault places too much under the description of power. As a consequence, 'distinctions between just and unjust social arrangements, legitimate and illegitimate uses of political power, strategic and co-operative interpersonal relations, coercive and consensual measures – distinctions that have been at the heart of critical social analysis – become marginal' (McCarthy 1994, p. 254). Quite simply, power is trying to do far too much and without a more careful distinction between authority, force, violence and legitimacy, there is a certain one-dimensionality about Foucault's approach.

This hints at perhaps the two main problems with Foucault's theory – the problem of normativity and the problem of social structure. His theory of power tends to focus on social relations at a surface level without getting to their underlying conditions. Nor does he allow for any underlying normative basis to society. Against this it might be said that ultimately social cohesion can only be provided by relatively enduring social structures and a relatively stable form of consensus. These are issues that need to be addressed in the conclusion.

Chapter 8

CONCLUSION:
UNCERTAINTY AND DIVERSITY

———◦—◦———

1. DEFINING THE TERMS

It should be clear by now that although the concepts of conflict, cohesion and consent are widely used and widely applicable, they are not easy to define. Indeed a decent account of these terms should not try to define them too thoroughly, but let them speak for themselves in the different contexts in which different thinkers use them. The terms clearly are intermeshed and derive their meaning in relation to each other. They are often used interchangeably in so far as they describe aspects of the same process. To give too precise a definition would clearly be a mistake, but our study allows us to make the following generalisations:

Conflict may refer to struggle, force, coercion and contestation. In a way, this term is the easiest to define, but considerable problems arise when we try to account for the origins and role of conflict. So in Marx we may find a discussion of class conflict, economic conflict, or a conflict of interests. However, we can also find a conflict between more abstract things like capital and labour or the forces and relations of production. Weber, in discussing conflict, talks about such things as social status or stratified social groups. In Gramsci the discussion concerns hegemonic blocs and wars of manoeuvre, for Pareto conflicts take place among elites.

Consent and **consensus**, which are used interchangeably here, refer to processes of agreement, legitimation, compliance and assent. However, this consent must be seen in its wider context – that it is not something voluntary (although this is occasionally suggested by Weber's writing) but takes place under definite conditions. And if consensus is seen as existing between conflicting interests, as is suggested by Gramsci's conception of hegemony, then this process must involve negotiation and compromise, but maybe also manipulation and duress.

Cohesion may be taken to mean the degree to which such differences can be overcome and the system integrated. It may refer to the way that a social system hangs together, or else may refer to the solidarity of a social group. In the work of Parsons and Durkheim it relates to social norms and values, but it may have a more structural or material dimension as in the structural Marxism of Poulantzas, who talks of the unity of the social formation and the state as a factor of social cohesion. For Gramsci, cohesion refers to the historical bloc (unity of structure and superstructure), for the Frankfurt School it relates to the integrated society, while Foucault talks of the cohesive role of discourse and disciplinary practices.

2. DEFINING THE THEORIES

Marx

In Marx, the discussion of conflict, cohesion and consent takes place at the level of the system rather than in relation to individuals. Therefore the production of social cohesion and the generation of consent seem to be built into the capitalist system. This is especially so with the process whereby workers consent to sell their labour power, which in turn reproduces capitalist relations and generates ideologies that justify this process. Therefore, if workers consent to the rule of capital, this is not so much because they are coerced into doing so, but more because the mystifying character of the wage-relation conceals the process of exploitation.

If the capitalist system generates its own cohesion and consent, it also generates its own conflicts. The breakdown of social cohesion and consent is often seen as a result of the inherent failings of the capitalist system itself rather than anything more political or conscious. In fact it could be said that social consent flows from social cohesion – or the ability of the system to maintain itself – and that consent only becomes an issue once cohesion has broken down.

But Marx's political writings display a greater belief in the role of agency and history is defined in terms of class struggle. To try and reconcile these positions we might say that the system produces its own cohesion and consent but that this is not stable. History is the history of conflict, but only when conditions allow. Cohesion and consensus may be challenged during particular moments of crisis, and under these conditions we may make our own history.

Gramsci

Gramsci examines more subtle mechanisms of social control and consensus. Hegemony corresponds to the construction and maintenance of consensus throughout civil society. A ruling group must seek legitimacy through the construction of a hegemonic bloc that offers intellectual and moral leadership. The dominant group exercises its power through the state. Against competing groups it must conduct a war of positions. Therefore hegemony does not flow automatically from the economic position of the dominant group, but needs to be constructed and negotiated. This process requires the forging of unity between the components of the ruling bloc, and winning the consent of the wider layers over which hegemony is to be exercised. The state helps forge a unity between the different components of the ruling bloc and acts as the institutional terrain for this process of construction, negotiation and contestation.

In contrast to Marx, cohesion and consent need to be more actively built. But then this itself is a product of the inherently conflictual nature of society. The distinction between the more coercive aspects of class domination (as represented by the repressive bodies of state power) and the consensual aspects of wider society is indicated by Gramsci's distinction between the East and the more developed West. To distinguish between cohesion and consent we might say that consent is the active hegemonic project, but this must take place within the cohesion of the system. The historical bloc and passive revolution show how consent must be won by relating to wider socio-structural issues such as developments in production.

Ideology plays an important role in Gramsci's work, both as an unconscious layer of everyday life and in a more positive sense as something capable of mobilising and articulating different social interests. Ultimately, Gramsci is an advocate of conflict. But he realises, like Machiavelli, that if that conflict is to be won, consent must be developed.

Functionalism

Society is seen as a bounded, self-maintaining system while social institutions and practices are seen in terms of their function in performing a social requirement. Functionalist sociologists look at how social equilibrium is maintained and how society meets its needs and requirements.

Durkheim's approach contains a dual focus on normative and structural factors. Social order comes from a core of institutionalised values that are held in common by members of a community. This leads to the widespread view that functionalism advocates a theory of social consensus. But as has been argued, the institutionalisation of common values can be seen in terms of social cohesion or the maintenance of the system, but less so in terms of a more active process of social consent.

There is some room for conflict within a functionalist perspective. But this is seen in terms of something pathological or a deviation from the norm. The aim in both Durkheim and Parsons is to return to a state of order and conformity. Where conflicts emerge, they are not something in fundamental contradiction with the system as they might be in Marx, but are a secondary or dysfunctional effect. In particular, problems are caused by the growth of new divisions of economic functions which have outpaced the development of corresponding forms of moral regulation. Whereas for Marx economic conflict is a fundamental aspect of capitalist society, for Durkheim it is the product of unregulated economic expansion.

Parsons adds to functionalist theory by looking at the functional prerequisites of the system, which are that it must adapt to its environment, mobilise its resources to achieve its goals, maintain internal coordination of its parts, develop ways of dealing with deviance, hold itself together and maintain itself in a state of equilibrium. Something either contributes to the maintenance of the system or else it is dysfunctional in undermining the effectiveness and integration of the system. Such a focus clearly indicates the dominance of the issue of cohesion within the functionalist perspective.

Weber

Weber has a conflict-based theory of history, so forms of domination can be seen in terms of different struggles that occur. His notion of class encompasses those struggles that take place in the market sphere. Conflict can arise from class differences over interests and things like the distribution of property and resources. In particular, conflict is related to the distribution of life chances. Class arises out of our market situation and class consciousness may develop in relation to either competition or a common situation with others – perhaps leading to the formation of a party to defend class or status position. But Weber's account does not constitute an economic theory like Marx's and is more of a sociology of economic behaviour. The economic sphere is not the sole determinant of social relations and class conflict is not the inevitable consequence of economic development. Any conflicts that emerge are historically contingent and may be due to a range of stratified characteristics such as occupation, background, ethnicity or gender.

Weber's views on legitimation would seem to offer a good account of consensus and the way in which different forms of society rely on different forms of legitimation – traditional, charismatic and legal–rational. The problem, though, is that due to the influence of Nietzsche the concept of legitimation is conflated with that of domination. Nietzsche's influence is also apparent in Weber's pessimistic account of modernity, where the individual spirit is crushed by the process of rationalisation. The cohesion of the social system strengthens in accordance with the development of rational administration and governance, the advance of technology, and the development of a disciplined labour market. Bureaucracy develops as a means of coordinating and administering the complex spheres of modern social life. The rationalisation process brings with it a new level of social cohesiveness. The different social spheres – the economy, state, politics and culture – are all interrelated and interdependent. This view of the integrated society influences the Frankfurt school.

Critical Theory

The early Frankfurt theorists see monopoly capitalism as bringing about increasing domination and centralisation and they examine these effects in the cultural sphere. Therefore, whereas Marx argues that social cohesion is maintained through the driving force of economic production, Adorno and Horkheimer look at society as an integrated totality and shift emphasis to the role of cultural reproduction. It is argued that the masses are pacified through the gratification of their material wants and the stunting of their critical faculties. The culture industry provides mindless entertainment and utilises psychological techniques of repetition and recognition to manipulate our desires.

Through this combination of material satisfaction and cultural impoverishment the masses are pacified to the extent that Adorno and Horkheimer can see little prospect of progressive social conflict. Marcuse is more optimistic in so far as he can see some hope in the emergence of new social movements. But generally, the Frankfurt theorists see consensus as a process of pacification rather than interaction. Social cohesion is considered almost total with society having reached a new level of integration.

The critical theorists are a strange breed, for unlike most Marxists they seem to minimise the role of conflict. While Habermas challenges the view that the masses are passive and uncritical, he does so not through the notion of conflict, but through the idea of consensus. This is achieved at an ahistorical transcendental level – consent is something innate in the nature of human societies.

Habermas wants to move away from the pessimistic view of Adorno and Horkheimer by arguing that as well as instrumental reason, there is such a thing as communicative rationality, which is a necessary condition for meaningful social life. The intersubjective lifeworld provides a set of background understandings that give coherence to our social actions and forms the horizon within which communicative actions are always already moving. Conflicts emerge between the interests of the lifeworld and those of the system. The problem is that in understanding this relation, consensus is seen as prior to conflict. So it is argued that social institutions are corrupted by capital and the media. But could it not be that social institutions – those of the post-war welfare state, for example – are, from their inception, the expression of the conflict between interests and groups, that they do not have a prior universal basis but are themselves the very expression of past conflicts?

Foucault

Foucault certainly rejects the universalist approach to social institutions, seeing them in their social and historical specificity. It may also be possible to say that these institutions embody conflict in so far as they are produced through strategic interaction, although it is far from clear how this works.

Foucault has a strong emphasis on social cohesion, not as an overt force, but as a subtle process that works through different practices, techniques, and methods. In Foucault's work the unity and cohesion of the social is provided first by discourse, then by discipline and surveillance.

Foucault's notion of disciplinary regulation can be seen as an alternative to the idea of consensual agreement. In disciplinary society social cohesion is based on the conformity to social norms and on the correction of deviants through a combination of coercion and persuasion. In a society that places emphasis on changing people's behaviour and establishing societal norms, disciplinary techniques are linked to the process of normalisation. Foucault's work does introduce the idea of social norms and meaningful agreement, but only in the context of routinised behaviour, and making disciplinary modes of power appear natural.

Foucault rejects theories of consensus such as might be found in models of legitimacy or sovereignty since these imply subjectivity, consciousness and agreement. This leaves very little room for agency and the danger is that agents become passive constructs. Their needs, wants, ideas, values and actions are the product of the dominant discourse and disciplinary power.

In his work on power Foucault argues that the social is a terrain of continual strategic interaction and struggle and that wherever there is power there is opposition. The trouble is that by denying the importance of classes or the state or underlying economic relations, it is never clear exactly what power is exercised for, nor what resistance is exercised against. Despite the claim that resistance and struggle occur, it could be argued that Foucault's work on disciplinary power still overemphasises its monolithic and cohesive nature, offering little space for difference, dissent or alternative strategies.

Postmodernism

For postmodernists such as Lyotard the issue of consensus is more bound up with the practice of science and the status of knowledge. Lyotard develops a critique of Habermas from a knowledge point of view, arguing that in Habermas's theory of communicative rationality 'such consensus does violence to the heterogeneity of language games' (Lyotard 1984: xxv). Rather than one privileged form of knowledge, Lyotard argues that there is a series of competing language games. If any of these gains ascendancy it is because of dominant power relations and a process of legitimation 'by which a "legislator" dealing with scientific discourse is authorized to prescribe the stated conditions . . . determining whether a statement is to be included in that discourse for consideration by the scientific community' (ibid., p. 8). The legitimacy of science is linked to the legitimacy of the legislator; science is linked to ethics and politics. We can see that Lyotard is advocating a version of Foucault's power and knowledge argument.

But postmodernism goes further than Foucault, so, for example, Lyotard's notion of language games argues that there is a collapse of all 'grand narratives' and we are left with a fluid reality made up of incommensurable language games, each with its own immanent criteria of rationality. The emphasis on the plurality of language games is symptomatic of postmodernism and is reflected in Baudrillard's claim that reality is largely linguistic or symbolic. For Baudrillard 'it is a question of substituting the signs of the real for the real' (Baudrillard 1994: 2) so that everything becomes an image or media fabrication and there are no real-world events, like the Gulf War, that exist outside discourse (Baudrillard 1991). Instead, events such as wars take place among TV audiences, the distinctions between truth and falsehood and fact and fiction are blurred and wars become performative and rhetorical constructs (see Norris 1992).

Postmodernism rejects the Enlightenment project and its notions of truth and progress. All forms of knowledge that claim truth are to be rejected, with truth considered to be a contingent matter. With no grand narratives, culture is said to comprise multiple, diverse discourses. Since the world can be known only through these discourses and since there is no distinction between sign and reality, the world becomes uncertain and fragmented. Lyotard argues that this age is marked by the transformation of culture and crisis of narratives. The postmodern refers to the condition of knowledge in the most developed societies. Although Lyotard's main concern is with the status of knowledge, he does make claims about the nature of society. The postmodern society is postindustrial, where knowledge becomes the new focus of production. The transformation of knowledge has an effect on public power and institutions. There is a decline in old institutions, political parties, the state and traditions and the development of new networks of language games.

In the introduction these ideas were mentioned as reinforcing the fragmentations and divisions within society without offering any emancipatory potential. Lyotard's view of the postmodern society celebrates rather than challenges its atomised and fragmented nature. The postmodern condition is in fact reinforced as a reality by those theories that comment on it. The postmodern emphasis on uncertainty, diversity and fragmentation is in fact a new way of imposing social cohesion and consent. Postmodern ideas constitute an ideology of inaction that lends support to new forms of governance based on the individualisation and atomisation of social agents. It tells us that progress and emancipation are utopian ideals and that collective social identities like class are a thing of the past. Such notions are of course hugely beneficial to the rulers of society, as they demobilise any potential opposition. In fact we might claim that postmodern ideology can be used as a tool of governance. Although postmodern theories derive from Foucault, Foucault's own theories of governmentality can be used to explain the role postmodernism plays in individualising social regulation and making it appear as something inevitable and irresistible.

It was noted that the postmodernist position was strongly challenged by Habermas. But ironically, two theorists he influences – Giddens and Beck – express views that are rather similar to the postmodernists'. The next section will look at how their theories of reflexive modernity and risk society also legitimate uncertainty and diversity as the basis of a new social order.

3. CONTEMPORARY THEORIES

We can see with the theories covered a clear periodisation of capitalist development. With Marx we have an earlier phase of capitalism, a liberal phrase with miserable social conditions and the emergence of imperialism. Gramsci looks at a more developed phase of capitalism with the emergence of new production techniques such as Fordism and a more interventionist state. Weber is also concerned with new features of modernity, the growth of bureaucracy and processes of rationalisation. This is taken on by Adorno and Horkheimer to look at the totally integrated society and monopoly capitalism. For them capitalism has stabilised itself through total administration.

If we apply these to the post-war order we can explain developments such as the welfare state, Fordist production and the development of the international system. This period might be defined according to its mode of production, regime of accumulation, state regulation, hegemonic bloc, system of legitimation or else its forms of governmentality. The post-war period, perhaps more than ever before, maintained a strong degree of social cohesion and consent.

Yet this society began to change. Foucault might help us to understand this at the level of governmentality and the shift to a more flexible form of regulation that places greater emphasis on the role of the individual. Others look into the changing nature of the production process. Daniel Bell (1973) introduces the idea of the postindustrial society marked by a decline in manufacturing and dominated by a new professional class. Social divisions are based on culture rather than economics, and the elite is determined by its access to knowledge. Since Bell's time the communications revolution has progressed further and new theories have developed to exploit the themes of the knowledge economy and communications revolution. Another approach would be to stress the post-Fordism angle. The economic uncertainty of the 1970s showed Fordist methods to be too rigid. The term post-Fordism is used to describe new production methods and management techniques. The manufacturing process has been made more flexible, accompanied by state strategies of economic deregulation and liberalisation. The consequence of these processes is a new, more uncertain and diverse society with a flexibilised workforce and social and spatial fragmentation and dispersal. Yet even with these new levels of uncertainty and diversity there is still a strong sense of social cohesion and consent. Indeed, it might be argued, these are the new forms.

Postmodernism is one way of describing these processes while leaving everything as it is. Indeed, in Lyotard's words: 'All we can do is gaze in wonderment at the diversity of discursive species' (1984: 26). Anthony Giddens and Ulrich Beck offer a slightly different view. They examine the passage from pre-modernity to modernity to what is now not so much postmodernity as radical or reflexive modernity. Their position, it is claimed, entails neither the modernist uncritical acceptance of social institutions nor the postmodernist abandonment of them. It is necessary to acknowledge the reshaping of civil society and the development of new social networks. Given that there is now less security and more uncertainty and risk, this period is characterised by its reflexivity. We have not moved beyond modernity but we have become more aware of the reflexivity within modernity itself.

According to Giddens, we have entered the period of high modernity, cut loose from its moorings in the reassurance of tradition and characterised by the separation of space and time. There is the development of disembedding mechanisms that lift social activities out of their localised context. These social practices must now be constantly reexamined in light of new information. The production of systematic knowledge becomes integral to system reproduction (Giddens 1990: 52). However, these knowledge claims are circular in that modernity involves the institutionalisation of doubt (ibid., p. 176).

The idea of reflexivity is linked to risk. The globalising world creates a new intensity of pressures and an expanding number of contingent events. The globalisation of the world economy requires more flexibility of the state, civil society and personal life. Giddens fully accepts that globalisation is a real fact and indeed that economic globalisation has been a success. But a failure of its steering mechanisms has led to inequality (Giddens 2000: 124). How close this sounds to the view of Durkheim and the need to socially and morally regulate the expanding division of labour! The market economy can only function effectively within a developed civil society. Giddens argues for active, reflexive citizenship and life politics based on increasing individual autonomy and the negotiations between risk-taking individuals and the wider society. In particular, Giddens links the risk society to the opportunities opened up by sweeping changes in science and technology. He calls for a new society of 'responsible risk takers' in government, business enterprise and labour markets. This is a feature of a new world, a world of states without enemies, where new questions like risk management, democratic devolution and the renewal of the public sphere become increasingly important (Giddens 1998).

This can be developed further through an examination of Ulrich Beck's theory of risk society. He argues that modernisation does not have to be a negative process, as with Weber, Adorno or Foucault. Rather, the process of rationalisation can be radicalised and it offers us new possibilities based on a new relation between social structures and agents. As with Giddens, the best way to understand this is as unstoppable global forces combined with the individualisation of responsibility. On the one hand, 'the unleashed process of modernization is overrunning and overcoming its own coordinate system' through such things as the separation of nature and society and a new understanding of science and technology (Beck 1992: 87). But this also means that

> people will be *set free* from the social forms of industrial society – class, stratification, family, gender status of men and women . . . reflexive modernisation dissolves the traditional parameters of industrial society: class, culture and consciousness, gender and family roles. It dissolves these forms of the conscience collective, on which depend and to which refer the social and political organizations and institutions in industrial society. (Ibid., p. 87)

In contemporary society, the social production of wealth is accompanied by the social production of risks. Beck defines risk as 'a systematic way of dealing with hazards and insecurities induced and introduced by modernization itself' (ibid., p. 21). This process is globalised with development destroying boundaries and producing new antagonisms. Society demands a reorganisation of power and authority.

According to Beck, 'the risk society controls new sources of conflict and consensus' (ibid., p. 47). However, these are no longer class-based, for we are now witnessing a classless form of capitalism. Nor is the workplace any longer the main site of identity formation. Instead, new social lifestyle and group identities emerge based around the individualisation of social risks. It is argued that whereas in class positions being determines consciousness, in risk positions consciousness determines being (ibid., p. 53). If risk society entails uncertainty it also creates a greater diversity of identities and conflicts, ideologies and alliances (ibid., p. 101).

Beck argues that 'risks become the motor of the *self-politicization* of modernity in industrial society' (ibid., p. 183). This is also a process of individualisation so that 'the individual himself or herself becomes the reproduction unit of the social in the lifeworld' (ibid., p. 90). Use of the term 'lifeworld' indicates the influence of Habermas, an influence that can also be found in the work of David Held and his notion of cosmopolitan governance. Held, like Giddens and Beck, stresses the link between processes of globalisation and processes of individualisation and his theory of cosmopolitan governance stresses the theme of autonomy above all others (Held 1995). Giddens, we have seen, talks of the constitution of the self as a reflexive product. These writers are all concerned with the politics of individualised lifestyles, with people made to plan and conduct their own life.

In contrast to the postmodern theories, Giddens, Held and Beck hold an optimistic view that sees the potentials of present society. But both approaches can be said to share the assumption that society is becoming ever more fragmented and differentiated and that social life is more uncertain and diverse. In a sense, both approaches celebrate such a situation. They describe society as it presents itself to us rather than attempting a critical analysis of it. From a Foucauldian perspective we might therefore suggest that such theories are themselves a part of the governance process, a process that seeks the ordering of society along individualised lines. This is clear when we consider the relationship Giddens has to Tony Blair and Third Way politics. But it is also evident in the way all these theories attack the politics of collective agency. Beck's classlessness of social inequality and capitalism without classes is all very well until we consider how we might attempt to act in such a society. Given that the globalisation process is described in terms of powerful forces beyond our control, the fragmentation of collective agency leaves us with little power to resist. While it may seem that increased uncertainty and diversity undermine social cohesion and consent, they in fact reinforce it. For the theories of Giddens, Beck and the postmodernists act as ideologies of inaction, accepting the present neo-liberal order as given, while guarding against conflict by questioning the role of collective agency.

Beck and Giddens argue that collective agency is replaced with individual freedom. But as Slajov Žižek suggests:

> The freedom of decision enjoyed by the subject of the 'risk society' is not the freedom of someone who can freely choose his destiny, but the anxiety-provoking freedom of somebody who is constantly compelled to make decisions without being aware of their consequences. (1998: 151)

It is easy to get this impression with Giddens, that globalisation is an inevitable process sweeping all before it. Giddens uses the terms 'juggernaut' and 'runaway world' to describe the globalisation process.

This all suggests that the movement is irresistible and that the best we can do is apply some steering mechanisms.

Matthew Watson highlights the political aspect to these globalisation theories in that the issue of globalisation has been used as a rhetorical device to discipline people's expectations of what is feasible and to rein in social and welfare commitments and economic expectations. They encourage a political fatalism in terms of what is possible for economic and social regulation and discourage our expectations of the state and social institutions (Watson 1999: 127). But this does not mean that these theories advocate the removal of governance. On the contrary, they reinforce its new individualised form.

This is where the understanding of modernity derived from Foucault – despite its postmodern leanings – shows its superiority over the tradition derived from Habermas, since it focuses on the world as it is, on actual social practices and institutions and methods of government, rather than using an ideal type that is imposed on society with a utopian vision of how social life (or reflexive modernity and cosmopolitan democracy) might develop and liberate us. Further, a critical Foucauldian perspective would be able to say how theories about reflexive modernity are themselves an aspect of governmentality, ensuring the neo-liberal ordering of society and its workforce. What these theories do is celebrate the individualisation of governance, while all talk of reflexivity and risk-taking is founded on a fundamental assumption – not just that capitalism, but the neo-liberal variant of it, is here to stay.

Theory today lacks a critical edge. In fact it is often a part of the same process it describes.

4. CONCLUSION

Conflict, cohesion and consent are intertwined. Consensus presupposes possible conflict, cohesion is maintained only for so long as conflict can be contained. Social cohesion and consent are therefore about the overcoming or deferral of conflict. In part this comes from the system, in part it comes from a more conscious intervention. Owing to developments at a systemic level and supported by the mainstream theories of our time, cohesion and consent are being renewed. Strange though it might seem, in this period, fragmentation is the new form of social cohesion, uncertainty the new form of social consent.

REFERENCES

Adorno, T. (1987) 'Late Capitalism or Industrial Society?', in V. Meja, D. Misgeld and N. Stehr (eds), *Modern German Sociology*, New York: Columbia University Press, pp. 232–47.

Adorno, T. and M. Horkheimer (1986) *Dialectic of Enlightenment*, London: Verso.

Alcoff, L. (1990) 'Feminist Politics and Foucault: The Limits to a Collaboration', in A. Dallery and C. Scott (eds), *Crises in Continental Philosophy*, Albany: State University of New York Press.

Alway, J. (1995) *Critical Theory and Political Possibilities*, Westport, CT: Greenwood Press.

Anderson, P. (1976) 'The Antinomies of Antonio Gramsci', *New Left Review*, 100: 5–81.

Anderson, P. (1979) *Considerations on Western Marxism*, London: Verso.

Anderson, P. (1992) 'The Origins of the Present Crisis', in P. Anderson, *English Questions*, London: Verso.

Baudrillard, J. (1991) 'The Reality Gulf', *Guardian*, 11 January.

Baudrillard, J. (1994) *Simulacra and Simulation*, Ann Arbor: University of Michigan Press.

Beck, U. (1992) *The Risk Society*, London: Sage.

Bell, D. (1973) *The Coming of Post-Industrial Society*, London: Heinemann.

Benjamin, W. (1973) 'The Work of Art in the Age of Mechanical Reproduction', in W. Benjamin, *Illuminations*, Glasgow: Fontana.

Bottomore, T. (1966) *Elites and Society*, Harmondsworth: Penguin.

Dahrendorf, R. (1959) *Class and Class Conflict in Industrial Society*, Palo Alto, CA: Stanford University Press.

Durkheim, E. (1964) *The Division of Labor in Society*, New York: Free Press.

Durkheim, E. (1982) *The Rules of Sociological Method*, New York: Free Press.

Durkheim, E. (1995) *The Elementary Forms of Religious Life*, New York: Free Press.

Durkheim, E. (2002) *Suicide*, London and New York: Routledge.

Engels, F. (1976) *Anti-Dühring*, Peking: Foreign Languages Press.

Engels, F. (1978) *The Origin of the Family, Private Property and the State*, Peking: Foreign Languages Press.

Foucault, M. (1971) *Madness and Civilization*, London: Routledge.

Foucault, M. (1974) *The Order of Things*, London: Routledge.

Foucault, M. (1976) *The Birth of the Clinic*, London: Routledge.

Foucault, M. (1979) *Discipline and Punish*, Harmondsworth: Penguin.

Foucault, M. (1981) *The History of Sexuality, volume 1: An Introduction*, Harmondsworth: Penguin.

Foucault, M. (1985) *The History of Sexuality, volume 2: The Use of Pleasure*, Harmondsworth, Penguin.

Foucault, M. (1988) *The History of Sexuality, volume 3: The Care of the Self*, Harmondsworth, Penguin.

Foucault, M. (1989) *The Archaeology of Knowledge*, London: Routledge.

Foucault, M. (2001) *The Essential Works 3: Power*, Harmondsworth, Penguin.

Giddens, A. (1990) *The Consequences of Modernity*, Cambridge: Polity.

Giddens, A. (1998) *The Third Way: The Renewal of Social Democracy*, Cambridge: Polity.

Giddens, A. (2000) *The Third Way and Its Critics*, Cambridge, Polity.

Gouldner, A. (1971) *The Coming Crisis of Western Sociology*, London: Heinemann.

Gramsci, A. (1971) *Selections from the Prison Notebooks*, London: Lawrence and Wishart.

Gramsci, A. (1977) *Selections from the Political Writings (1910–1920)*, London: Lawrence and Wishart.

Gramsci, A. (1995) *Further Selections from the Prison Notebooks*, London: Lawrence and Wishart.

Habermas, J. (1984) *The Theory of Communicative Action, volume 1*, Cambridge: Polity.

Habermas, J. (1987a) *The Theory of Communicative Action, volume 2*, Cambridge: Polity.

Habermas, J. (1987b) *The Philosophical Discourse of Modernity*, Cambridge: Polity.

Habermas, J. (1988) *Legitimation Crisis*, Cambridge: Polity.

Habermas, J. (1989) *The Structural Transformation of the Public Sphere*, Cambridge: Polity.

Habermas, J. (1991) 'Legitimation Problems in the Modern State', in J. Habermas, *Communication and the Evolution of Society*, Cambridge: Polity, pp. 178–205.

Held, D. (1995) *Democracy and the Global Order: From the Modern State to Cosmopolitan Governance*, Cambridge: Polity.

Hirst, P. (1976) *Social Evolution and Sociological Categories*, London: George Allen and Unwin.

Horkheimer, M. (1972) *Critical Theory: Selected Essays*, New York: Seabury Press.

Horkheimer, M. (1987) *Eclipse of Reason*, New York: Continuum.

Jameson, F. (1990) *Late Marxism*, London: Verso.

Joseph, J. (1998) 'In Defence of Critical Realism', *Capital & Class*, 65: 73–106.

Joseph, J. (2002) *Hegemony: A Realist Analysis*, London and New York: Routledge.

Laclau, E. and C. Mouffe (1985) *Hegemony and Socialist Strategy*, London: Verso.

Larrain, J. (1983) *Marxism and Ideology*, London: Macmillan.

Lenin, V. I. (1961) *Collected Works, volume 27*, Moscow and London: Progress.

Lukács, G. (1971) *Lenin*, Cambridge, MA: MIT Press.

Lukes, S. (1973) *Émile Durkheim: His Life and Work*, Harmondsworth: Penguin.

Lyotard, J.-F. (1984) *The Postmodern Condition: A Report on Knowledge*, Manchester: Manchester University Press.

McCarthy, J. (1994) 'The Critique of Impure Reason: Foucault and the Frankfurt School', in M. Kelly (ed.), *Critique and Power: Recasting the Foucault/Habermas Debate*, Cambridge, MA and London: MIT Press.

Machiavelli, N. (1988) *The Prince*, Cambridge: Cambridge University Press.

McNay, L. (1992) *Foucault and Feminism*, Cambridge: Polity.

McNay, L. (1994) *Foucault: A Critical Introduction*, New York: Continuum.

Marcuse, H. (1966) *One-Dimensional Man*, Boston, MA: Beacon Press.

Marcuse, H. (1969) *Eros and Civilisation*, London: Sphere.

Marsh, D., J. Buller, C. Hay, J. Johnston, P. Kerr, S. McAnulla and M. Watson (1999) *Postwar British Politics in Perspective*, Cambridge: Polity.

Marx, K. (1952) *Wage Labour and Capital*, Moscow: Progress.

Marx, K. (1963) *The Poverty of Philosophy*, New York: International Publishers.

Marx, K. (1973a) *The Class Struggle in France*, in K. Marx, *Political Writings, volume 2: Surveys from Exile* [SE], Harmondsworth: Penguin.

Marx, K. (1973b) *The Eighteenth Brumaire of Louis Bonaparte*, in SE.

Marx, K. (1974a) *The Civil War in France*, in. K. Marx, *Political Writings, volume 3: The First International and After* [FI], Harmondsworth: Penguin.

Marx, K. (1974b) *Critique of the Gotha Programme*, in FI.

Marx, K. (1975a) Preface (to *A Contribution to the Critique of Political Economy*), in K. Marx, *Early Writings* [EW], Harmondsworth: Penguin.

Marx, K. (1975b) *Critique of Hegel's Doctrine of the State*, in EW.

Marx, K. (1975c) *Excerpts from James Mill's* Elements of Political Economy, in EW.

Marx, K. (1975d) *Economic and Philosophical Manuscripts*, in EW.

Marx, K. (1975e) *A Contribution to the Critique of Hegel's Philosophy of Right*, in EW.

Marx, K. (1976) *Capital, volume 1*, Harmondsworth: Penguin.

Marx, K. (1981) *Capital, volume 3*, Harmondsworth: Penguin.

Marx, K. and F. Engels (1965) *The German Ideology*, London: Lawrence and Wishart.

Marx, K. and F. Engels (1973) *The Communist Manifesto*, in K. Marx, *Political Writings, volume 1: The Revolutions of 1848*, Harmondsworth: Penguin.

Merquior, J. G. (1980) *Rousseau and Weber: Two Studies in the Theory of Legitimacy*, London: Routledge and Kegan Paul.

Merton, R. K. (1957) 'Social Structure and Anomie', in R. K. Merton, *Social Theory and Social Structure*, New York: Free Press.

Michels, R. (1915) *Political Parties*, Glencoe, IL: Free Press.

Miliband, R. (1973) *The State in Capitalist Society*, London: Quartet.

Mommsen, W. (1974) *The Age of Bureaucracy*, Oxford: Blackwell.

Mosca, G. (1939) *The Ruling Class*, New York: McGraw-Hill.

Neumann, F. (1966) *Behemoth: The Structure and Practice of National Socialism*, New York: Harper.

Norris, C. (1992) *Uncritical Theory: Postmodernism, Intellectuals and the Gulf War*, London: Lawrence and Wishart.

Pareto, V. (1976) *Sociological Writings*, ed. S. E. Finer, Oxford: Blackwell.

Parsons, T. (1954) *Essays in Sociological Theory*, New York: Free Press.

Parsons, T. (1977) *Social Systems and the Evolution of Action Theory*, New York: Free Press.

Parsons, T. (1991) *The Social System*, London and New York: Routledge.

Partridge, P. H. (1971) *Consent and Consensus*, London: Macmillan.

Poulantzas, N. (1973) *Political Power and Social Classes*, London: New Left Books/Sheed and Ward.

Poulantzas, N. (1978a) *Classes in Contemporary Capitalism*, London: Verso.

Poulantzas, N. (1978b) *State, Power, Socialism*, London: New Left Books.

Roderick, R. (1986) *Habermas and the Foundations of Critical Theory*, London: Macmillan.

Smart, B. (1983) *Foucault, Marxism and Critique*, London: Routledge and Kegan Paul.

Smart, B. (1986) 'The Politics of Truth and the Problem of Hegemony', in D. Couzens Hoy (ed.), *Foucault: A Critical Reader*, Oxford: Blackwell.

Soper, K. (1993) 'Productive Contradictions', in C. Ramazanğlu (ed.), *Up against Foucault: Exploration of Some Tensions between Foucault and Feminism*, London and New York: Routledge.

Thompson, E. P. (1993) *Customs in Common*, Harmondsworth: Penguin.

Thompson, K. (1986) *Beliefs and Ideology*, Chichester and London: Ellis Horwood and Tavistock.

Trotsky, L. (1974) *The First Five Years of the Communist International, volume 2*, London: New Park.

Watson, M. (1999) 'Globalisation and the Development of the British Political Economy', in D. Marsh, J. Buller, C. Hay, J. Johnson, P. Kerr, S. McAnulla and M. Watson, *Postwar British Politics in Perspective*, Cambridge: Polity.

Weber, M. (1978) *Economy and Society*, ed. G. Roth and C. Wittich, 2 vols, Berkeley: University of California Press.

Weber, M. (1991) *From Max Weber: Essays in Sociology*, tr. and ed. H. H. Gerth and C. Wright Mills, London and New York: Routledge.

Weber, M. (1992) *The Protestant Ethic and the Spirit of Capitalism*, London and New York: Routledge.

Weber, M. (1993) *Basic Concepts in Sociology*, New York: Citadel Press.

Williams, R. (1982) 'Base and Superstructure in Marxist Cultural Theory', *New Left Review*, 82: 3–13.

Zeitlin, I. M. (1981) *Ideology and the Development of Sociological Theory*, Englewood Cliffs, NJ: Prentice Hall.

Žižek, S. (1998) 'Risk Society and Its Discontents', *Historical Materialism*, 2: 143–68.

FURTHER READING

Adorno, T. (1991) *The Culture Industry*, tr. and ed. J. M. Bernstein, London: Routledge.

Beetham, D. (1985) *Max Weber and the Theory of Modern Politics*, Cambridge: Polity.

Beetham, D. (1987) *Bureaucracy*, Buckingham: Open University Press.

Bellamy, R. (1987) *Modern Italian Social Theory*, Cambridge: Polity.

Bendix, R. (1966) *Max Weber: An Intellectual Portrait*, London: Methuen.

Calhoun, C. (ed.) (1992) *Habermas and the Public Sphere*, Cambridge, MA: MIT Press.

Cook, D. (1996) *The Culture Industry Revisited: Theodor W. Adorno on Mass Culture*, Lanham, MD: Rowman and Littlefield.

Craib, I. (1984) *Modern Social Theory: From Parsons to Habermas*, Hemel Hempstead: Harvester Wheatsheaf.

Fenton, S. (1984) *The Origin of the Family, Private Property and the State*, Peking: Foreign Languages Press.

Fontana, B. (1993) *Hegemony and Power: On the Relation between Gramsci and Machiavelli*, Minneapolis: University of Minnesota Press.

Foucault, M. (1988) *The History of Sexuality, volume 3: The Care of the Self*, Harmondsworth: Penguin.

Freund, J. (1968) *The Sociology of Max Weber*, Harmondsworth: Penguin.

Habermas, J. (1978) *Knowledge and Human Interests*, London: Heinemann.

Held, D. (1980) *Introduction to Critical Theory*, Berkeley: University of California Press.

Hindess, B. (1996) *Discourses of Power from Hobbes to Foucault*, Oxford: Blackwell.

Horkheimer, M. (1974) *Critique of Instrumental Reason*, New York: Seabury Press.

Jessop, B. (1982) *The Capitalist State*, Oxford: Martin Robinson.

Joseph, J. (2000) 'A Realist Theory of Hegemony', *Journal for the Theory of Social Behaviour*, 30, 2: 179–202.

Layder, D. (1994) *Understanding Social Theory*, London: Sage.

Lenin, V. I. (1965) *The State and Revolution*, Peking: Foreign Languages Press.

Löwith, K. (1982) *Max Weber and Karl Marx*, London: George Allen and Unwin.

Lukács, G. (1968) *History and Class Consciousness*, London: Merlin.

Meisel, J. H. (ed.) (1965) *Pareto and Mosca*, Englewood Cliffs, NJ: Prentice Hall.

Miliband, R. (1977) *Marxism and Politics*, Oxford: Oxford University Press.

Outhwaite, W. (1994) *Habermas: A Critical Introduction*, Cambridge: Polity.

Parkin, F. (1982) *Max Weber*, London: Tavistock.

Parsons, T. and E. Shils (eds) (1951) *Toward a General Theory of Action*, Cambridge, MA: Harvard University Press.

Rasmussen, D. (1990) *Reading Habermas*, Oxford: Blackwell.

Slater, P. (1977) *Origin and Significance of the Frankfurt School*, London: Routledge and Kegan Paul.

Thompson, E. P. (1968) *The Making of the English Working Class*, Harmondsworth: Penguin.

INDEX

215